MEMOIR

OF THE

DUCHESS OF ORLEANS.

BY THE

MARQUESS DE H——.

TOGETHER WITH

BIOGRAPHICAL SOUVENIRS AND ORIGINAL LETTERS.

COLLECTED BY

PROF. G. H. DE SCHUBERT.

TRANSLATED FROM THE FRENCH.

SECOND EDITION.

PHILADELPHIA:
PORTER & COATES,

TRANSLATOR'S PREFACE.

The character of the Duchess of Orleans is one of such remarkable loveliness, and shines with such radiant lustre in the midst of the French Court, and in the subsequent trials to which she was subjected after the downfall of Louis Philippe, that it is worthy of the most careful study. While translating her most interesting Memoir by the Marquess de H———, which had such well-deserved success in France and England, another work upon the same subject and of additional interest, by her tutor, Prof. de Schubert, fell into my hands. The style of the two authors is so different, and her character looked at from such different points of view, that it has been deemed advisable to unite the two Memoirs in one volume, for the reason that the originals are not likely to fall into the hands of the general reader. The following interesting account of Prof. de Schubert and his Life of the Duchess may be found in Monsieur Girard's preface to his able French translation:—

"In 1816, Prof. de Schubert was appointed preceptor to the children of the Duke of Mecklenburg Schwerin. Endowed with a superior mind, extensive information, and a profoundly religious and sympathetic character, he needed a sojourn of only three years in that household to render his memory ever precious. Shortly after leaving Ludwigslust to occupy the chair of natural science at the University of Erlangen, the young princess Helen solicited a correspondence with him, which only ended with her life. After a sojourn of eight years at Erlangen, Prof. de Schubert became a professor in the University of Munich, and received the honor of a membership with the Academy of Sciences.

"The long career of Prof. de Schubert has been marked by numerous publications upon the natural sciences, theological questions, instructive biographies, narrations, etc. All the works of the former Professor of Ludwigslust much interested the Duchess of Orleans, who gratefully acknowledged them; those which most attracted her were upon his religious views, containing his profound meditations upon the nature of the soul and its relations with God. By the side of the interesting biography of the Marquess de H——, this work appears to offer a triple source of interest. First, the more complete information concerning the education of the princess up to her marriage. Second, the publication of about twenty-four letters or fragments of letters written in German, addressed to Prof. de Schubert, the grand duchess, or a youthful friend. Finally, and most important, the exclusively religious point of view of the author, which is in perfect harmony with the convictions of the Duchess of Orleans."

CONTENTS

PART I.

MEMOIR, BY THE MARQUESS DE H - -

PART II.

BIOGRAPHICAL SOUVENIRS AND ORIGINAL LETTERS COLLECTED BY PROF. G. H. DE SCHUBERT.

PAGE

I

The princess Helena Louisa Elizabeth, of Mecklenburg Schwerin, born at the castle of Ludwigslust, on the 24th of January, 1814, was the daughter of Louis Frederick, hereditary grand-duke of Mecklenburg Schwerin, by his second wife, Caroline of Weimar. The princess Caroline was both charming and intellectual, and her father, Charles Augustus, grand-duke of Saxe-Weimar, the friend of Goëthe and Schiller, was one of the most distinguished princes in Germany ; her mother was the princess Louisa of Weimar, of whom Madame de Staël has left such a fascinating portrait. "She was," wrote she, "the true model of a woman destined by nature for the most illustrious rank ; without pretension or weakness she inspired both confidence and respect. Her soul was penetrated with the heroism of chivalric times, without being disrobed of feminine gentleness."

1*

The princess Helen was only two years of age when the grand-duchess Caroline died, in the prime of life. While dying, it is said she requested her husband to grant another mother to her children, and designated her cousin, the princess Augusta of Hamburg. Never was maternal devotion better directed. The princess Augusta became grand-duchess of Mecklenburg in 1814, and being soon after left a widow, consecrated all her best affections to her cousin's children. She retired from society that she might devote herself more entirely to their education, and chiefly to that of the princess Helen, who attached herself to her from the very first, and never ceased to love her with the tenderness of a daughter.

One takes pleasure in recognizing in this graceful child all the qualities that she afterwards exhibited. The perfect simplicity of her character was doubtless maintained by her entire forgetfulness of self. Indeed, a special charm attaches itself to those natures that never vary, independent, if one may so speak, of their intrinsic value; one always finds in them the freshness of childhood. On the contrary, virtues acquired during the course of life are rarely allied with complete self-abnegation; for the efforts they have cost are recalled continually, and make one look upon them with a sort of complacency, in spite of oneself. The princess Helen, at the age of four years, manifested a tender, generous concern for the sufferings of others, and was strong in bearing her own, as we have since seen. "She was never egotistical," say those who had charge of her early education, "and was at that age inspired with a never decreasing devotion to others, which renders her tenacious of life even at this hour. She was benevolent, if one may so speak, even towards God; ever ready to act from love to Him, rather than from a sense of duty. Upon one occasion, some one expressed surprise at the readiness with which she yielded a childish fancy; she replied in a low tone, 'our Lord has said, Whosoever shall compel thee to go a mile, go with him twain.'"

Before she was permitted to visit the poor and to direct the charitable establishments founded by her mother, which she did at a later period with remarkable judiciousness, her instinctive charity exercised itself upon the families of her dependents; she made their children come to her, and taught them what she had learned herself. This gentle, frail little creature, inspired the tender respect of her pupils, large, robust children of Thuringia, who kneeling before her, gravely answered her questions, and oftener left her rewarded than punished. The presents that were hung yearly for her upen the Christmas tree, were soon found in the hands of her playmates, who were made to promise never to admire them in her presence, lest the articles to which she attached the most value, should be the first cheerfully sacrificed. Her desire to please and to be surrounded by happy faces, which in some children is only a graceful form of *coquetterie*, arose from a deeper feeling; without suspecting it herself, she early became attractive to all who approached her.

Her masters, charmed with her avidity for knowledge, were often forced to interrupt their recitals, in order to check the impression made upon her delicate organization, by a touching history or heroic trait. Her constitution was too feeble for a nature whose sudden and fine impulses betokened an affinity with the Southern races, while their duration and length convinced one of her German origin. At twelve years of age, she lost a friend who had shared her studies and resided near her for several years; her grief was so great that she became seriously ill. At this epoch her countenance assumed a melancholy expression, naturally entirely foreign to it, but which a long succession of afflictions afterwards rendered habitual.

In the spring of 1827, the grand-duchess took

her for the first time to Weimar. Up to this moment she had educated her in almost entire solitude. Living for the greater part of the year in the country, either at Doberan, on the borders of the Baltic, or at Plushon, which belonged to the hereditary grand-duke, the young princess knew, out of her own family, only her professors, men of rare merit in Germany, and the excellent and distinguished women whom her mother had placed over her when she was eighteen months old, and who up to her marriage never left her. To this contemplative life she owed an intellectual cultivation rare in any woman, and simple tastes which were sources of a thousand delights in the course of her changeful destiny. Accustomed to live in a sort of intimacy with Nature, she penetrated the beauty of its varied objects as well as its completeness ; a bright day, a walk in some beautiful place, or the sight of flowers that she loved to gather, afforded her joy in childhood, and gave her moments of pleasure in after life.

The princess Helen was not surprised by the new movement which presented her at the court of Weimar ; with a mind already open to all intellectual pleasures, she found herself everywhere at ease, and seemed to have passed her life in the midst of those to whom she was presented. The remembrance of that little girl of thirteen years remained in their minds, like a charming, poetic apparition. "I see her still," writes one, "clothed in red, without any other ornament than her pretty brown hair; lively as a bird, yet dignified in all her movements, and I recall the tender pride with which the aged grand-duke of Weimar fixed his eyes upon her.

A journey to Switzerland, whither she went to join her brother prince Albert, alone interrupted the regularity of her life from 1827 to 1830. Upon leaving the great sand plains of Mecklenburg, with its marshes and monotonous sombre woods, the first sight of the splendors of Swiss scenery, filled her with emotions too deep for utterance. One day she was surprised in tears at the Falls of Schaffouse, gazing at the foaming waters sparkling in the golden sun-beams.

After a new sojourn at Doberan, the princess Helen returned with her mother to Ludwigslust, where she received confirmation in the parish church on the 30th of May, 1830. The inhabitants of the community who had known and cherished her from her birth were present at the ceremony, and united their fervent prayers with those of their "good Helen," "*unsere gute Helene.*" When she kneeled before the altar, after the pastor laid his hand upon her and pronounced the Benediction according to the Lutheran rite, all joined with emotion in singing the canticle she herself had chosen :—*O herzlich lieb habe ich o Hen.*

"From the depths of my heart, O Lord, I love thee."

We perhaps dwell too much upon details whose sweet simplicity contrasts with the more severe reality of scenes that have impressed the memory of the princess Helen upon us :—it is not simply because we take a sad pleasure in dwelling upon the peaceable events of a life so full of agitation, but because some remarkable traits in her character here strike us most forcibly. Habituated to the courtesy of patriarchal simplicity, to respectful confidence on the part of the people, and to the paternal protection of princes, surrounded by warm hearts and acquainted only with sentiments to which her heart found no difficulty in responding, she might have been less competent than most persons to understand the varied society and different countries to which she found herself transported. Her vivid imagination might have been more easily excited than most others, but she had that faculty in a high degree which belongs to character as well as mind :—rapid intuition of diverse situations and intelligent comprehension of them, nay more, deep admiration of all that awakened the idea of a great work to be accomplished, of a noble cause, of lofty thoughts, whatever might be the form under which they presented themselves. It was owing to this quickness of comprehension and the gift of assimilating sympathies with all that caused the hearts of others to throb, that in the forest of Doberan, a princess of sixteen years of age, acquainted only with France through her books and what her masters taught her, was qualified to take an ardent interest in the events of 1830, and to distinguish them with marvellous sagacity from those of an ordinary revolution. In this contest wherein she saw a people in arms not to attack, but to maintain the laws against the power that sought to overthrow them, all her interest from the very first was upon the side of the people; she daily awaited the arrival of the French journals with as much impatience as if she was agitated concerning personal events, copied the articles that chiefly interested her, and, in short, watched the political movement, apparently so foreign to her own interest, with singular emotion. This first enthusiasm awakened in the name of France and liberty left its deep traces in her mind, and the name of the Orleans family was impressed upon her heart long before she divined that it would one day be her own

From this moment, French literature assumed an interest altogether new in her eyes. She directed her studies chiefly in that language, and spoke from preference that tongue she had been habituated to speak from infancy.

But soon some personal disquietudes succeeded the disinterested emotions the events of France had awakened within her. The grand-duchess was taken seriously ill, and sent to Tœplitz in such a feeble state, that it was feared she would die before reaching the end of her journey. Her daughter seated by her side watched her with tender anxiety, though without fearing she might be left an orphan for the second time. God spared her such a grief. The sojourn at Tœplitz, to which she attributed the establishment of her mother's health, perhaps exercised a decisive influence over her destiny. The princess seldom left the sick chamber, and received only a very few persons; but none who once saw her remained indifferent to her charms. The French minister, Monsieur Bresson, without having yet been introduced, had occasion to meet her, and never lost the impression she made upon him. It was also at Tœplitz that the king of Prussia, already allied to her family by the marriage of one of his daughters to the hereditary grand-duke of Mecklenburg, saw her for the first time. At first attracted towards her by the superiority of her intellect, rendered still more striking by her extreme youth, he found daily increasing pleasure in conversing with her, and expressed an attachment for her that never afterwards diminished.

Among the many manifestations of kindness she then received, we should regret to pass in silence one more precious than all others, for it is pleasant to think that two persons, separated on earth by diverse fortunes, yet worthy of each other through true elevation of character, meet at one date in life, and become drawn together by a common sympathy, notwithstanding the difference in age and position.

The dauphiness came with King Charles X., to inquire concerning the health of the grand-duchess, who was still confined to her chamber. The princess Helen received her, and was the bearer of her mother's thanks. The rapid intuition of her heart led her to perceive true moral greatness of character even when concealed by austere simplicity of manners. The calm dignity impressed upon the features of the dauphiness unveiled to her an abyss of continued struggles and conquests. She in turn so much inspired the admiration of the noble exile that her sweet image remained impressed upon her years after their meeting. When some of the French visited the dauphiness at Prague, she first questioned them concerning the young duchess of Orleans, whose name she was convinced needed only to be mentioned. "Is she happy ?" she asked with much earnestness ; "I sincerely hope so, for I knew her and know how well she merits happiness."

The year 1832 was a memorable one to the princess ; marked by one of those great griefs that can never be effaced. While visiting a ruin in the environs of Jena, her brother prince Albert had a dangerous fall. In accordance with his own request he was conveyed to Mecklenburg, to his own family, where he languished several months before he died. His sister watched him with tender care, but cheered by no hopes of recovery. During these days and nights of anguish, she stifled her own grief that she might aid him in bearing his sufferings, and lead him to die with resignation at the early age of twenty-two years. Perhaps it was in this great struggle that she learned to control her deepest emotions, to suffer with apparent serenity, concealing her extreme sensitiveness within her own soul and to be mistress of herself at all times. Seven years later, when full of happiness, she writes :—"This date will remind you of the great trial that marked it. The Lord has richly blessed me since that sad epoch; he has been a friend and protector, granting me happiness I never conceived of; although my youth never recovered from the shock it then received, tears have borne their blessed fruit; I felt it would be so then, and thanks be to God, I feel it now. I have learned to love his holy will, even when it tries me, and to resign myself to it, cheerfully."

She passed the winter following her brother's death in entire solitude. She devoted herself to reviving her mother's fortitude, and only sought distraction in frequent visits to the poor. The more she suffered herself, the more she sought to diminish their sufferings by abundant alms.

The praise of a princess' generosity, it seems to me, is a eulogy of little value; to give, is a thing so easy, that it is sometimes asked how it may be distinguished from an amiable fancy; but thanks be to God, He has not granted the privilege of exercising true charity, *only* to the poor, because they only can give what costs them a sacrifice. To be prodigal of time, attention, and interest, to diffuse joy wherever she passed, to lead the poor to think that she thought of their pleasures as well as their misery, was the princess Helen's privilege and pleasure; hence we dare praise her generosity, without the fear of bestowing eulogy too trivial. After her long season of mourning, it was not without a struggle that she submitted to the wishes of her family to return to Schwerin, and take part in the fetes given at that court, in honor of th fiftieth year of the reign of the aged duke, her grandfather. One hesitates to repeat compliments current in the society of princesses;—yet it is nevertheless true, wherever she presented herself, she was beloved, and the particular interest manifested in her, arose from the special concern she took in the most ordinary actions of others. The benevolence of her youthful countenance with its pensive expression, surprised and charmed, old and young, great and small; all felt her sweet and cheering influence; an interview with her increased one's yearning for what is good; in short, whether she entered a cottage or parlor, countenances brightened like sunbeams at her presence. Those who knew her can testify, how much more delightful life seemed in her society, and how the thought of her was mingled with their hopes and remembrances, and how a shadow seems now to be cast over their brightest dreams for the future.

II.

Who has not experienced a melancholy emotion, upon seeing a vessel launched into the broad sea, and been tempted to seize the hand about to detach the cable ; however smooth the surface of the water, however luminous the horizon, the imagination pictures an o'erclouded sky and angry waves.

The moment seems about to arrive when the fate of the princess Helen is to be decided, and one experiences a like emotion ; one hesitates to leave the peaceful dwelling, where she has yet known nothing of life but its joys, or griefs mingled with consolations that God never fails to send with trials coming directly from his hand. Yet now, the story of her life becomes a part of our own history, and her happiness and sorrows commingle with ours.

In the spring of 1836, the duke of Orleans and the duke of Nemours, left France for the first time since 1830, and went to Berlin, where the aged king received them with his accustomed cordiality; becoming subsequently charmed with so much real merit and grace, he regarded them with paternal affection, and frankly expressed his regret that he had no more daughters upon whom to confer happiness. The image of the young princess Helen, whom he had known at Tœplitz, then presented itself, and he felt that she alone was worthy of such accomplished princes.

He was conscious that many varied qualities ought to be found in the future duchess of Orleans. None but of royal blood could be presented as daughter-in-law to the queen, Marie Amelia, and must be as well educated for France, as if born there. A person well known for superiority of intellect and virtue could alone call our princess by the name of sister. In short, it would be necessary for her to rise above all the narrow restrictions and puerile contempt that the government of the king then inspired in Europe, and boldly face all chances and even dangers she would have to encounter as the wife of a French prince.

The king of Prussia saw these qualities so rarely united in the princess Helen of Mecklenburg and in her only ; his tenderness for her and the royal prince made him earnestly desire their union. He took a personal interest in these two destinies, that no resistance on the part of his own family could shake. Though the king had revealed his wishes to the duke of Orleans, when he visited Berlin, and had latterly spoken much of them, the duke wished to satisfy himself that the king's affection had not blinded him with regard to the merits of the princess, and that she was such an one as he had painted before determining to seek the hand of one whose external circumstances corresponded with his desires. His loyalty led him to consider his marriage as a duty both to his family and country, and regarded the event as one of the most serious in his life ; without being willing to sacrifice any of the exactions of rank, he determined not to surrender any conditions of private happiness and domestic union. He revealed his plans to none of the king's ministers, before seeking to form his own judgment of the intellectual and moral qualifications of the princess ; having satisfied his own mind, he made Monsieur Bresson his ambassador to the court of Mecklenburg, with power to ask the hand of the princess Helen.

It is said that her brother, grand-duke of Mecklenburg, was at first ill disposed towards this alliance. It would be unjust to charge him with opposition simply on account of his views concerning the events of 1830, and the house of Orleans; his deep anxiety for his sister's happiness led him to fear her departure to a country so fatal to its princes. Have we now, right to blame him? We may admire the still more exalted ideas and equal tenderness of the duchess of Mecklenburg, aud the noble aspirations of the princess Helen. All that was said of the duke of Orleans doubtless fascinated the young girl's imagination, and the thought of sharing the throne of France enhanced the glory of the future; but these were not the most lively motives that agitated her mind. In short, she did not deem happiness (though she deeply enjoyed the measure of it God granted her) of so much importance as others of more ordinary minds; it was not her first aim; or rather, happiness, in her eyes, did not consist in the tranquil possession of the good things of this world, but in the exercise of all the noble faculties of the soul and mind, and in the accomplishment of a "noble and important work." Hence she felt attracted to France and the house of Orleans, by what would repel one of less decision of character. The trials to which the king and his sons had been continuously exposed, seven years before, were not unknown to her; she knew in what anxiety the days of the queen had passed, in consequence of the dangers to which the princes voluntarily exposed themselves in Africa, and were subjected to in their own country. Her share of these perils and cares, she determined to accept with a firm will. She resolved to devote her life to the prince, whose noble character inspired her confidence, and to aid him in the accomplishment of his great work.

It appears that the duke of Orleans divined what was passing within her mind, and that he intuitively replied to her thoughts in the letter addressed to Monsieur Bresson, but destined for the princess Helen; in this epistle he unreservedly exposed all the objections to their union, arising from the solicitude of the Mecklenburg family. "I received strength from that letter," said the princess, "to march against all foreseen difficulties." From that moment she no longer hesitated, and with the support of her mother's approbation, indulged in her unfolding hopes, and fixed her thoughts upon the future country of her adoption.

The marriage contract was signed on the 5th of April, 1837, and on the 15th the duke of Orleans' bethrothed, left Ludwigslust with her mother, who desired in person to present her to the queen. From the dawn of day the vestibules and stairways of the castle were crowded with old servants and youthful companions, seeking a farewell sight of the princess. Upon seeing the way strewn with flowers, she bowed and smiled, though in tears. Bouquets were thrown by beloved hands into the carriage, and it was with difficulty that she made her way through surrounding groups. Four verses of her own composition, traced upon one of the windows of the palace, reveal the deep emotions of joy and sadness she experienced at the moment of her departure.

So lebe wohl, du stilles Haus
Ich zieh betrübt aus dir hinaus
Und blüht mir fern ein shönes Glück,
Ich denke gem an dich zurück.

May 14, 1837.

She received touching marks of affection throughout the whole route ; deputies from among the peasants and lords of Mecklenburg presented their earnest wishes for her happiness. King Frederick William desired that the princess and her retinue might halt at Potsdam, and there received them with his ministers and the royal family. When the time of departure arrived, the king manifested much emotion, and solemnly blessed the young girl, over whose future destiny he had exercised some influence.

On the 22d of May the ambassador appointed to accompany the princess to Paris, arrived at Fulde, and was presented. The king placed the duke de Broglie at the head of this embassy, in order that his venerated name might be associated with the event of his son's marriage ; few possessed such a rare combination of worth and talent. The princess was capable of appreciating the king's choice and duly expressed her thanks.

It was upon the 25th of May, a delightful spring day, that she passed the frontier, under a triumphal arch, bearing the inscription, *France*, in large floral letters. Without dwelling upon the ordinary official receptions from Forbach to Fontainbleau, we must notice the effect everywhere produced by the princess' appearance. She was doubtless agitated by conflicting emotions. As she wrote at a later date, some sad presentiments mingled themselves with her hopes, some regrets for her native country, with a sincere love for that of her adoption. But her deepest emotions were always concealed by a benign dignity. She was neither intimidated nor exalted upon suddenly finding herself the object of universal attention. Her replies were not dictated but inspired by the emotions of the moment, and were always suitable.

It was chiefly at Metz, the first French garrisoned city, that her unconstrained tact and noble, yet not haughty, bearing made the most decided impression. At Forbach she only encountered a rustic population ; the courtesy and cordiality of the mayors of the Alsatian villages, almost reminded her of the good Mecklenburgers and their familiar amicability. Metz was altogether a French town, ill-disposed to foreign manners, and always more ready to criticise than approve. In a few hours before her departure she entirely captivated the idle, curious multitude. The officers of the garrison, who were presented to her shortly after she alighted from the coach, and before she had taken any repose, declared that they should have been intimidated in that young girl's presence, if they had not been fascinated by her modest grace.

Indeed, the indescribable charm of her countenance pleased from the very first. If no particular feature attracted attention, the eyes of all were fascinated by the symmetry and beauty of her whole person, and an interest excited, impossible to be withdrawn. Her benevolent smile and ever varying expression, sometimes joyous, sometimes full of affection and emotion, reflected her soul and deepened the impression made by every word she spoke. Though her uncommon dignity constantly reminded all of her rank, which she seemed unconscious of, we may say the feeling she inspired was that of sympathy. At a later period, when grief under all its forms had tried her, the extreme mobility of her countenance was lessened by an habitually gentle, pensive expression, that even when most animated, seemed to solicit a hopeful word.

The arrival at Fontainbleau was characterized by one of the most striking spectacles the place had ever witnessed. It was one of those rare moments when the country and ruling power were in harmony, and when political interests were commingled with the private happiness of the House of Orleans. The marriage of the prince royal seemed to silence all disquietude for the future, and the nation seemed sailing into an era of prosperity; the public satisfaction was marked by a general elation, and the princess's cortege was welcomed with repeated cries of "long live the king." The interior court was filled with troops, while an immense multitude surrounded the railing. The king and princes stood in waiting at the foot of the grand staircase; near him the duke of Orleans, who had just returned from Chalons, where he had his first interview; at the head of the stairway stood the queen, with the princesses, ladies of honor, and invited guests; and a little distant a group of distinguished men who had played a part in political scenes and were illustrious in France, either from rank or talent.

The young princess alighted from the coach with uncommon grace, while all eyes were fixed upon her. She knelt at the king's feet, and kissed his hand with tender deference, then cast herself into the queen's arms with so natural an emotion that none could look on with indifference.

"It was a touching scene," writes one upon returning from Fontainbleau. "The young princess has truly a royal bearing ; though so youthful and even childlike in her appearance, she seems to govern all around her. Her countenance admirably accords with her intellect and character ; it is an index of her soul ; her eyes are radiant with intelligence and animation ; it would be impossible to conceive of more dignity and ease of manner, void of boldness. The princess's attention did not seem in the least distracted by the profusion of rich attire, jewels, and laces. There was some anxiety felt concerning the arrival at Paris in the midst of these displays and vanities. But all were orderly and animated. At the moment of entering the Tuileries she arose with childlike curiosity in the calèche to catch a coup d'œil of the place, and the impression her appearance made upon the spectators was a most happy one. She never lost self-possession for a moment, and I believe that God reigns in the very depths of her heart. She impresses the imagination like those princesses in fairy tales led by good genii into brilliant palaces."

III.

The years immediately following the marriage of the duchess of Orleans, were blessed with every joy that earth could afford. She found complete happiness in the bosom of her family, in the éclat of a brilliant court, and in the sincere homage paid not only to her rank, but to her virtues ; with every hope for a cloudless future, there was nothing to mar her enjoyment, and she appreciated it with all the fulness of her lively yet reflective nature.

Upon the 30th of May, the anniversary of her wedding, she thus writes to the friend of her childhood : " To-day, my heart is more filled with happiness and gratitude than ever. One hails the anniversary of such a day with ever new emotion. How different is this from that of the past year ! Behold all my hopes realized, and new ones attracting me to the future : a deep and true affection, that I did not then surmise, filling my heart, my position in accordance with the desires of my family, established upon a solid foundation, and an approaching hope, binding me to the hearts of the country, all these are subjects of gratitude ; a few of them we anticipated, but they are more numerous than your fond heart and mother's ever conceived, and more than I had ever dreamed of. It is two o'clock. At this moment, a year ago, I was in the midst of the pomp and glory of the wedding festival. What gifts were showered upon me. Since then, thanks be to God, I have learned to regard luxury with sufficient indifference, excepting what is granted me, according to its true value. Then the evening, with its successive ceremonies, that agitated my mind, yet fixed my happiness. Oh what remembrances ! what difference ! Let us together thank God, who has loaded me with benefits, and placed such a noble, important aim before me in life. It seems as if God is granting me too much happiness ; I feel it surpasses all that I merit, yet accept it with gratitude, since He sends it."

And when these hopes were realized, what a hymn of joy is contained in these few lines written shortly after the birth of the young Count Paris ; her maternal transports mingle themselves with the most exalted feelings of her new duties towards France

"How merciful God is!" exclaimed she; "you raise your heart with mine in devout thanks; it has sounded the depths of my happiness. Yes, your child is the happiest of mothers; her heart is too small to retain its delights. A new world is unfolded t me; a child to cherish with the hopes of a people to be realized in that child. The task is great, is noble;—may God grant us his wisdom, his light."

Her passionate interest in the glory of hei country, if possible, surpassed her personal joys. The march of public events and literary movements engrossed her mind. In associating with the royal prince who was ever ready to pay homage to men of distinguished talents, she gathered such a circle around her as she would wish her son to move in.

In the midst of most diverse opinions, she was pre-eminently capable of increasing the number of those personally friendly to the royal family. Full of affectionate submission to the wishes of the king, she avoided with scrupulous delicacy every thing that might attract particular homage to herself, or grant any license to parties ever ready to imagine a diversity of opinions between the heir to the throne and the head of the State. Denying herself the pleasure of assembling friends of her own choice around her, lest malevolence might attribute the act to political intrigue, she made no distinction between her own manner of living and that of her sisters-in-law. She passed a portion of each morning with them in the queen's apartments. While at their work, the king often joined them, and read aloud the most remarkable writings of the day. In the evening the princess royal remained with the queen until her hour for retirement, then withdrew to her own apartments, where she read alone with the prince. Domestic life was animated by her vivacity, and she never sought to distract her mind from its sometimes monotonous duties by puerile pleasures. Indulgence in a refined taste for the arts often relieved the weariness of court life. Sometimes the finest artists of the Conservatoire were summoned to execute the music of the great masters at the Tuileries, and they still recall the pleasure with which the king listened to those ancient airs, souvenirs of his youth. Sometimes the duke of Orleans reproduced the splendor of former times at Chantilly. The duchess in her youth and beauty presided at these fêtes, yet she always feared becoming too much engrossed in the current of happiness, and was disquieted by so gay a life. On the eve of a fancy ball to be given at the Marsan Pavillon, she called a friend and besought her to tell her with all sincerity whether she thought her culpable in encouraging too frivolous, perhaps dangerous amusements. With charming naïveté, she both asked and feared a reply.

This incident, trivial in itself, reveals the depths of the duchess of Orleans' nature. She always experienced these scrupulous emotions, even when most absorbed in the excitement of the moment. Every thing in life interested her ; yet she constantly looked beyond the delights of the world towards heaven. While reviewing a past year, her soul thus expresses itself in devotion and prayer. "How quickly this year has passed away ! (1840) ; it has been rich in benedictions. May God grant us faithful, thankful hearts ! Let us serve Him in thought, word and deed. May he be with all our beloved ones, lead them to himself, protect and bless them. Ah ! how ready the heart is to make renewed vows each returning year. At this solemn hour, God and our beloved ones alone fill the thoughts."

The baptism of count de Paris took place in the month of May, 1841. "The spring has again returned in all its glory," she writes ; "it will be the most beautiful ornament of the anticipated fête ; the hours to be passed at Notre Dame on the second Sabbath of May, will be filled with emotion, prayer and hope. I desire to have my mind freed from all minor distractions. Yet I am tormented with anxiety, lest my child should be restless, afraid, or perhaps obstinate in that solemn hour. Read, I pray you, what Fénélon has written on the subject of Baptism ; those pages are beautiful and instructive."

Upon the 3d of May, she thus writes :—"Nothing could have been more beautiful or more solemn than yesterday's fête ; nothing more pure and touching than the sight of my little angel presented at the altar ; naught more profoundly moved than my poor maternal heart at that moment. If I was not deceived, the eyes of all present were filled with an expression of tender affection for the child. The prayers of the baptismal ceremony are beautiful, and I found them in accordance with my feelings as I followed them."

The birth of a second son, the duke de Chartres, increased the happiness of the royal family. A new horizon was arising to the duchess of Orleans, and while it filled her heart with joy, also gave rise to serious thought. There was no simple pleasure to which she was indifferent, and none which did not awaken some serious feeling.

A few abstracts from letters written at this period enable us to lift the veil from that pure, ardent soul.

"You know," writes she, "that nature has always a great influence over me. I find that we cannot sufficiently identify ourselves with it by observation. God speaks to the heart in its admirable manifestations. I think it good to cultivate a taste for it in the minds of children ; in admiring Nature, they learn to adore the Creator. You are right in believing that I do not allow a fine sunset or moonlight to pass by, without leading the hearts of my children to Him, who made these wonders of Nature. The emotion of the beautiful must be developed in these young minds.

"Yesterday I summoned up all my resolution to separate Robert from me, and to leave him in his new lodgings near Paris. It was a sort of triumphal promenade that wrung my heart. Paris ran joyously on before me while I led the little one ; my mother and attendants followed me. I had the pleasure of putting the poor child to sleep. I earnestly recommended him to Madame G—— who has charge of the dormitories, and gave Paris his supper ; he is as lovely as an angel. I love such an evening ; it calms the agitations of the heart. I now enjoy few such, for I endeavor to satisfy the demands of society as far as possible."

"The minds of children expand more freely when alone with their parents. I endeavor to be alone with my son as much as possible. To-day I went with him to Neuilly; I reclined upon his couch, and he slept in my arms while I showered a thousand caresses upon him. You should see how affectionate and thoughtful he is. Oh! the happiness of a *bourgeois* mother."

She again writes upon the return of the duke of Orleans from his last voyage to Africa.

"(June, 1840.) Congratulate me upon the return of my protector, my friend, my life. His absence seems to have been a long dream. Yesterday was a delightful day. I can only compare it with Paris' birthday. My heart was full of gratitude and palpitated with joy. Some visitors came, then we were left alone for a few moments. The little one was in my bed-chamber; the door was half open; he entered a little timidly, yet gave his hand to his father, who thinks him much grown. The family withdrew, and we dined together alone. The little one trotted around the table, singing, laughing and delighting his father's heart. It was a precious evening of intimate communion."

One of those events that painfully and frequently reminded France of the estimation in which the life of her king was held, interrupted the peaceable current of domestic joys.

"Providence has again protected us in a very

visible manner," writes the duchess of Orleans, after an attempted assassination; "the king, queen, my aunt, and all accompanying them, were spared; and we have seen the frustration of the eighth infernal attempt against so precious a life. A sense of the goodness of God has supplanted the first emotion of horror at such a crime. His grace fills my soul. I cannot sufficiently thank Him for preserving us from so frightful an evil. We immediately set out to join the family at St. Cloud. There above all, upon seeing the king and embracing him with my whole heart, did I fully realize God's goodness in preserving him to us. You will understand how fully my heart joined in the *Te Deum*, at the chapel of the castle." At another time, upon receiving intelligence of a like event, she entered the apartment where the Count de Paris was taking a lesson, and exclaimed, with great emotion, "kneel with me, and thank God."

These and like past experiences, impressed her still more sensibly with a feeling of the instability of all things, and a vague fear of being too completely happy. A letter written from Dreux, on the 7th of July, 1841, expresses in a touching manner, the almost superstitious feeling that sometimes oppressed her.

"I there saw, for the first time, my poor sisters-in-law's tomb, and the vaults wherein we all shall one day be received; how many tears will fall there —how many of my own, perhaps, may be shed, before my ashes are there deposited. These thoughts filled me with reflection, and led me to consecrate myself anew, and with full confidence to resign myself into the hands of God."

Nevertheless, the year 1841 ended in the plenitude of terrestrial benedictions. There was every reason to hope for a like future. The duke of Orleans, who had been ill for some time after his return from Africa, was entirely restored. The enthusiasm with which he was received while travelling with the duchess through the interior of France, bore testimony to his increasing popularity The king, perceiving his great capabilities, initiated him more and more into his confidence, and thus increased the hopes of all for the future.

"The prince," writes the duchess of Orleans, "to my great satisfaction, finds his duties greatly multiplied. I say, to my great satisfaction, though they often separate me from him, for I am ambitious for his advancement, and when I see his success in every thing he undertakes, and the increasing confidence placed in his judgment, even of those things near to the king's heart, I am proud of him and this pride sometimes suffices in lieu of himself."

IV.

Some anxiety was mingled with these happy presages. The duchess's health, of which she never was careful, began to fail, and her physicians insisted upon her trying the waters of Plombières. It was difficult to persuade her to this decision. She would be obliged to leave her children just at the time of the year when she could most freely enjoy their society in the lovely retreat at Neuilly, where their domestic life was less interrupted by duties to the world.

"If you knew," she writes before her departure, "how much I enjoy the beautiful summer weather in the country, and still more my children, who are so pretty, fresh and rosy, passing their days in the open fields. They are like little flowers in the midst of o'ershadowing plants."

She always yielded to the entreaties of her

friends, but now sought the consolations of religion with even more than her ordinary fervor, as if she would gain strength for unknown trials. On the 3d of July she left happy Neuilly with the duke of Orleans. They were accompanied by General Baudrand, M. de Montguyon and Madame de Montesquiou. While crossing the outer boulevard they passed a cemetery; the entrance to it was bordered with little shops, where crowns and funeral ornaments were offered for sale. "I despise those merchants who speculate on grief," said the prince ; and casting his eyes on the various inscriptions, he continued, "all possible wants are anticipated ; there, is a crown for a young girl, here, one for a little child." These words much moved the princess, her thoughts were doubtless of her absent children. The prince seeing her eyes fill with tears, smiled, took her hand in his and said, "No, that shall not be for a child, it shall perhaps be for a man of thirty-two years." She quickly raised her head and affectionately reproached him for dispelling one sad image by another still sadder." He soon succeeded in withdrawing her from sad thoughts, and their journey was cheerfully ended.

"I am so happy," said she, one evening, "that I have no desire to be restored to health. If I had not this trial, I should probably have one still more painful; physical pain, of all sufferings, is most supportable. I only go to Plombières because my friends desire it."

Although the duke of Orleans had expressed his desire that the princess might be spared the fatigue of public receptions, the department of Vosges received them with great acclamations. Triumphal arches were everywhere erected, and the carriage was surrounded by an animated multitude. They arrived at Plombières on the 5th of July; the duke spent the following day in examining the princess's establishment, and with tender care providing it with every thing that could render her sojourn agreeable. He recommended her many times to the care of those who were to remain with her, reminding them that she was ever negligent of her health, and ready to abuse returning strength.

Towards evening, the prince accompanied her through the pretty valley of St. Loup, and seeing her forming a bouquet of wild flowers, gathered a bunch of scabious plants and presented it to her. This ill-omened gift did not then attract attention, but was afterwards remembered by those who saw him present it.

Early on the morning of the 7th of July the prince departed. With much emotion the poor princess exclaimed, "Our separation will happily not be long; but the first moments are always painful."

On Thursday, the 14th, the weather was fine, and the duchess, desiring to test her strength, proposed a walk in the Gérarmé valley, where a peasant family of musicians had lived for several generations, and still took pride in exhibiting a piano made by the grandfather. The princess reposed a long time in the lowly cabin, where a young shepherd played all kinds of airs upon an old guitar, which she gaily tried after him, to the great delight of the poor family. It was late when they returned to Plombières. The princess was to receive several guests at dinner. Excited by her walk, and with a handful of flowers, she hastened up-stairs to arrange her toilette. Madame de Montesquiou had scarcely commenced dressing when a domestic came to say that General Baudrand wished to see her immediately. Astonished at this request, she made her repeat it twice. "Madame, he desired you to come down with all haste." "But, Monuier, you seem greatly agitated." "Madame, I conjure you go down quickly." "Oh! mon Dieu, what has happened? Has the king been assassinated?" "Madame, you might divine all; do not remain so near the princess; hasten down."

She found the general with a letter in his hand,

neither able to speak or rise from his chair. He handed her the fatal letter, containing only these words: "The prince-royal is dead." Had the duke of Orleans been assassinated? Had he perished in quelling a revolt, or been smitten by a sudden illness? These four words only apprised them of the irreparable evil, and they must announce it to the princess without any preparation or consolation. Time was flying, while the valet, with watch in hand, was exclaiming, "there is only a quarter of an hour to dinner; no one yet knows the news, and it is still possible to hide it for a while from the princess." This idea was speedily rejected; the prefect and physician were summoned. The latter insisted that she should at first be only apprised of the prince's serious illness. "Her life is dependent upon you," said he to the prefect; "you are responsible for it." It was finally decided that the prefect should prepare a telegraphic dispatch announcing the prince's alarming illness at Paris. A few moments longer deliberation and the princess would have left her apartment.

Madame de Montesquiou, imploring God for the strength she so much needed, ascended the stairs leading to the princess's apartment; upon reaching the glass door that separated it from the hall, she paused a moment; through the light curtains over the pane she saw the princess finish her toilette, turn her graceful figure and joyous face towards the door, and finally open it. Immovable against the wall, she could not summon sufficient courage to speak the words that would destroy so much happiness. "What! are you dressed?" said the princess gayly. But approaching nearer, she added, "What is the matter with you? you are very pale; what has happened to you? any misfortune in your family? are your children or husband ill?" Madame de Montesquiou pressed her hand in silence, yet the princess seems to feel no presentiment." "No, Madame, at length replied Madame de Montesquiou, I have suffered no misfortune, yet am not less unhappy—I have news for your royal highness." These words made her recoil. "Great God! what has happened? my children, the king?" "Alas! madame, the prince-royal is very ill." "Oh, my God! he is dead! I am sure of it! tell me" . . . —then falling upon her knees, she cried, "My God! have mercy on me; do not let him die! Thou knowest I could not survive him!" After remaining a few moments in prayer, she asked to see the dispatch and read it several times. "This is not the ordinary form of a telegraphic dispatch," she said, a doubt seeming to cross her mind, which was quickly dispelled by the prefect.

Then she burst into tears. She soon arose with determination, saying, "I will set out this moment, perhaps I shall still arrive in time to watch beside him." Orders were given for her departure. Some moments she yielded to hope; "perhaps I shall find him almost well; oh! then I shall be well reproved; but happy in being so." Then again her fears would arise—"He is so afraid of disquieting me; he must be very ill, from his thus apprising me." And her tears again began to fall.

At eight o'clock in the evening, the party left Plombières, surrounded by a deeply agitated multitude; every one sobbed in taking leave of the princess, who bade each one a touching adieu. They were obliged to pass the streets still adorned with flowers. The princess prayed and wept in uninterrupted silence. At midnight they reached Epinal. Madame de Montesquiou pressed her face against the window, trembling lest some public demonstration of grief should apprise the princess of her misfortune; but the multitude, filling the streets, were silent. In the darkness she could see the commander of the division advancing towards the door; without daring to ask any questions, she said in a low voice, "we are returning to Paris." He made no reply, and she understood by his gravity that he knew perhaps even more than she

They continued their route. In about an hour, it was announced that a coach was coming from Paris. " Open, open ! " cried the princess, but they retained her in the coach. At this moment she saw two men advancing towards her, and recognized M. Chomel, physician to the royal family. At the sight of him she uttered a piercing cry. " Monsieur Chomel ! ah ! my God ! the prince." " Madame, the prince is no longer living." " What do you say ? no, no, it is impossible. What illness could have thus smitten him ? Tell me, give me the death blow." " Alas, madame, an unparalleled catastrophe—a fall from his carriage. He did not recover consciousness ; a few German words pronounced from time to time, were his only signs of life ; doubtless a message for your Royal Highness." " No it cannot be," she exclaimed ; " I do not believe it ! " Then sobs stifled her words. Turning towards Madame de Montesquiou she asked, " But the illness of which you spoke ? " " Madame, that was only told to prepare you." " What ! you knew of his death ! what courage you had," she added, with that delicacy of feeling that always characterized her.

In profound darkness they were nearly an hour upon the route ; the princess sank back in the coach and continued to weep while her suite vainly endeavored to restrain their own grief; then sobs would break forth, in spite of themselves, which alone interrupted the silence of the night.

When day dawned, she exclaimed: "What a day is this for me!" then pressing General Baudrand's hand, added, "Oh! my dear General, you can understand my grief better than any other; you knew his worth, guided his early years, loved him so much! Oh! I have lost all; and France, also, has lost one whom she idolized, who knew her so well. But you do not know as I do—how good he was; what patience, what gentleness he possessed, what good counsels he gave me! No, no, I cannot live without him." One sought to draw her thoughts towards her children. "My poor children!" she exclaimed, in this first moment of grief; "he has all my heart, I can think only of him."

At four o'clock in the morning, her sisters-in-law met her; she threw herself without speaking into their arms, and seated herself beside them in the carriage. From that moment she seemed absorbed in one thought alone; that of contemplating once more the dear features she should no longer see living. The mournful procession paused, only for a few moments' repose, at one of the small villages.

After two cruel nights, they reached Neuilly about nine o'clock on the morning of the 16th of July. The king and the royal princes were awaiting the duchess, at the Eu Castle. They led her into a saloon, where she could only at intervals utter a few broken words. "Oh! my dear Helen," said the king, "the greatest of misfortunes has befallen me in my old age." "My dear daughter," resumed the queen, with gentle authority, "live for us—for your children."

After a few moments the princess left the saloon, supported by the king and the duke de Nemours. The queen and her children followed weeping. She directed to the chapel where the remains of the royal prince were deposited. The coffin, alas! already closed, stood covered with black in the centre of the chapel. She knelt beside it, fixed her eyes upon the long velvet pall, and after a short prayer, she arose strengthened, and returned to her apartments, where she clothed herself in the weeds of widowhood, which she never afterward laid aside.

Those who then saw her, were struck with the palor of her countenance; life seemed to have left her, and she remained for so long a time in a state of stupor, that fears were entertained for her frail health.

TRANSLATOR'S NOTE.

The following full account of the death of the duke of Orleans, published at the time in Galignani's *Messenger*, will doubtless be of interest to the reader. If this misfortune had not befallen the generally beloved duke of Orleans, how different might have been the destiny of Louis Napoleon:

Yesterday, July 13th, at 12 o'clock, the duke of Orleans was to leave Paris for St. Omer, where he was to inspect several regiments. His equipages were ordered and his attendants in readiness. Every preparation was made at the Pavillon Manan for the journey, after which his royal highness was to join the duchess of Orleans at Plombières. At eleven the prince got into a carriage, intending to go to Neuilly, to take leave of the king, queen, and royal family. The carriage was a four-wheeled cabriolet, or calèche, drawn by two herses, driven by a postilion. It was the conveyance usually taken by the prince when going short distances round Paris. He was quite alone, not having suffered one of his officers to accompany him. On arriving near the Porte Maillot, the horse rode by the postil ion, took fright, and broke into a gallop. The carriage was soon taken with great velocity up the Chemin de la Révolté. The prince seeing that the postilion was unable to master the horses, put his foot on the step, which was very near the ground, and jumped when about half way along the road, direct from Porte Maillot. The prince touched the road with both feet, but the impulse was so great that he staggered and fell, with his head upon the pavement. The effect of the fall was terrible, for his royal highness remained insensible on the spot. Persons instantly ran to his assistance and carried him into a grocer's by the wayside. In the mean time the postilion succeeded in getting command over his horses, turned the carriage round, and came to the door of the house where the prince was lying. His royal highness never recovered his senses. He was placed on a bed in a room on the ground floor, and surgical aid sent for The royal sufferer was bled, but it produced no good effect. Th news of the accident was conveyed to Neuilly. The queen immediately set out on foot and the king followed. His majesty was to be in Paris at 12 o'clook, to hold a council of ministers. His carriages which were ready, soon overtook their highnesses, who entered them with Madame Adelaide and the princess Clementine. He proceeded to the house into which the duke of Orleans had been taken. He, by that time, was nearly lifeless. It may be easy to imagine, but it is impossible to describe the grief of their majesties and royal highnesses at the spectacle they beheld. Dr. Pasquer, the prince royal's first physician, had just arrived, and was soon compelled to announce that there was an effusion upon the brain, and every moment the danger seemed to increase. A few words pronounced by the prince in German, gave a momentary hope, but it as quickly vanished. Marshals Soult and Gerard, the Ministers of Justice, Foreign Affairs, the Interior, the Marine, Finances, and Public Works, were admitted into the death-chamber of the royal duke. At two o'clock, as the case became more desperate, the king sent for the duchess de Nemours, who had remained at Neuilly. She came attended by her ladies in waiting. No pen can paint the afflicting scene presented by the chamber when the duchess of Nemours entered, and added her bitter tears to those of the rest of the family. The queen and princesses were on their knees by the bed-side, praying, and bathing the head of their departing son and brother with their tears. The princes were speechless and sobbing almost to suffocation. The king stood by, silent and motionless, watching with painful anxiety every fluctuation in the countenance of his dying heir. Outside the house, the crowd continued every moment to increase, every one was overwhelmed with consternation. The curé of Neuilly and his clergy instantly obeyed the king's summons. Under the influence of powerful medicaments the agony of the dying prince was prolonged. Life withdrew, but very slowly, and not without struggling powerfully against so much youthful strength. For a moment, respiration became free, and the beating of the pulse more perceptible. As the slightest hopes are grasped by hearts torn with despair, this scene of desolation was interrupted by a momentary calm, but the gleam soon passed away. At 4 o'clock, the prince showed the unequivocal symptoms of departing life, and in another half hour, he rendered his soul to God, dying in the arms of the king, his father, who at the last moment pressed his lips on the forehead of his lost child, hallowed by the tears of the afflicted mother, amid the sobs of the whole family. The prince being dead, the king drew the queen into an adjoining room, where the assembled ministers and marshals threw themselves at her feet, and endeavored to offer consolation. Her Majesty exclaimed, "What a dreadful misfortune has befallen our family, but how much greater for France." Her voice was then stifled by sobs and tears. The king seeing Marshal Gerard absorbed in grief, took his hand and pressed it, with an expression that showed his sense of his bereavement, but at the same time, a firmness and magnanimity, truly royal. The mortal remains of the prince were placed upon a litter and covered with a white sheet. The queen refused to get into her carriage, declaring her resolution to follow the corpse of her son to the chapel at Neuilly, where she desired them to be deposited. Consequently, a company of the 17th Light Infantry was hastily marched down from Combeine to line the procession on each side, and thus those men who had shared with the prince in all his dangers of the passage of the Iron Gates and the heights of Mongara, in Africa, served as the escort of his now lifeless body. Several of the men wept and called to mind the brilliant valor with which the duke of Orleans had assailed the enemy, and at the same time, the mild and delicate beneficence with which he had ever tempered the necessary rigor of command. At 5 o'clock, the mournful procession moved towards the Neuilly chapel. General Athalin walked at the head of the bier, carried by four non-commissioned officers. Behind, followed the queen, princess Adelaide, duchess de Nemours, princess Clementine, duke d'Aumale and the duke de Montpensier. Then came Marshals Soult and Gerard, the ministers, the general officers, the king's household and princes, with an immense number of other persons. The sad procession moved along the Avenue de Sablonville, and crossing the old Neuilly road, entered the royal park and traversed its whole length to the chapel. Here their majesties, the princesses and princes, after prostrating themselves before the altar, left their beloved child and brother, under the guardianship of God. In the evening the royal family remained in seclusion, except that the king conferred with his ministers. At 7 o'clock, Monsieur Bertin de Vaux, royal physician, set out for Plombières, where the duchess of Plombières had gone for the benefit of the waters. Amidst all their own affliction, during this disastrous day, the thought of the deprivation sustained by the duchess, was never out of the minds of her royal relations, and her name was repeatedly invoked in their lamentations. At length it was resolved that the duchess de Nemours and the princess Clementine should go to her with letters from the king and queen, and commenced their journey at 9 o'clock; they met the duchess returning to Neuilly.

V.

ALL these broken hearts were at length sustained by courage and faith.

"Yes, the Lord who smites," she writes five months after the sad event, "is a merciful Father; I have an unalterable conviction of this, even when I do not experience His consolations. I am in the midst of a contest that exacts blind faith; sometimes this faith is very strong, and then love and hope lighten my heart like a ray from above; but again, I feel all the weakness of my poor human nature and cannot raise my heart to God. What patience God has with us! How could we bear the burden laid upon us without Him?"

On the 14th of July of the same year, she writes from Dreux: "The date of this letter will sufficiently apprise you of my anguish in tracing these lines; but let not your heart be troubled; suffer not on my account."

"Thank God for me; He has wonderfully sustained me; He has granted me his peace, his presence; he has caused me to inhale the perfume of eternity, and strengthened and revived my poor, withered, stricken heart; my soul is filled with gratitude to God, whose mercy has caused such sweet consolations to spring up in the very bosom of death, and pours itself out in constant prayer. Upon returning here, I cried unto God: 'let me not falter; leave not my soul to be shipwrecked in despair, upon his tomb, where I realize the nothingness of life, and the mystery of eternity.' God had mercy upon me; he granted me grace to weep sweet tears, and I had almost said, tears of joy. My heart was filled with the thought of eternal felicity, and seemed already raised above the world, above my grief; it seemed already in harmony with that beloved soul, and to be enjoying his happiness. Peace, joy, light, mercy;—praises to the thousand times merciful God! Such are the experiences of my soul; thank Him, who has granted me such realization of his love, in the midst of death. The preceding days were terrible. Therefore I did not write to you. The 6th was the anniversary of the happiest day of my life; the 7th, that of his departure from Plombières; the 10th, was spent in prayers and tears at the chapel erected upon the spot where the happiness of my life was destroyed; the 11th, was the day of the solemn inauguration; finally, the 12th, the time of our pilgrimage to Dreux: I suffered a thousand deaths, and was fearfully depressed, till at the grave I again found the Lord. Now, I am at peace with Him, with my cross, with my future upon earth. Upon the Sabbath, at 10 o'clock, I shall take the communion in Paris, and beseech God to establish my soul in this peace, in this faith, in this love that nothing ought longer to trouble."

But this faith and love, had its rise and fall; if God sometimes granted her soul wings to mount and renew its strength, when again drawn towards the earth, the burden seemed still more weighty;—with heaven shut out, grief returned with all its rankling distress, remembrances and languor;—a familiar face, a date, sufficed to reawaken her anguish.

"Ah! what have I not suffered in speaking to W—— of the sacrifice his wife has made for him. How happy I deem her in being able to show him that she loves him more than all the world, and that to follow him she is ready to leave what is next dearest to her, her children. How I envy her!

But why should my tears fall at each event in life, at each foreign circumstance? My grief is like a glass, in which every object is reflected."

"1843. My sister-in-law is married. You will imagine that I had not courage to be present at the ceremony. I have been several times to St. Cloud, to see my good Louise. I love her so much, that I would go any distance to see her. The warm affection of the queen and Victoire did me good. I felt that each one of the family, suffered on my account. My heart was in the past, at Fontainbleau. A voice seemed to speak within my heart, of consolation, of eternity, of reunion. I passed the night in writing and thinking. My decision sometimes to appear in the parlor, cost me much anguish. The condolence of a general, yesterday, completely unnerved me: this often happens. I do not long remain in company, but I see the king and queen are pleased with the part I have taken, and this ought to be an indemnity for my sufferings."

"I have been obliged to receive the ministers and royal household with Paris; the reception was in the evening, in the very apartments where *he* appeared so often. They were brilliantly lighted as on former occasions, and presented the aspect of a fête; but alas, what a fête. In the midst of the crowd, there was but one thought, one regret; above all the surrounding group arose the noble cherished portrait of the prince painted and placed in my saloon by Monsieur Ingres; all my acts must pass under his eyes."

"There is nothing new in our sad and quiet home. The beautiful spring days make my children smile, and me weep. This season, he loved so much; we walked together, and rejoined the children at Neuilly. There he made me bouquets of the earliest flowers, and would not place them in his button-hole, as formerly, but said, 'they are not sombre enough for a man who has passed his thirtieth year.' He made the children play out of doors the whole day, and when I sent for them to come in, said to me smiling, 'you think the children are only well off, when under your own eye.' We dined at five o'clock in order to ride out after dinner. We passed the evening in the fragrant garden at Neuilly, making large bouquets. We returned at nine o'clock, and conversed upon the light or serious subjects of the moment. The politics of the day led to the favorite topic, the moral greatness of France, its defence, its isolated position, the moral valor of the people, etc., etc. I was struck with the indefatigable ardor of his mind, and the calm, admirable *sang-froid*, with which he judged his country, its position and future. . . .

"It is again spring, with the sweet air he loved to breathe, its flowers, its birds which he noticed, and to which he called my attention; then the happy children running in the fields; but every thing is changed. The world is no longer the same to me; the heavens, the sun, no longer smile upon me; or rather, their glory oppresses me, and I would hide myself, that I might not see this spring-tide, that newly awakens my grief."

And a few weeks later: "You are right in believing that the return of this month in which ended the happiest day of my life (not the happiest in itself, but in its promises) has not passed without the most harrowing comparisons. Six years ago this evening, I saw the sun set for the last time upon my native land. The confidence which inspired me through all the journey, then for a moment failed. I do not know if you remember the pains you had to revive my drooping courage. I shall never forget the impressions of that last evening in Germany. In the midst of animating hopes, I experienced an unaccountable grief which I attributed to the solemnity of the moment, but which seems to me now, like a presentiment of misfortune; but if my trials have been great, my happiness has been without parallel. I endeavor to be thankful, not only for the remaining good, but for those I have already possessed."

An accident, threatening the life of the entire royal family, interrupted the course of these sad days, in which she "passed from one degree of grief to another." In the account given to her friend, she paints her lively gratitude to God, for saving her beloved ones, as by a miracle; yet the bitterness of remembrance is mingled with her expressions of thanksgiving.

CHATEAU D'EU.

Yesterday the king wished to go out in the char à banc; I asked permission to accompany him with my two children; this request I had never made before. The king placed himself upon the first seat with Aumale and Paris; the queen, myself and Robert upon the second, François and Clementine upon the third; then Joinville and Auguste. The king descended to a little village upon the banks of the sea, where he visited a battery and made Paris fire a cannon, to which he applied the lighted match with a courage that enchanted everybody. He remounted the char à banc to return to Tréport, where he proposed to visit another battery. To reach Tréport, it is necessary to cross a bridge over a foaming torrent; the queen begged to alight, declaring that it was dangerous to cross so frail a structure; I had passed upon it when my horses began to be frightened; I besought the king to let me alight. "Nonsense," he exclaimed, "go on!" The cannon fired at the same moment, the sluice opened, the horses pranced, and the three were precipitated into the abyss. The char à banc would have been dragged in, if the postilion, of the thill-horses had not held them with a rare *sang-froid*, when they were even upon the very brink of the precipice. The band happily broke and the char à banc was arrested. I cannot tell you what I experienced in that moment which seemed to me a century. The king and my sons safe, I should have feared nothing, I would willingly have remained within. My heart was deeply affected in seeing all that I loved saved I thanked God; nevertheless, there was a little bitterness intermingled with this prayer; it was not entirely pure from murmuring. Why was this protection that kept us, *then* denied? Why now escape a danger a thousand times greater than that which was so fatal in its results? Not even a horse was wounded! That fall of twenty five feet into a gulf of whirling waters, without receiving a scratch! and then so light a fall that was so destructive! The more one thinks, the more one murmurs. I do not wish to feel so, yet my poor heart is thus constrained against my will.

After the accident, the king returned with us upon foot, to the Tréport battery. An immense crowd followed him with acclamations of joy ; every one seemed happy ; I only wept in the midst of this cortège, remembering another, when the king also upon foot, giving his arm to the queen, followed the victim of a like disaster."

As we have foreseen, her children only bound her to life ; "they only," said she, "make me live, and sometimes conceal the dregs of the cup from me. A vail of melancholy is cast over everything but the joyous life of my children.

"To-day being Paris' birthday, I invited the poor childen from Eu and Tréport, here, which gave them great pleasure. I also endeavored to throw aside all sorrow ; I made myself a child, and took a childish pleasure in the enjoyment of those around me."

She mingled her life with that of her sons, and the slightest circumstance drew her thoughts instinctively towards them.

"I have lately been with the queen to visit Monsieur Scheffer. His St. Augustine truly edified me ; it is a masterpiece. Nothing could be more sublime than St. Monica's countenance ; one would believe her to be already in heaven ; her expression is full of God ; I was deeply touched, especially, when I pressed Paris' hand within my own."

The absorbing interest of her mind, was the education of her sons as their father would have desired them to be educated, and to work for the happiness of France, which she could only do through them. It was touching to see so great a mind absorbed in the most tender care of their health, plays, and early studies; nothing seemed trivial to her, for she always bore in mind the great end she wished to attain. Thus, the attention she gave to politics, the assiduity with which she followed public discussions, and the just disquietude she felt concerning the state of the public mind, towards the close of the year 1847, were only varied forms of her ever maternal vigilance. She had that sort of sympathy with France, which does not necessarily imply approbation, but comprehension of the ideas by which a country is agitated. From the first, she felt the threatenings that preceded the storm, and though she like others could not render an exact account of the extent and nature of the danger, she long experienced the anxiety that agitated the minds of many upon the first days of February, and which quickly spread to the court.

She writes in 1847: "There are subjects in the order of the day, that make me blush to open the journals. I am sad from the very depths of my heart at the general discontent of the public mind, and the discredit it reflects upon the higher classes.

"The moral evil does not manifest itself in sudden agitation or outbreaks, but in the weakness of the rulers and indifference of the people. A reaction must take place. A skilful hand is necessary to suppress the disease, a sympathetic heart is needed to heal it. Alas!, my thoughts dwell only upon one prince who understood this epoch, whose delicate soul felt the reaction of his country's moral sufferings. He would have known how to temper them, and to inspire the country with a new elation; his decision would have seconded his intentions; his wisdom would have directed the right; France has need of him, but God has taken him from her!

"What will our future be? This thought agitates my nights and troubles my solitary hours. The evil is profound, because it attacks the morality of the population. Is it momentary, or is it the indication of weakness? I do not know how to judge, but I pray God to send a reviving breath over our withered France."

However exorbitant the claims of the contending parties might be, the duchess of Orleans desired that they might at least be examined, and was afflicted at seeing the king's ministers fully confident that reason and right were on their side, without due deliberation. But her fears and preferences for a policy that she believed best calculated to establish the throne and to calm hostile passions, she loyally laid before the royal family, but did not permit them to extend beyond her own immediate circle. If she was mistaken in believing that it was possible to prevent the disasters of 1848, it must be granted that the measures of many others were at fault. Malevolence only can reproach her with having foreseen them, and the only reply worthy of her, would be the simple narration of her actions, words and even gestures, in that journey on the 24th of February, when the suddenness of the shock revealed the depths of each heart. It is a pity to pass in silence the rarest examples of dignity and courage, in those sad times. One can scarcely refrain from pausing before the majestic figure of the queen, so bold in danger, so submissive in misfortune ; or not render homage to the prince who so nobly sacrificed his rights, confronting all perils, without other ambition than that of saving the widow and children of a tenderly regretted brother. But since it belongs to us only to review the facts so many times related, and it is our aim to present the character of the duchess of Orleans, we must follow her alone in the midst of the general disorder; it is her alone we must see at the Tuileries. If we have had the happiness of attaining our end, the duchess of Orleans will not appear on that 24th of February different from what she was on the preceding evening or the morrow, and circumstances alone will have served to manifest her noble qualities. There is always the same mélange of feminine delicacy, decisive action, and exquisite sensibility.

VI.

The night preceding the 24th was one of great anguish for the princess; the bravest began to be disquieted: "We have not even had strength to pray," said she; and, indeed, what at first seemed only a ministerial crisis, suddenly assumed the aspect of a revolution. The less they were prepared, the greater was the disorder; each moment bore away the hope a previous one had excited; the most popular names, even, succeeded to the power;—from Guizot to Thiers; from Thiers to Odilon Barrot. The reform—that last concession which one would believe magical in its calming effect, since it had suppressed factitious passions—had been promised and the news spread from rank to rank of the national guard, and produced a powerful effect upon the groups pressing round the entrance to the Tuileries. The king, in the midst of the counsels and contradictory rumors borne to him in the unaccountable confusion, decided to make a last effort. Followed by his sons and aides-de-camp, several of whom had not even time to put on their uniform, he mounted a horse and reviewed the troops ranged round the interior court and upon the Place du Carrousel. The queen and princesses, near the duchess of Orleans and her young sons, are at the windows, following him with anxious eyes. Many cries of "long live the king," for an instant reanimate their hopes; but soon they are dissipated by shouts of "long live the Reform!"* The king is not deluded. He feels the coldness with which he is received by the national guard, and the abandonment of those upon whom he ought to be able to rely; his countenance expresses neither fear nor agitation, but the calm melancholy of a man wounded to the very heart. He returns to his apartment, and while he is reflecting for a few moments with his head buried in his hands, an officer precipitately enters, exclaiming:—"Sir, there is not a moment to lose; give orders, or abdicate." It is about eleven o'clock in the morning. The king, after a moment's silence, says: "I have always

* For an interesting account of this crisis, see vol. 12th of the London Illustrated News, published in 1848.—*Translator.*

been a pacific king ; I will abdicate." Then arising, he opened the door to the saloon where the queen and princesses were assembled, and repeated in a firm tone : "I will abdicate."

At these words, the queen and princesses rush towards him, and conjure him to retract those fatal words. The duchess of Orleans bows respectfully before him, and takes his hand, which she kisses with tenderness ; "Do not abdicate, sir, do not abdicate," she exclaims, bursting into tears. But the king, without replying, returns to his cabinet, followed by the princesses, and slowly writes the act of abdication, which he finally reads in a loud voice : "I abdicate the crown, which the national voice called me to wear, in favor of my grandson, the count de Paris. May he succeed in the great task that falls upon him to-day !" "May he resemble his grandfather !" exclaims the queen. The duchess of Orleans renews her passionate entreaties with the king ; she begs him "not to lay a burden upon his grandson that he has not sufficient power to sustain himself." Her maternal instinct told her too well, that to tear the crown from the king, was not to give it to her son. When she can no longer hope to obtain any thing by her prayers, and the king has finished the last letter of his name, she throws herself, weeping, into the queen's arms. For a few moments they hold each other's hands in silence. These moments are short;—the king is pressed to depart; words of adieu are exchanged in haste. He leaves, followed by the queen and several of the princesses.* The duke de Montpensier does not

* The following is Lamartine's account of the king's departure from the palace:

"The king took off his uniform, laid his sword upon the table, put on a plain black coat, and gave his arm to the queen, leaving the palace to the new *régime*. The silence of this last moment was only interrupted by the stifled sobs of the spectators. Without any striking prestige as a king, this prince was beloved as a man; his long experience inspired men's minds with confidence, while his attentive affability attached him to the hearts of all. His old age, deserted for the first time by fortune, excited commiseration. Political superstition stood aghast at the sight of this last fugitive from the throne. It seemed as if with him the wisdom of the empire was retiring. The queen, leaning upon his arm, seemed proud to fall at her post with her husband and monarch who had been, and who remained without a throne and without a country upon earth. The aged couple, inseparable in prosperity and in exile, presented a most affecting spectacle. Even republicans would have dropped a tear at the departure of this father and mother, driven from the hearth where they thought to leave their children. The spectators kissed their hands and touched their dress. . . . At the moment of crossing the threshold of his cabinet, the king, turning back to the duchess of Orleans, who had risen to follow him, exclaimed, "Remain here, Helen!" The princess threw herself at his feet, conjuring him to take hesitate to leave his sick wife under the care of a friend, that he may protect his father's departure.

The king, in quitting the Tuileries, believed that his absence would appease the tumult, and leave his grandson upon the throne, under the direc-

her with him. She forgot royalty, and thought only of the father of her husband. Her entreaties, however, were in vain. . . . . A messenger had been sent to order one of the royal carriages, but the mob had already burnt them on the Place du Carrousel, and the groom who had gone to order one, had been killed by a discharge from the insurgents. It was, therefore, necessary to abandon this mode of departure. The king left by the door of a subterraneous passage, which leads from his apartments to the garden of the Tuileries. He crossed on foot that same garden which Louis XVI., Marie Antoinette, and their children, had crossed in their flight to the National Assembly,—that path to the scaffold, or to exile, which monarchs never retrace. The queen comforted her husband with a few words, uttered in a low tone. A group of faithful servants, of officers, women and children, followed in silence. Two little hackney carriages, engaged by an officer in disguise, on the public stand in the street, drew up at the exit of the Tuileries, at the bottom of the terrace. Here the nerves of the queen, over-excited by the prolonged crisis she had suffered, altogether failed her at the last moment; she gasped, tottered, and fell. The king was obliged to raise her in his arms, and place her in a carriage, which he himself immediately entered. The duchess de Nemours, the ornament and beauty of the court, bathed in tears, entered the second carriage with her children, seeking with a restless eye for her husband, who was

tion of his daughter-in-law; but events marched more quickly than his imagination could follow. Scarcely had he left the palace, when royalty itself was in doubt. The insurgents approached the railings of the interior court, and threatened to break

still engaged amidst the difficulties and dangers of his duty. A squadron of cuirassiers surrounded the two carriages, which set off at full speed along the Quay de Passy, towards St. Cloud. The duke de Nemours remained to the last to secure the safe departure of the duchess of Orleans. Whilst the evacuation of the palace by the troops was thus effected, a small number of officers and counsellors, some devoted to the dynasty, some to the person, and some only to the misfortunes of a lady, were in consultation round the duchess of Orleans and her children. . . . The report of three cannons shook the windows of the apartment. It was the artillery of the palace which was firing on the people as they issued from the quay to the Carrousel. The princess sent General Gourgaud to stop the firing, and the artillerymen extinguished their matches in token of peace. General Gourgaud returned, and M. Dupin followed him. M. Dupin was one of the great authorities of public opinion. Whatever course he took, multitudes followed in his steps. . . . . The duchess saw him enter the apartment, the presage at once of strength and peace. 'Well, sir,' cried she, 'what are you come to tell me?' 'I am come to tell you, madam,' replied M. Dupin, in a saddened but hopeful tone, 'that perhaps the part of a second Maria Theresa is reserved for you.' 'Direct me, sir' replied the princess; 'my life belongs to France and to my children.' 'Well, then, madam, let us depart; we have not a moment to lose. Let us go to the Chamber of Deputies.'

them. The crowd, which had quickly pressed into the king's saloon, dispersed, and the duchess of Orleans was only surrounded by her household (not one composing it abandoned her for a moment) and a few deputies, who pressed her to take the regency,

This, in fact, was the only course for the duchess to take. The cause of the regency, already lost in the streets, might be retrieved in the chamber of deputies, if that body in discredit among the people, by courtliness of spirit, had preserved sufficient ascendency to arrest the fall of the monarchy. The presence of a woman, the grace and innocence of a child, were more powerful attractions than any speeches. The bloody mantle of Cæsar, exhibited at the tribune, was less affecting than the tears of a young and beautiful woman, presenting her orphan child to the representatives of a chivalrous people.

It has already been stated that the king and queen, with the duchess de Nemours and her children, seated themselves in two hired coaches, on the Place de la Concorde. On reaching Saint Cloud, the king took court carriages and proceeded to Trianon, where he stopped for a few moments, as if to allow time for fortune to overtake him, and arrest his flight. . . . . When evening set in, the king departed, taking the road to Dreux, which place he reached early in the night. . . . He informed the Mayor and sub-prefect that it was his intention to remain four days at Dreux, and there to await the decision of the chambers respecting his future place of residence, and the position which the nation might thenceforward allot to him. . . The king retired to rest at two o'clock; while he was sleeping a friend arrived from Paris and announced the proclamation of as the last chance of saving the monarchy. "It is impossible," she replies, "I cannot bear such a burden; it is beyond my strength; no one is prepared to see me regent; I myself less than any one."* While she is speaking, the sound of guns is heard;

the republic. . . . A council, composed of members of the royal family and their friends, was held at the king's bedside. It was determined that the members of the family should effect their escape separately and in different directions. The fugitives were disguised in clothes of the plainest possible description. (The account, from page 302 of Lamartine's Works, of several pauses and incidents on the route, is most interesting, but too lengthy to be here introduced.) Through friendly mediation, it was arranged that the king should embark at Havre, on board of one of the vessels employed in the conveyance of cattle and provisions from France to the English coast. Adverse winds prevented the carrying out of this plan. . . . The king and queen departed from Havre in a steamer, and landed at Newhaven, where he was informed that the hospitality of his son-in-law, the king of the Belgians, had assigned the place of Claremont as his abode."

* Monsieur Lamartine, in his "History of the Revolution of 1848," expresses his opinion that it was the duchess of Orleans' desire to hold the regency, and that "Louis Philippe and his ministers perished under the unforeseen consequences of wresting the regency from the young mother of an infant king." "If," continues Lamartine, "if instead of laying before the people that ambiguous abdication, which made no provision for the regency, and which suffered contending parties to catch sight of the duke de Nemours behind the formal abdication, if M. de Girardin, the bearer of the intelligence, had

a few minutes more, and the Tuileries will be invaded. She must fly, to save her life and children, or face the perils of the day, in order to preserve the crown for the count de Paris, and to defend the rights of France. Placed between these two alternatives, her duty appears clearly defined ; she is neither in hesitation or trouble. Taking the hands of her two children, she crosses the long gallery which separates her from her apartment, and pauses before their father's portrait : "It is here that we must die," says she, calmly ; she then gives orders for the doors to be opened, ready to submit, with her children, to a frightful death, if her tranquil courage cannot conquer the mobile mind of

represented before the imagination and the heart of the nation a young mother reigning by popular favor in the name of her son ; if this beloved princess, untainted with the shadow of a charge, had herself appeared in the court of the palace, and presented her child to the adoption of the country, there is no doubt nature would have triumphed over the people. But the duchess of Orleans, even at this last hour, was, as it were, in exile with her children in the apartments of the palace assigned to her. . . . In M. de Girardin's interview with her, not a word, from her, indicated a mortified ambition, or a concealed sorrow. Her griefs were unmingled, not only with all political intrigue, but even with the feelings of ambition. She exhibited the calmness and disinterestedness of a mother who entirely forgets herself amidst the recollections of her husband and her hopes for her son."

the defying multitude, whose shouts already reach her.

At this moment, two deputies hastily entered, and in the name of the duke de Nemours, besought her, without delay, to join him at the bridge across the garden ; he had watched over the king's departure, and returned to lead her safely out of the Tuileries. She recognized in them aid from heaven ; she had no time for questions, and was almost borne onward by the multitude, seeking to protect her against the bayonets pointed towards the Place du Carrousel. As she passed through the garden-gate, the mob were taking possession of the Tuileries.

Upon reaching the Place Louis XV., the princess perceived the duke de Nemours upon horseback ; but separated by the crowd, she could not communicate with him. She was ignorant of the measures he had taken to conduct her to St. Cloud. Her instinctive courage pressed her towards the Boulevards ; there she would find herself confronting the true people of Paris, now nothing more than a troop of rebels. Perhaps she might perish there ; yet perhaps her presence might bring them to reason. Monsieur Dupin seeks to turn from this direction. A voice cries, " A la Chambre !" all repeat " A la Chambre." Believing herself to be following the direction of the duke de Nemours, she permits herself to be led towards that quarter. He himself in the distance sees her, without the power to detain her, and nothing remains for him but to follow. The crowd, well disposed at this moment, cry, "long live the duchess of Orleans!" "long live the count de Paris!" while it forms like two walls, between which the princess advances, holding the count de Paris by the hand, while Monsieur Scheffer, an officer of the national guard, follows, bearing the little duke de Chartres, who is ill, in his arms. At this moment, Monsieur Odilon Barrot was seeking in the Tuileries for the duchess, in order to lead her to the Hôtel-de-Ville; but he could not force an entrance, and returned to the chamber, which he reached after her.

When the princess entered the assembly, the disorder was extreme; the deputies were pressing to the tribune; a strange crowd filled the passages, obstructing the progress of the royal cortège. Some cry, "away with the princes; we will have no princes here!" others cry still louder, "long live the duchess of Orleans! long live the count de Paris!" She takes her place near the tribune, and remains there, with her two children at her side; behind her are the persons of her suite, struggling to keep the multitude from gathering around her. Monsieur Dupin ascends to the desk, and announces that the act of abdication is to be borne by Monsieur Barrot to the chamber; in the meantime, he insists that the unanimous acclamations with which they have welcomed the count de Paris as king, and the duchess as regent, be clothed in a legal form. At these words, violent protestations burst forth from a part of the chambre and tribune. The president commands all foreigners to withdraw, and entreats the princess to retire, "out of respect to the law." "Sir," she replies, "this is a royal session." Several of her friends seeing the tumult increase, entreat her to withdraw. "If I withdraw from here, my sons will never return again," she responds, while remaining immovable at her place. But the crowd presses, the noise increases, and the heat becomes so excessive that the princes can scarcely breathe. The princess permits herself to be led through the left gallery, extending round the semicircle, to the higher seats, facing the tribune, and there seats herself, with the duke de Nemours and her children. At this moment, Monsieur Odilon Barrot, returned from the Tuileries, obtains a hearing, while he proclaims, "the crown of July rests upon the head of a child." Then are heard acclamations of "long live the count de Paris!" The duchess arises as if about to speak. Upon one side of the chamber the cry is, "Speak, speak!" while the other silences the voice. She utters these words: "We are come here, my sons and myself—" but is quickly interrupted. She makes a new effort to make herself heard, but in vain, and resumes her seat. Several orators succeed one another, in a confusion impossible to describe. Finally, Monsieur de Lamartine advances towards the tribune. His first words revive the hopes of the princess' friends; but with her sweet and gentle smile, she makes a motion of her finger that shows them she does not share their illusion. Towards the end of the discourse, violent blows reverberate through the hall; the doors of the journalist department, upon the right of the tribune, are forced open by armed men, who precipitate themselves into the apartment with loud vociferations; they level their loaded guns, and walk from one side of the chamber to the other till they perceive the royal group, at which they aim. The majority of the deputies withdraw. The duchess of Orleans and her sons find themselves discovered; there remains between them and the bullets only a remnant of the deputies, who have stationed themselves before them. From the calmness of her countenance, one would judge that she was incurring no danger; leaning over the nearest seat, she gently rests her hand upon the shoulder of an attendant, and says in a low voice which betrays no emotion, "what do you counsel me to do?" The reply is, "Madame, the deputies are no longer here, we must go to the presidency in order to rally the 'chambre.'" "But how shall I reach there?" she responds, without moving or appearing agitated by the bullets flying over her head. "Follow me," replies Monsieur Jules de Lasteyrie. From seat to seat, they descend to the left end of the hall, where they find themselves in a passage reserved for delegates, leading to a dimly lighted corridor; two folding doors separate it from the hall; one is open. Monsieur de Lasteyrie forces a passage through the crowd with his arms; perceiving a company of national guards without the door, he commands them to hastily rank around the duchess of Orleans, which they immediately do."*

But in the meanwhile, the crowd is again formed; the princess and her children are forced against the closed door, and can advance no further. She however disengages herself, but before she is able to seize the hands of her sons, they are in the darkness violently separated from her, and she is dragged to the very hall of the presidency. There, not

* In her exile the duchess of Orleans sent a souvenir to each of these brave men men who, in accomplishing their duty contributed to the preservation of her life upon that day.—AUTHOR'S NOTE.

finding herself followed by her children, she utters a despairing cry that resounds through the hall above the noise of the tumult. Only these words are heard, pronounced with singular energy : "My chil dren ! my children." The children were detained in the narrow passage. The duke de Chartres, overthrown and for an instant lost under the feet of the crowd, is recovered and borne to the apartment of one of the hussars. A workman in his blouse, seized the count de Paris and carried him by force in his arms, doubtless in order to defend him, but in the midst of the noise, disorder and darkness, each mistrusted his neighbor. The unhappy child is torn from him and borne, or rather thrown, from arm to arm till he reaches the corridor, where Monsieur de Montguyon lets him down through a window into an interior court, and leads him back to his mother.

Scarcely has she seen him, and been assured that the youngest one is in safety, than all traces of emotion disappear. The sight of her son at once restores her presence of mind, and passing instantly from violent despair to entire self-possession, she again seeks counsel from those around her. A reunion of the dispersed deputies was not to be dreamed of ; the President's hall might perhaps be invaded like the Court of Justice ; the Hôtel-des-

Invalides is the nearest place; there she may at least find a temporary asylum, and deliberate upon the measures best to be taken. A carriage is found at the gate; the princess enters it with the count de Paris, escorted by two national guards; Monsieur de Lasteyrie, takes the reins from the coachman's hands, in order to hasten departure. Monsieur Mornay reaches the entrance to the Hôtel-des-Invalides almost as soon as the duchess. The princess ascends to the governor's apartments. By a seeming fatality, Marshal Molitor is ill and cannot leave his room. There are only a very small number of old soldiers around, and it is feared that they will refuse to obey the orders of those unknown to them. "Let orders be given in my name," says the princess, without hesitation. The marshal expresses his fears for her safety and that of her sons; he represents the isolated position of the Hôtel-des-Invalides, and its ill defence from within. "No matter, sir," she replies, "it is a good place to die in, if we are not to see to-morrow, or to remain in, if we can defend ourselves."

The duke de Nemours, with several others, has rejoined her; they consult how troops may be reassembled for defence, or how it is possible to return to Paris. The princess seeks to communicate her ardor for resistance, listens to their advice with calmness, and replies as frankly and with as much authority as if she was in peaceable possession of the regency, holding council at the Tuileries. Among those who accompanied her, some remain near her, while others hasten to different ministers and promise to return with the latest news.

During those hours of anxious waiting, neither body nor soul sinks under the weight of fatigue and emotion. She is scarcely seen to repose for a moment. It is not the excitement of imminent danger that inspires her courage, but a clear and precise view of duty, with all its risks. About midday, Monsieur Biesta arrives from the minister of the interior, with the message from him for the princess, that in spite of all his efforts, he can only summon a very small number of national guards, and that the mob are gaining ground and approaching the Hôtel-des-Invalides. Others return from the minister of war, and also report that there is no longer any thing to hope for, that the insurgents already know her retreat, and that her life and that of her sons is in great danger. "Is there no one here who advises me to remain?" asked she; "if there is so much as one person, only one, who counsels me to remain, I will do so. I think more of my son's life than of his crown; but if his life is necessary to France, a king, even a king of nine years of age, must know how to die."

However, at six o'clock in the evening, Monsieur Barrot, who had remained all day at the ministers', and had not for a moment paused from his generous efforts, reaches the Hôtel-des-Invalides; he relates what had passed at the Hôtel-de-Ville, and affirms that all is going wrong, that to-morrow it will be impossible to renew the contest, but that now they must retire from a place that will be the first point of attack, and which it is no longer possible to maintain without troops or munitions. The princess is entreated to leave the Hôtel-des-Invalides secretly, and to conceal herself in the neighborhood, where she can return on the following morning if it becomes possible to organize a defence. But at no price would she expose the old soldiers to dangers she would not share herself. "I will remain altogether, or withdraw altogether," is her reply. When it was at length decided to leave the place, she was conjured to disguise herself in some simple dress, that attention might not be attracted towards her. She rejects this idea with a measure of indignation. "If I am taken," she exclaims, "I will be taken as a princess;" and they were only able to prevail upon her to tear off the lace that covered her robe. But she was happily not recognized in the short transit from the Hôtel-des-Invalides to "la rue de Monsieur," which she made upon foot, leaning upon the arm of Monsieur de Mornay. The count de Paris, holding the hand of Monsieur de Lasteyrie, followed a few steps behind her; from distance to distance, others of the suite dispersed, that no suspicion might be excited; then came the duke de Nemours, who never lost sight of her. At his earnest prayers, the duchess of Orleans consented to leave Paris, with her son, that same evening, upon condition that she might await the results of the morrow at a château upon the environs. Upon entering the carriage, she turned towards one who had been with her all that day, and said: "Upon one word, to-morrow, or in ten years, I return here." The noise of wheels at night, in those deserted streets, attracted the attention of a few insurgents; they called out for an arrest, and aimed at the coachman; but he spurred the horses across a barricade, at the risk of shattering the carriage, and thus left Paris.*

* "The duchess of Orleans had friends at Lille, and the numerous force garrisoned in that city might, by her presence, have been won from the republic, and urged by enthusiasm to defend the cause of a woman and a child. The thought of showing herself to the troops, and claiming the throne for her son, occurred to the duchess during this last night of her stay in France; but the crime of civil war stood between the throne and this thought, and the duchess of Orleans renounced it. . . .

Reaching the deserted château at night, the princess first thought only of refreshment and repose for her exhausted child ; even this was difficult to obtain, for they did not dare light a fire, lest the smoke might betray their presence to the inhabitants of the village. She finally laid down beside him, and when she saw him quietly sleeping, for the first time experienced a feeling of fear.

Some will perhaps remember the frighful tempests in the month of February, at the moment when the king vainly endeavored to embark for England. The princess mistook the sound of the wind for that of the beating of drums, and expected every moment to see the chamber where her child was reposing, invaded. The night and day of Friday was spent in like anguish. Upon Saturday, the 26th, the duke de Chartres was restored to her, and though still ill, was so happy at seeing his mother and brother, that the countenances of all three were somewhat brightened.

At Ems, she was met by her mother. Whilst her memory reverted to the pure but short-lived happiness she had enjoyed in France,—to her bereavement, her sorrow, and the ruin of her fortune through the faults of others,—she tranquilly resigned herself to the doom pronounced by her adopted country, where, among persons of all political parties, the name of the duchess of Orleans will ever be associated with sentiments of admiration affection and respect."—TRANSLATOR.

Evil tidings arrived at the same time from Paris. Monsieur de Mornay announced that they must not lose a moment, but regain the frontier, and brought a passport to Germany, which he had obtained with great difficulty. The princess still resisted ; she consented to leave Paris, but was unwilling to leave France. The count de Paris also repeated his wish to remain in his own country, and his words seemed to his mother like a warning from heaven. Her friends still insisted upon her departure ; she must go and make preparation. At the end of several moments, Monsieur de Montesequion who had returned from giving his last orders, found her upon her knees, praying aloud ; the count de Paris was kneeling beside her, and the duke de Chartres, upon his bed, had his little hands clasped together. He made a memorandum of her words ; they were : "My God, protect France, protect my poor children, protect the generous host who has not shrunk from offering us hospitality in these dangerous moments ; let this act bring upon the family a shower of benedictions, and forbid that the remembrance of our sojourn with them should ever be unwelcome."

A driving rain, violent wind, and complete darkness, rendered her departure lugubrious enough. Few words were uttered ; she only pressed the hand of her hosts, and took the rings from her own fingers and placed them upon theirs.

All the way from Pontoise to Beaumont, the railroads were disconnected and the bridges on fire. They were obliged to take the post to Amiens. At Lille they were obliged to wait several hours for the Belgian convoy. The princess and her children remained in the coach. Some one recognized them, but no one betrayed them.

In crossing the frontier, the duchess of Orleans burst into tears; monsieur de Mornay, who had accompanied her, could not restrain his own. "Our tears are very different," said she to him; "you weep for joy, that we are saved, while I weep for grief at leaving France, that France upon which I call down all the benedictions of heaven. In whatever place I may die, France knows well, the last throbbing of my heart will be for her.

"When the thought passes through my mind that I shall never see France again," said she, many years after, "I feel as if my heart would break."

VII.

It was not the duchess of Orleans' nature, to be long overcome by grief. Her courage quickly returned; not that courage for action to which she was no longer called, but that cheerful resignation, at times almost serene, which she had besought of God daily for ten years, and most frequently obtained.

"Perhaps this trial," said she, upon reaching Cologne, "will be useful to my sons: in exile they will receive such an education as their grandfather received. Who knows but it may be of more value to them than any other?

She had, as one would imagine, brought nothing away from Paris; the little money gathered up in their hasty departure, had been exhausted in the journey; she passed the first days of her exile in the veritable want of all things. Her mother's family, it is true, were eager to offer her hospitality, and more than hospitality—all that watchful affections could desire. She was deeply touched, but declared it was impossible for her to accept any thing further than a shelter for herself and family. It was only upon this condition that she established herself at Eisenach, early in May. There she lived in the most simple manner, till she was certain of the fortune that remained to her; she felt this trial less than all others. Indeed she did not dwell upon it; the queen of Belgium in her anxiety for her, sent a mutual friend to Eisenach to see that her sisters and nephews were in want of nothing. She found her in a large room without fire, clothed in the light apparel she wore upon leaving the Tuileries. The heat of a stove made her sick; a fireplace was a thing unknown in that part of Germany; the princess turned these trials into pleasantry. What mattered they to her?

A less lofty, gentle soul, would have suffered a thousand accessory pains, which, preöccupying the mind, sometimes oppresses it more than the misfortune itself. Returning as an exile to the place from which she had departed in the buoyancy of hope; passing, in a few hours, from the highest to the most humble position; from incessant excitement to the monotonous repose of a small village ; sinking, after the agitation of those latter days, into a forced inactivity, she had certainly sufficient cause for *ennui*, —that weariness of life which troubles the harmony of the soul, and seems, for a time at least, to take away its strength ; but the princess was as indifferent to trivial chagrins as to trivial pleasures. She suffered deeply, as she had enjoyed deeply, and her heart, far from neglecting consolations cordially offered, accepted them with simplicity, almost with delight.

Nothing could be more touching than the welcome with which the inhabitants of Eisenach received the princess ; their discreet sympathy was expressed in a thousand ways. Their hearts were penetrated with a respectful, tender pity. When she passed through the streets, they scarcely fixed their eyes upon her, lest they might reawaken her grief ; the thought of all was, how they might divert and soften it. When the spring returned, her chamber, despoiled of all other luxury, was always supplied with flowers ; the wealthy inhabitants contributed their exotics, the poor their wild flowers ; all sent their tribute.

" A truce to complaints," writes she on the 20th of May, 1848 ; " we are in a peaceful valley, where anarchy, which elsewhere rumbles, is still silent.

You are apprised that I have accepted the hospitality offered by my uncle with such paternal goodness. Our habitation is just what we need ; the house is charming, the country magnificent, the brave people discreet and full of delicate sympathy. I bless God for having granted me this asylum ; but sometimes the separation from all those who are dear to me ; the great distance from that family I love so dearly, from that mother whom I venerate, from that sister, angel of consolation,—anxiety for the future, poignant remembrances of the past, trouble my soul, and make me almost overlook the blessings God still grants. Sometimes I feel as if shut up in the very ends of the earth, dead yet living, overpowered. with thirst to devote myself to that country I love so much, and riveted by a chain that wounds at each respiration. My existence is but a continual mental contest, in which I am animated by one single desire :—the salvation and happiness of France. This prayer calms me ; I can have no more ardent wish for the country I love so passionately. . . . . We must not fall back upon ourselves, but advance, unfalteringly, fixing our eyes on high, from whence strength and consolation will not always be denied."

While she was writing, a bloody contest was again rendering the fate of this country, so ardently beloved, doubtful. The four days in June, during which this struggle lasted, were more painful for her to endure than those of her own peril; the acute suffering, mingled with the accents of patriotic pride, are revealed in her letters at this time.

"O, my dear friend," she writes on the 9th of July, 1848, "what anguish, what torture did I endure during those four days of suspense, when the fate of France, the fate of entire society, was being decided at Paris! when our friends were upon the brink of a precipice; when the family of those so devoted to us in exile were running the greatest dangers. I could only cry out to God. God has saved France, spared our friends; I bless him for it, yet feel my heart oppressed with sadness. What a victory! what an epoch we live in for witnessing like contests! But what energy was displayed in resistance! what heroism, what constancy! If it was necessary to shed blood, we ought to bless God that it was not in the name of one of us that it flowed. Men actually in power have saved France; they reëstablish order, they take wise and energetic measures, but I fear their time will not be long; I fear that the country is destined to pass through many successive crises before it rests upon stable, solid foundations. Poor France! great in its misfortunes, as in its glory!"

In the beginning of the summer of 1849, the duchess of Orleans left Eisenach for England. In the midst of all the emotions of such an interview, her joy in finding herself with her family was great. The tone of her correspondence during this visit indicates a calm and comparatively happy state of mind. Let us not pass over a single expression of delight sown here and there in her letters.

"Your letter found me in the midst of the family circle," she writes from St. Leonard's. "Our passage was rough; the wind was so high, and the sea so tempestuous, that our arrival was greatly delayed, besides making us horribly sick. Except N——, all succumbed to this frightful malady, which I deem worse than death, because it stupefies while it harasses. My children did not suffer long; one was patient and grateful to all who took care of him; the other could ill restrain his anger against an evil he could not conquer. Instead of landing in London at seven o'clock in the morning, we did not reach it till four in the afternoon. My sister Louise had been waiting for us at the station for eight hours! You can imagine what this interview was for me. It is impossible to describe it. I found them better than I had hoped; but, alas! that impression has been quickly dissipated; her parched skin and emaciation afflict me exceedingly.

Chomel arrives this morning, and will enlighten us concerning the extent of the evil. God grant that he may not augment my fears! But I do not know how to be sufficiently grateful to God for restoring our mother; she is better than she was the moment I left her, and is so affectionate, so tender, so angelic towards me. We found her, with all the family, waiting with feverish impatience at another station. Father was moved and tender; brothers and sisters well. Father is thin, but looks well; he is a little feeble in the evening when drowsiness oppresses him, but possesses a strength and clearness of intellect, with a magnanimity of heart, admirable in one so sorely tried. Upon arriving here, we found several visitors; finding myself thus in the bosom of my beloved family, and surrounded by old faithful friends, the illusion was for the first days complete, and bore me above the pain of such sweet impressions. Little by little, we feel anew all the bitterness of our actual situation. The reunion and intimate converse with so many noble and beloved ones, still consoles and softens many griefs I had the joy of witnessing the general surprise at the appearance of my children, especially Paris. The king, mamma, my brothers, and everybody, find him greatly improved, and take great interest and delight in him. Mamma is very happy in seeing these two poor little ones again, and her *chevalier* still holds a large place in her heart; but she expresses an infinite tenderness for Paris, who replies to all her manifestations of interest with less reserve than his nature has hitherto admitted of. He is in a stage of development, with which Monsieur Reguier is well content. The voyage, and many things he has seen, doubtless contributed to this."

Upon the eve of returning to Eisenach, she writes: "Our domestic life is very sweet. I am much with the queen, hence with the king, whose affectionate tenderness increases from day to day, and makes me shrink from the moment of separation. I hope to make frequent sojourns with the family; the first will be upon my dear child's receiving his first communion."

The duchess of Orleans finally returned to Claremont after a sojourn of several months at Eisenach, and devoted herself entirely to the religious education of her son. She remained with him in his catechetical exercises with the Abbé Guelle, followed him in his retirement, and when she could not join in his exercises, united herself to him by prayer. The Lutheran doctrine concerning the Holy Eucharist, approaches ours nearer than that of any other Protestant communion. At the momont of her son's entrance upon Christian and Catholic life, the feeling of the differences of worship, always painful to her, was perhaps less sensibly felt than at other times, because she was impressed with a sense of union upon the point then most occupying the hearts of both.

Without permitting ourselves to enter into the details of a mother's intercourse with her child (edifying as it might prove) we must give her own touching account of the ceremony witnessed by so many friends from France.

"At eight o'clock, on the morning of the 20th of July, 1850, we went with the king and queen, followed by all the family and numerous faithful friends, to the little French chapel in London. Paris was placed at the foot of the altar, between the king and myself, before a prayer desk, surmounted by a lighted torch. He bore in his left hand a white scarf, emblem of purity. Before mass the Abbé Guelle addressed a beautiful and touching exhortation to him; then mass was said, by the bishop of London, Doctor Wiseman, a priest highly honored by the French clergy. Before the time for communion, the bishop made an equally fine address, and then the Abbé Guelle led the dear child to the altar. He knelt and received the body of his Lord with an edifying and devout respect.

On returning to the prayer-desk, he passed near the king, who raised his hands to bless him. Then the dear child turned instinctively towards me, with a look that I shall never forget and know not how to describe. The bishop then made another addres to him, and mass being finished we left the chapel full of emotion. Paris' demeanor was surprising for his age ; full of earnestness and dignity ; every one remarked it ; not only the king, who said it was one of the most delightful days of his life, not only the queen and my brothers who were deeply moved, but disinterested strangers were struck with the manner of that pure, pious, grave, yet artless child. Every one wept from sympathy and tenderness. Poor Robert was deeply affected during the ceremony. At two o'clock, we found all again in the chapel, except the king, whose health requires great care. The bishop was again present. Vespers were chanted, the Abbé Guelle made a touching address, then Paris at the foot of the altar, read anew the vows of baptism in a clear, firm voicc. Finally, we returned with our hearts full of thanksgiving to God who loves and blesses children."

Upon returning from a journey to St. Leonards the duchess of Orleans found the king's health so enfeebled that she thought no longer of leaving him. She was living near him at Richmond, where he died upon the 26th of August of that same year (1850), in the full possession of his faculties, and in the serenity of an upright man. He received the sacraments of the church, surrounded by his family, to whom he had ever been a tender father. His life ended like his youth, in exile; but his riper years were not useless to his country, and the eighteen years of peace, happiness, and liberty, France owed to him, should have led her to a different course with regard to him. His last breath was spent in enjoining upon his children the duty of not separating themselves from the queen. They all replied, gathering around him: "She will be always our first thought, and we will never leave her." Soon they were again called to be united around another death-bed, and to weep over one of the most remarkable and beloved of beings. Her majesty, the queen of the Belgians, in a few weeks followed the king. Every one will recall the effect produced by her death, in Belgium, the mourning worn by the entire population, even in the most miserable hamlets and her venerated memory already passed into tradition; but the vacancy left in her family by her loss, can never be defined.*

The duchess of Orleans writes on the 12th of

* For a fuller account of the death of Louis Philippe taken from London News, see p. 118.

October:—"It would be impossible to describe the desolation felt by us all, after the loss of our second Providence upon earth. God has taken our angel from us; He knows what is best, but His designs are impenetrable. Each day we understand more and more the greatness of our loss. We weep not only for a friend, but a support. Since that tutelary angel no longer watches over me, I feel anew the isolation of my existence, and in mute affliction, fear to love those ardently who still remain to me upon the earth; for the fourth time in my life God has taken those objects from me that possessed all my affection. This sad thought makes me sometimes shudder for my children, who may, perhaps, some day, share the fate of other objects which my love has cherished. Do you blame me for these thoughts? Be indulgent; look upon them only as the result of a succession of misfortunes; help me to pray God to lessen the bitterness of the cup He gives me to drink. If you could see our mother! if you could hear her words of submission and faith that astonish us! She is truly a noble woman. She lives only for heaven. Her only thought is of seeing her children and self prepared to enter there. She is far above human suffering, for God sustains and strengthens her. . . . Alas! I despair of imitating her, and pray God to pardon me for the degree of sadness into which this affliction has plunged me."

Two years passed without any release from the monotonous sadness of an exile aggravated by such severe misfortunes. The days of the duchess of Orleans were passed either at Eisenach or in England; it was in the latter place that she received the news of the 2d of December.

As long as the fate of France remained uncertain, and the form of government, and the family to whom it should be intrusted was only a secondary question, while the rights of society itself were in danger of being misunderstood, she followed the contest with anguish, but, as we know, also with hope; and this vague hope, which she did not even desire to see promptly realized, sufficed to animate her patience, to color the distant horizon, and to give her wings to cross the intervening space.

Upon the 2d of December, surprise, uncertainty, with regard to the course best to follow, and anxiety for her friends, aroused all the powers of her soul; but when she understood that a new period, of indefinite duration, was about to open, she was seized with a profound and almost bitter sadness. She who was mistress of herself in danger, and tranquil in the greatest misfortunes, resigning herself into the hands of God, was now seeking Him, without experiencing His peace. She wished to be submissive, but her heart revolted. "Every thing is against me," said she. "Yes, even the Christianity of the admirable queen. I am irritated with her for not being indignant. She has a word of indulgence and charity for every one. I cannot . . ." here tears overpowered her. Were they tears of disappointed ambition? No, if by that word is understood sordid desires and selfish purposes; yes, if it implies the sadness of a soul devoured by the ardor of a hopeless devotion and profound melancholy concerning a destiny impossible to accomplish, and an aimless future opening to her sons; hopeless for their country and their cause.

With this multitude of ideas and divers impressions, was mingled a measure of disquietude for her friends who were suffering for a cause, in behalf of which she had no new sacrifices to offer. Her foreboding imagination exaggerated the pains of their exile. She saw them, for long years, away from their families and country, deprived of all things. The desire of despoiling herself for them and of manifesting her sympathy, became almost a constant thought. One of these exiles related with a smile, though deeply moved, that he had received, early in January, a packet containing bills of varied value, with pieces of gold for all countries. She hastily gathered up what she found at hand, thinking that he and his companions in exile, driven precipitately from France, without time to arrange their affairs, might be in need of money.

The decrees of the 22d of January found her indifferent as far as they concerned herself; they would have been rather a sort of consolation, if her natural generosity had been less active. "As to what concerns us," she writes several days before the publication of the decrees, "you know that we are, thanks to God, raised above all expectation. The humiliation of our country, and persecution of our friends, is what we feel most. Inasmuch as the decree has not been issued, I pray you to use freely some of the means I have given you; I cannot altogether renounce the only solace that remains to us in misfortune."

Several months thus rolled away, in this difficult period, which she ever painfully remembered. Before her sons she maintained self-possession; with them she was cheerful, and with marvellous judgment knew how to prevent them from forgetting that they were away from their own country, in a time of serious trial, yet to create a pure atmosphere around them, guarding them against *ennui*, so hurtful to the development of children, and more injurious to their faculties than great misfortunes. But when she was alone, assured that her children were engaged either in work or play, she was assailed by a thousand mournful thoughts, that a word caused to flow forth like a wound roughly opened. One day, in taking leave of a friend, whom she was questioning with a benevolent interest concerning his family, she asked, "What is your daughter's name?" He replied, "She bears the name of your royal highness, Helen." At these words she burst into tears. "Ah, why have you called her Helen? that name bears misfortunes," and remained several moments without speaking.

In order to calm her mental agitation, she had recourse to forced active physical exercise; it seemed as if she sought fatigue of body in order to gain repose of soul; long walks, and incessant motion, served better to distract her thoughts than reading and music, which she nevertheless loved and appreciated; she acknowledged frankly, that a fixed attention upon subjects foreign to her habitual reflections was impossible. No book settled her mind, and even prayer could not pervade it. It was not that "God was not always in the depths of her heart," but that she feared to seek for Him there. The profound depths where His image still was, seemed hidden by the whirling of the surface of the waters.

She felt the need of external distraction, to escape reflections. She desired to travel, in order for some time to escape "the heavy and enervating atmosphere of England, that was killing her." The close of the year 1851 and a portion of 1852, she divided between Germany, whither her mother naturally attracted her, and Switzerland, which she loved in remembrance of her childhood; but this course, undertaken with every advantage for the young princes, threatened to become fatal to her. On the environs of Lausanne, where the route bordered a stream greatly increased by rains, the carriage upset and rolled into the water. In a moment the princes disengaged themselves and with one bound leaped upon the bank; but as they sought for their mother, to their affright they could perceive only her hair floating above the waters. She had fainted, and was half borne down under Madame de V—— who had also swooned. They had the greatest difficulty in drawing her out. Scarcely had she come to herself, when she uttered a cry of joy at the sight of her children saved and uninjured. The terrified expression of her children at the thought of their mother's danger, made a more lively impression upon her than even the accident itself. Of her dislocated shoulder, and fearful pains endured during her return in a *carriole* to

Lausanne, she spoke lightly. But she remembered with emotion, the care of her sons and friends, and the prompt arrival of the queen from England. This shock was nevertheless a severe test to so nervous a temperament; the patience of her soul triumphed over it. Though confined to her bed in a strange house, where she was in need of a thousand things, notwithstanding the care of her hosts, who were moved with pity and sympathy for the lovely invalid, she was always cheerful.

As soon as the duchess of Orleans was in a state to leave Lausanne, she set out for England. Towards the beginning of autumn, she rented a dwelling in Devonshire, the most southern province in England, where the aspect, on a bright day, was somewhat like Italy; but the fog that she sought to flee from thither pursued her. From the month of November till the following April, she saw the beautiful view from Kitley, with its noble forests and grand lake leading to the sea, only through a thick gray curtain and heavy rains. Those monotonous wintry days and long evenings were well calculated to oppress a spirit of less energy. She bore the trial patiently; and maintained a cheerful bearing by occupying herself continually with the thought of others, and by seeking to enliven the circle around her. Her energy never decreased.

She would cross the muddy roads to the environs, visit poor families, and interest herself in country occupations for the sake of developing a taste for them in her children, and of overcoming the ill consequences of an isolated education by actual observation and natural impressions.

"Kitley is becoming charming," she writes in the commencement of April. "Spring invests it with new attractions; the roads are bordered with blooming hedges, rippling waters, and shady woods. It is a wild place, where the work of man is little seen, yet an agreeable one to live in. I have made the acquaintance of several families in the neighborhood, who are amiable and intellectual."

She went to see them, invited them often to Kitley, in order to make them more at ease, and spoke English to them, though forced to smile at her own faults. Nothing could be more cordial than her welcome as a hostess. Several notes written each evening after a visit to her, present her to us under a new aspect, and give a pleasant impression of the perpetual attention she lavished upon her guests. We see in her what is rarely to be found in a woman, the desire to please without the slightest thought of self.

"Monday, 20th of June, 1853. I had arisen and was arranging my toilette when I heard a gentle knock at the door. It was the princess, already dressed, come to see if I wanted any thing, or was fatigued from my journey. She sat down, and we had commenced a conversation, when some one announced that the physician was there. She left me hastily to accompany him to the sick bed of a *femme de chambre;* the latter is German; the physician speaks English only; she went to translate the physician's questions and her replies. After several moments she returned; we resumed our conversation, which was several times interrupted by necessary household orders; then the hour for a history lesson, at which she was always present, recalled her to her children. At noon we assembled around the table; no luxuries here nor elsewhere; all was simple and pleasant. It seems to me that there is a certain elegance in the arrangement of every thing here. No little superfluity or those exaggerations of comfort which indicate too great concern for mere material gratification. The domestics appear as part of the family; they are evidently not chosen for their good appearance, but for their faithfulness. This domestic life pleases me altogether."

"21. We left for Kitley in the middle of the day, and returned at nine o'clock in the evening, overcome with hunger and fatigue, but charmed with our journey. The princess' horses were sick, as often happens, for want of proper care. We went out in a small establishment, and the princess and myself could scarcely refrain from laughing, when we met Lord Mount Edgecombe's steward at the entrance to his park, mounted upon a magnificent English horse, ready to escort the princess, and making all sorts of apologies, with great gravity, for his master's not coming in person. His respectful bearing contrasted strongly with our poor equipage, but I thought to myself, no one glancing within could ever mistake the rank of the occupant. She would appear what she is even in a peasant's garb and cart. While returning by water, the boat inclined for a moment towards one side ; the princess uttered a cry of terror ; I smiled in remembering to how many more serious dangers she had been exposed without shrinking. I remarked that she never spoke a word concerning those moments of her life."

"22. A rainy day. Impossible to move. Kitley enveloped in a shroud of fog. I have not experienced a moment of *ennui.* We have commenced reading *Polyeucte.* She appreciates all its beauty duly ; but two scenes placed us, as it were, in Paris. The future, the past, the present of France, the difficulty of resigning herself, the problem of detachment and perpetual trouble, were all discussed, and the poor *Polyeucte* remained open on the table."

She asked me to play upon the piano. "Music," said she, "soothes my too poignant thoughts; it varies my feelings, without wounding them. I so much wished that Paris might be fond of it, that I had teachers for him when he was seven years of age; but that led him to a dislike for it. I wished to hasten the time for every thing, and to have him become a man."

"23. Went to Torquay; in descending towards the sea, we met an old vendor, whom the princess had engaged a year before to polish the varied colored stones found upon the strand. She recognized him, and stopped the coach in order to say good morning, and make several purchases; the poor man's face became radiant with delight. She returned to Kitley loaded with presents for all. The only luxury she permitted herself, was that of giving to others.

"In the evening, several of the princes' young comrades arrived. The rooms were all occupied; the princess had beds prepared in the library, one of which she occupied herself."

Sunday. "This morning, upon returning from mass, I found her more than ordinarily sad. I proposed to read aloud some religious work. 'I was going to make that request,' she replied. We ascended to her simply furnished room, with its portraits and souvenirs, and read several pages. 'I can scarcely fix my attention,' she exclaimed, at the end of a few minutes. We had been speaking of her children, and resumed the subject; 'I desire to attract a serious society about them, in order that they may form the acquaintance of distinguished men and women; not frivolous, worldly women, but mothers of families interested in their children, living good and natural lives. Sometimes an agitating thought passes through my mind. I am in feeble health; I may die. I can make the sacrifice for myself, but think with alarm of my children!!' A cloud passed across her face, and a quick apprehension oppressed me, but only for a moment, she appeared so well.

"26. I took leave of her this morning. She wished to rise early, in order that she might help me in my preparations for departure. We were all filled with emotion, even the children, whose imagination she had captivated as well as my own. Why? I cannot say. I have seen as remarkable natures, but life seems more delightful with her than with others. I do not know another hostess with whom I could converse for twelve hours without a moment's *ennui*.

I always have something to say to her, because her interest never flags. Nothing is a matter of indifference with her ; her soul is far too great for her feeble frame."

The close of the year 1853 was marked with such painful agitations for the duchess of Orleans, that we cannot pass it over in entire silence. Great reserve is enjoined upon even the subject of these agitations. But faithful to our design, we will seek only the reflection of the duchess of Orleans' inner life, her ideas and feelings. They have an eternal value, but will be appreciated according to the times and events.

Upon a question which could concern only a distant future, she thought differently from some of her friends ; opinions, which she could surrender without violence to duty, she gave up. Two thoughts directed her whole conduct ; the one concerning her country, the other her children. She believed herself bound to the former by the compact of 1830, which confided the deposit of its liberties to the Orleans family ; she believed it her duty to keep her children's future inviolate and fetterless. She did not feel free to dispose of what she regarded as a deposit in her hands, till the moment she was to render an account to her sons.

In view of an immediate and decisive action, if

she had felt assured of the assent of the country and the durable happiness of France under a free government, and if it had been presented to her as the result of its own concourse, she would have been ready, we dare affirm, to give up the preferences and souvenirs that bound her to the most lively impressions of her youth, and to sacrifice even her duties as mother and wife. These duties she could only surrender to one greater and more pressing. It would still have been her husband's will that guided her, since he desired her to subordinate her conduct to the wishes of France ; she would have taken nothing from the éclat of his name, since that name would have participated in the glory common to all the Bourbon family. There was no opposition of principles between her and her friends, only a different view of the times, opportunity, and means.

But when all thought of action was put aside, and France seemed tranquil, or at least silent, while the matter seemed only desirable or perhaps even useful to the interests of her sons, but without any immediate results for her country, she did not believe herself authorized, as mother and guardian, to dispose of the only good remaining to them ; namely, an independent future. It may doubtless be said that she was misled and deluded ; but in her delusion, there was nothing but what was generous, noble, and perfectly sincere. If she clung to them with a certain passionate persistency, it was because the most tenacious of all passions are those of a mother, above all when she acts in obedience to a will ever present, and fixed by death. But the more firm were her convictions, the more acutely she suffered ; she felt the need of communion with those whom she loved and admired, and whose titles she was proud of. Her tenderness, even, carried her beyond herself. In complete union, the slightest clouds might become great griefs, which would scarcely be noticed in relations less near ; the ardor with which she would seek to dispel them might increase them. At a distance, on the contrary, circumstances might dissipate the lightest clouds, and render the bonds more affectionate and sweet. This soon happened ; and the duchess of Orleans' last return to England, was the happiest and most exempt from agitation of the ten years of her exile ; while the joys of domestic life, which were ever so dear to her, were felt in their full sweetness.

The winter of 1856, which she passed in Italy, strengthened her feeble health. "The impression my journey left upon me," she writes from Genoa, "is that of delight. Follow my example ; come beneath this incomparable sky, where to live and enjoy is one and the same thing."

TRANSLATOR'S NOTE.

The following article on the death of Louis Philippe appeared at the time in the London News:

Louis Philippe died on the morning of the 26th instant, at Claremont, in the presence of the queen and several members of his family. He had been made aware of his approaching end early the previous day, and receiving the melancholy intimation with calmness, prepared for the final arrangements he wished to make. After a conversation with the queen, he dictated with remarkable clearness the concluding portions of his Memoirs, and then, having caused to be assembled his chaplain, the Abbé Guelle, and all his children and grandchildren who were at Claremont, he received with resignation and firmness the last rites of the Catholic Church. Towards seven in the evening, the debility that had oppressed him appeared to pass off, and fever came on, which continued during the night with great violence, but without disturbing his composure of mind. At eight o'clock in the morning he expired, in the presence of his devoted wife and of the following members of his family: the duchess of Orleans, the count of Paris, the duke de Chartres, the duke and duchess de Nemours, the prince and princess de Joinville, the duke and duchess d'Aumale, and the duchess Augusta of Saxe-Coburg. Thus ended the closing scene of the life of Louis Philippe of Orleans, once the sovereign of a great people, the soldier of one revolution, the conqueror of a second, and the victim of a third.

The following account of his life will doubtless prove interesting in this connection:

Louis Philippe was born in Paris, on the 6th of October

1773. The care of the young prince's education was assigned to Madame de Genlis, and ably and admirably did that eminent woman perform the duties intrusted to her. From her guid ance Louis Philippe immediately passed to the busy arena of active life. In 1791, war being declared against Austria, the duke made his first campaign, fighting with gallantry under Kellerman at Valmy and with Dumouriez at Jemappes. But the horrors of the revolution were progressing with gigantic strides; the unfortunate Louis XVI. was carried to the scaffold, and within a few months after, the duke of Orleans was seized on a plea of conspiracy against the French nation, and after a mock trial, consigned to the executioner. A short time previous to the death of his father, the duke de Chartres had effected his escape through Belgium into Switzerland, and was there joined by his sister Adelaide and Madame de Genlis. We can here only mention this romantic period of his life, and glance at his wanderings through Switzerland, Denmark, Lapland, Finland, America, and England. For one year he held the appointment of professor in the college of Reichenau, at a salary of £58, and for that sum undertook to teach history, mathematics, and English. He bore the name of Chabaud Latour, and none but the superiors of the institution were aware of his rank. The news of his father's execution reached him while quietly instructing the youth of Reichenau, and he instantly threw up his professorship, and after a protracted journey through Northern Europe, succeeded by the kind intervention of Mr. Morris, the American ambassador at Paris, in reaching the New World, where he landed in Philadelphia, 24th October, 1796, and was joined by his three brothers. They spent the winter in that city, and afterwards visited General Washington at Mount Vernon. Their residence in the United States was, however, short. Louis Philippe's two brothers died within a few years, one in England, the other at Malta. He accompanied his last remaining brother to Malta, and after his interment, sailed for Sicily, on the invitation of the king of Naples. There he gained the affections of the princess Amelia, and their marriage took place in November, 1809. In the year 1814, on the abdication of Napoleon, he returned to Paris, and for a short period was in the full enjoyment of all his honors. In 1815, Napoleon's escape from Elba called the duke of Orleans into active employment, and he proceeded, in obedience to the desire of Louis XVIII., to take the command of the Army of the North. In this situation he remained until the 24th of March, when he surrendered his command to the duke de Treviso, and returned to Twickenham. After the Hundred Days, the duke of Orleans obeyed the ordinance authorizing all the princes of royal blood to take their seat in the chamber of the peers; but subsequently incurring the jealousy and displeasure of the Court, he resought his old residence on the Thames, and dwelt there in seclusion until 1817, when he returned to France, and devoted himself to the education of his children, until the Revolution of 1830 broke out, ending in his elevation to the Throne of France. The circumstances of his reign until his final abdication of the Throne, and exile to England, are well known.

In the following extract will be found a detailed account of the last honors paid to the deceased ex-king:

The apartments at Claremont occupied by the ex-king and queen, were upon the ground floor of the mansion; they comprised the library, dining-room, gallery, breakfast-room, and the state bed-room, in which princess Charlotte died in 1817. After the arrival of the royal exiles, some changes were made in the appropriation of the apartments. The gallery was converted into a private chapel; the bed-room of the princess Charlotte became the cabinet of the ex-king, and the adjoining dressing-room the bed-chamber of the ex-king and queen. In this room Louis Philippe expired. His body was embalmed and placed in four coffins. The inner coffin, containing the remains, was of Spanish mahogany, lined with white satin, and covered with lead; the third coffin was of highly polished mahogany; and the outer, or state-coffin, was of the same material, covered with rich black Genoa velvet, thickly studded with silver nails, with ornaments and handles of the same metal, richly chased; on either side were the arms of the house of Orleans; the plate on the lid was surmounted with a regal crown, underneath which were three fleurs-de-lis. and the following inscription:

LOUIS PHILIPPE Ier.,
ROI DES FRANÇOIS,
Né à Paris
Le 6 Octobre, 1773.
MORT À CLAREMONT,
(Conté de Surrey, Angleterre,)
Le 26 Août, 1850.

In the centre of the royal chapel at Claremont, a platform was raised, upon which was placed, upon trestles, the coffin containing the body of the ex-king. The coffin was surrounded by twenty-four lighted wax tapers, and was covered with a black velvet pall, fringed with silver, and in the centre of which was a cross, extending the length of the coffin, worked in silver. The chapel walls were hung with black cloth, and the external light carefully excluded. On one side of the chapel a bench was placed for the accommodation of the ex-queen and the female relatives of the ex-monarch; but the space within the chapel

6

was so limited that none but the members of the late king's family and their immediate attendants could be admitted within its precincts. Seats were placed in an adjoining room, into which a small door opened from the chapel, for the strangers who attended the solemnity; but they could merely obtain a glimpse of the tapers burning on the altar, and occasionally hear the low tone of the officiating priest chanting the solemn cadence of portions of the mass for the dead. At nine, the ex-queen, with the princes and princesses, entered the chapel and took their places, the queen on the left, and the princes on the right of the *catafalque.* The king's former aides-de-camp stood behind the *catafalque.* After the service of the "lesser hours," mass was celebrated by the grand vicar, Dr. White, of the London district, assisted by the Abbés Tongel and Levasseur, of the French chapel in London, and by the Abbés Guelle and Crabot, respective almoner and chaplain to the king, and by the Abbé Coquerlan, canon of St. Deny's, who arrived on the previous day to perform the pious duty. After the mass, during which the prayer for the dead was chanted in full choir, the Abbé White gave the absolution. Immediately after the clergy, the queen passed around the catafalque, and sprinkled the coffin of her royal husband with holy water. At a quarter past ten o'clock the visitors were directed to form a line from the door of the chapel, along the vestibule, and the melancholy procession, which had been arranged within the chapel, passed between them, towards the final resting-place of the ex-king. Between Esher and Weybridge, the procession (in which were marked many persons of illustrious rank) was joined by many gentlemen on horseback, who fell in before the hearse, riding three abreast. The procession moved slowly towards Hersham, along the narrow lane overhung with elm, oak, chesnut and beach-trees. At Esher, the green was crowded with rustics. Many of the inhabitants evinced their respect for the ex-king by closing the window-blinds of their shops and houses. At Hersham the street was lined with persons, who received the sad procession with every demonstration of respect, many of the men remaining with their heads uncovered while the hearse passed. The procession having reached Weybridge, the mortal remains of the king, followed by the princes and all the attendants, were borne across Miss Taylor's garden to the chapel, where a long mass was celebrated by the Abbé Crabot. The ex-queen and princesses occupied the chapel gallery; their royal highnesses, the count de Paris and the duke de Nemours, were on the right of the coffin; the prince de Joinville and the duke d'Aumale on the left. After the mass, the body was removed to the vault, where it is destined to repose until France shall have opened its gates to the family of Orleans, and given the sons of the ex-king the right to deposit the mortal remains of their father in the tomb which he himself built in the sepulchral chapel of Dreux, and which already contains the relics of his sister and eldest son. After the last prayers had been pronounced, the princes once more sprinkled the coffin with holy water, and kneeling amidst the tears of all the attendants, fervently kissed the repository of the remains of their father. They were deeply affected, and it was not without difficulty that they were eventually induced to quit the vault.

The tomb in which the coffin is enclosed is a simple monument, covered with a large slab, attached by the upper end of the wall, and supported by two small columns. On the portion nearest the wall are sculptured, in relief, the arms of the ex-king, surmounted by a royal crown, and beneath the escutcheon is a Latin inscription.

Louisa Isabella, eldest daughter of Louis Philippe, was borr at Palermo, 3d of April, 1812. Her sister, duchess Mary of Wittemberg, the accomplished sculptor, was her junior by just one year. (The exquisite creation in marble of Joan la Pucelle d'Orleans was hers;) she died in 1839. They grew up in the closest affection, which was only severed by death. The care of their education was intrusted to Madame de Mallet, who, under the superintendence of their admirable mother, provided the most distinguished professors for the different branches of their education. They both derived the utmost advantage from them. The talent of the princess is stamped with lasting fame. She died in 1839. The worth of the princess Louisa, though not so dazzling, was no less solid. In her, the worldly wisdom of her father, and the Christian affection of her mother, appeared to combine. She was the favorite child of Louis Philippe, and he often acknowledged the benefits of her counsels. In the year 1832, on the 9th of August, she became the bride of Leopold, king of the Belgians, the sovereign of the people's choice and of their never-varying affection. Queen Victoria and Queen Louisa were intimate friends; they were frequently together, and when separated, corresponded. It is said that Queen Victoria wrote in French, that she might have the opportunity of addressing her friend with the "tu" and "toi," and other graceful familiarities of that language. After a union of eighteen years, so beneficial to her consort and his people, the queen of the Belgians, still young, and the doting mother of a youthful family, received the awful summons tc lay down her earthly crown, with calm fortitude and resignation, and departed amid many princely tears and the no less heartfelt sorrow of a people whom she loved so well. Queen Louisa leaves three surviving children; she died of phthisis, at Ostend, on the 11th instant, (1850.) On the night of the

9th, her majesty had a few hours' rest; but at six o'clock next morning her majesty fell into a state of general and fatal prostration. After a short time she, however, rallied and regained sufficient strength to converse with her confessor. Although greatly exhausted, she retained the possession of all her mental faculties, and at two o'clock, on the afternoon of the 10th, received the communion and extreme unction. Though a prey to the most excruciating pain, she could console her afflicted husband. She had previously taken farewell of all the members of her family, and just before expiring, affectionately pressed the hand of her royal consort, which grasped her own till life was gone. On the morning of her funeral, the king and the duchess of Orleans attended service in the English Protestant chapel at Ostend, and shortly after the duchess of Orleans left Belgium for London. The queen of the Belgians was buried according to all the rites of the Catholic church.

VIII.

SHE left Genoa in the spring 1857, and established herself at Thames-Ditton, a small village on the banks of the Thames, a short distance from Claremont and Twickenham. The duke and duchess de Montpensier, the princess of Coburg and children, joined the family circle. The accouchement of the duchess de Nemours was anticipated as a happy event; she had never been more beautiful and happy than since her exile. Complete union arising from sympathy of heart and mind, cast a gentle sweetness over the lives of all.

The family met every evening at one of the houses at Twickenham, Richmond, Thames-Ditton, or Claremont. Nothing could be more cheering or sacred than these reunions, where children of all ages, beautiful as angels and full of vivacity, though docile at the least signal, forced their parents to be cheerful. The queen bestowed a smile upon this little troop, and her eyes rested with pride upon each one of her daughters-in-law, come from countries so different, with accents so diverse, all united in the same devotion and love for herself.

For the royal family, that summer of 1857 was like a moment of respite in grief. Never, since 1848, had the duchess of Orleans spent such tranquil days; she felt it with gratitude.

"I feel inexpressibly happy," writes she, "in seeing my sons developing according to my heart's desire, strengthened in good, and in finding their young souls manifesting an almost paternal tenderness for me; taking care of their mother as if she had been confided to their solicitude, and in my ill health rendering me great assistance. The age of my eldest is, in my estimation, that most charming in the life of a man; he has all the candor of early youth, the rectitude of principles not yet shaken, with freshness of feeling and an ever-increasing decision and desire for constant advancement. Robert, though still young, manifests maturity with infantine purity, and his lively and sometimes vehement nature is moderated by daily increasing wisdom. You will say: you are blind concerning your sons. I assure you I am not: recognizing the benedictions God has accorded us in the midst of sufferings is not blindness. I shall always be very exacting, and desire that they should attain a very high end."

After so many trials and deceptions her intense prayer was at length granted. The work to which she had devoted her life fully succeeded, and an anxious affection was succeeded by a feeling of entire confidence. "I cannot express the change manifested in Paris," said she ; "I no longer protect him, it is he who protects me ; I love to see a conscience in him separate from mine. When he is not of the same opinion as myself, I am almost delighted. I dare say it, I have respect for him."

She was not alone in her judgment, and tha deference awakened by a profound and serious nature, was already mingled with the paternal affection he inspired in his uncle. The perfect union of the two brothers, betokened that their future would be what it ought.

The future always occupied her thoughts. Her ardor for all the lofty interests of this world had not diminished, but a life consecrated to duty always led her to a certain forecast. Her most lively desires and passionate affections were little by little despoiled of all that was purely personal.

"I feel as if the glimmer of entire detachment,'

said she, "would dispel even maternal ambition in my soul; but these moments are fugitive, the face of heaven is obscured and life returns." Then she added with her usual natural sincerity: "it is not detachment from the things of this world that is difficult; but the preference for things of heaven. Action distracts me, and the little things of life disturb me. How humiliating is the examination of one's self."

We recall the expression of her countenance; it was serious but not depressed. Notwithstanding the shocks she had received, she could still enjoy deeply, and many ties still bound her to earth.

"We to-day celebrated Paris' birthday," she writes. "God has granted him nineteen years. My heart seemed too small to contain so much joy, and this joy will never be disturbed by this beloved child. I am confident in saying that he will never, to the end of my days, disappoint my expectations. All the family were reunited at my house; the fête was beautiful and delightful."

They were again called to meet at Claremont. The duchess de Nemours had given birth to a princess; she was recovering rapidly; the child was beautiful as its mother, but the presentiments of those who were influenced by superstition, were confirmed, when, on the 10th of November, at the moment when the duke de Nemours was leaving the princess in health, and smiling with the thought of rising on the morrow, God suddenly called her, and that pure soul ascended to him with His name upon her lips.

The family can testify what depth of heart and ingenuous sympathy the duchess of Orleans manifested on this occasion. She had lost a beloved friend; her emotions were deep; but she felt that she must not allow herself to be overcome by them in the presence of others more directly afflicted, and set them an example of strength and submission. She was never weary of admiring what perfection faith added to the pure soul of the queen, who never rebelled at misfortune, but accepted it with tranquil dignity. She reproached herself for not being as resigned and weaned from the world as the queen. Her courage, nevertheless, was not less, but she was of a different age and nature, and called to other duties; she still had work to do in life. She thought depression fatal to young minds, and for their sakes sought always to rise above it. "I will not be discouraged," she would often say, with vivacity, "but take pleasure in surmounting difficulties." When one day glancing at the title of books upon her youngest son's table, her eye lighted upon Nicole's Essays: "Oh!" said she, "I do not like that book for young persons ; it detaches them too soon from life, and renders them incapable of action."

She constantly feared lest she and her children should lose the activity necessary to life; and those who knew her at this epoch, when sad impressions filled her mind, noticed greater energy of will. Were these vague feelings caused by her failing health ? Was she doubtful of the final triumph of purposes to which she had devoted her life, and consecrated to her sons' future ? What illusions had been dispelled ? Sometimes she would sadly ask if she should never see an end to the indifference manifested on the part of France towards opinions as well as persons. To her nothing was changed ; the two feelings that had sustained her, love for her country and faith in the advancement of the liberal cause, always remained ; but they were colored by graver tints. She judged events with more calmness and less confidence, foreboding even success with anxiety.

The news of the attempt on the 14th of January filled her with horror. She was alarmed and almost humiliated at the moral state of society in which such crimes could be committed without any public manifestation of emotion.

"That attempt," she writes from Richmond,

"was the most odious of all, and one is ashamed of humanity when seeing to what purpose the discoveries of sciences are applied. I have a horror of the fruits of such a crime. . . . One cannot think of what state our French society may be in, after this, without great emotion. The contest appears inevitable, and will be terrible. Our part is very plain and humble. We can only pray to God and exhort our sons ; thus we shall not be useless."

Religious thoughts, which always held the first place in the duchess of Orleans' heart, even when most distracted by the active duties of life, now pervaded it more and more. She was at once too serious and sincere to approach these subjects when absorbed by the occupations of the moment, or when she could not speak of them with complete freedom ; but the natural inclination of her mind always led her to them, and the more her hopes in life were blighted, the more she sought the resources of faith ; but what sufferings for her, even here ! The sombre form of Anglican worship did not please her imagination. . . . She could neither follow it in her own tongue, nor be reminded of the forms of her infancy and country. She could only in worship join with her sons in what was not interdicted by the doctrines she professed. Upon Catholic fête days she accompanied them to the church, read with them their religious works every evening, and her mind, always alert in seeking points of agreement, took great delight in these common occupations, and could sympathize in even the foundations of Christian faith. But she was too loyal to wish to find a complete union of sentiments where she knew differences ought to subsist. She had promised to make her sons fervent Catholics ; this she did, but remained herself a Protestant. It is not surprising that her melancholy feelings were rendered even more sensible upon the return of the Sabbath, for she was alone isolated in the midst of all those Christian groups. All spirit of controversy, God knows, was far from that sincere Christian soul, but how could she help lamenting being deprived in this world of a consolation granted to all of her dear ones—unity in one faith.

During these days, which were far from being thought the last of her life, the princess showed increasing fervor. She desired to form several exclusively religious relations, as if she would seek a momentary distraction from all political agitation, and prepare herself by the aids of religion for the last and perhaps most difficult act of maternal devotion. She was going to voluntarily separate herself from her sons, who were about to undertake a journey on the continent. It was not without anxiety that she saw the approach of their departure; but she well understood that the moment had come for her to trust to the results of an education in which no care had been spared; their decided characters no longer needed daily direction. Her work as a mother was finished. God spared her this separation, but revealed to her the moment of a longer and final separation.

In the beginning of the month of May, the princess was forced to leave the house she had rented at Richmond; she had great trouble in finding a habitation for the remainder of the summer, and was compelled to take the only one vacant at that time.

Cranbourn House is situated, like almost all the villas of Richmond, upon the banks of the Thames; but, as it is upon the declivity of the hill, and thickly surrounded by trees, whose shadows extend even to the windows of the basement, the aspect is sombre, and dampness more sensible than elsewhere. Upon arriving, the duchess of Orleans remarked that the entrance was gloomy, and that the railings, painted black, as was common in English places "resembled the entrance of a tomb."

She did not attach to this prophetic word any lugubrious impression, and soon gave a graceful, cheerful aspect to Cranbourn House; an abundance of flowers, filling the air with delicious perfume, quickly dispelled the first impression.

The duke de Chartres fell ill on the first days of May. The duchess of Orleans was not seriously disquieted. Yet she confided the care of him to no other person. She was constantly entering his chamber, and spent more than one sleepless night. Her agitation at first, then the joy of his recovery, enfeebled her frail constitution ; or rather it was already broken. These secondary causes, so weighty to those who survive, and which afford nourishment for grief, were in reality but small measures in the exact scales in which God weighs out our days. A succession of emotions, while exhausting her body, lent her a factitious strength even to the end. How many storms had passed over this tender plant ! These were the last gentle billows that were to bear her away.

Upon Sunday the 9th of May, she received a visitor from Paris, and conversed with great animation upon the state of France and its diverse chances for the future. Already suffering from a cold, she was obliged by Wednesday to keep her bed. Her feebleness was much greater than could be explained by the nature of the disease ; no one felt at all disquieted about her. A letter from the prince de Joinville, alone seems to testify to any apprehension of danger. But every one around her lavished the greatest care upon her ; her feeble health always rendered this necessary ; not one had any idea of alarm ; she, less than any one. Upon Thursday, Ascension morning, as Madame B——, who hardly ever left her, was preparing hastily for church in order that she might return before the duchess' time for rising, she reproachfully said : " Why do you rise so early ? Is it in order to pray for me ? " " Yes, as I do every day ; I ask God for the happiness of madame and her sons ; but madame will pardon me, I never dare express more definite wishes." " You are right," replied she ; " it is thus one ought to pray ; we know so little what is good for us."

Violent coughing, followed by faintings and nervous paroxysms, returned several times upon Saturday and Sunday. When scarcely recovered, she resumed conversation with her ordinary vivacity, and above all when her sons were in the room. Her physician besought her not to talk so much. " Let me at least look at them," she replied.

She would scarcely allow herself to be treated as ill, for fear of distressing those around her ; besides she then felt no pain. In a moment when the nervous paroxysm was most painful, she asked her friend to hold her hand in hers, for it soothed her ;

but immediately turning to her physician asked: "Is it contagious?" The first days she did not wish any one to watch with her; when she consented, the fear of fatiguing her attendants led her to desire a nurse. Her friends thought of sending to France for a sister of the "*Bon-Secours*" who had watched with the king in his last illness; but she, recalling the establishment of Deaconesses, also consecrated to the care of the sick, said: "I should like to be taken care of by that good sister, but I desire to do something for my persuasion, and think it will be best to apply to the Deaconesses" The letter, now written, did not reach Paris in time.

Upon Monday the 17th of May, about noon, she was oppressed with a sense of suffocation and weakness; she remained for some time motionless and almost without life. When they begged her to sit up, thinking she might breathe more freely in that posture, she replied with extreme slowness, "I can do so no longer." The crisis however passed, and she, so clear-sighted, saw no anxiety impressed upon the countenances of her friends. She was so tranquil, that the physician even was somewhat encouraged.

The day passed without any new drawback: she slept at intervals under influence of the remedies given for her cough. In this half sleep, she was heard to pronounce several words in a sort of cantilene rhythm ; all that could be understood were, "My parents are interred in a purchased piece of ground." But when she awoke, her mind was as clear as ordinarily. She asked for her sons, "It is a long time since I have seen them." Some one replied, "that they did not come into her room, in order that she might repose." She replied, "I do not wish them to think that I neglect them."

Upon Monday evening, the name of France was mentioned ; she said several words with a sort of exaltation ; then she was silent ; her feebleness was excessive. All retired early ; she took leave of her children with her accustomed words. "God bless you, my children." These accents are the last left in their memory. They left her without apprehension.

Nevertheless Monsieur de Mussy began to be alarmed at her constantly decreasing strength, even after she had taken some nourishment and a little wine. At this moment, thoughtful and grateful to others as usual, the princess addressed a maid waiting upon her, "You have also need of strength as well as me ; drink this wine," and passed her the glass.

She several times insisted that every one should retire. "I believe that I can sleep, *sleep well*," said she, dwelling upon the words. They withdrew As her friend retired behind the curtains of the bed and believed herself concealed, the princess called the physician to her and said, "Make her sit down, Monsieur Mussy; I see her in the glass always about."

Every quarter of an hour, potions and aliments were administered to strengthen her, and she never complained of being disturbed; but each time, gently repeated, "I am going to sleep so well."

The physician sought to feel her pulse. Astonished at so much care, she said, "You think me then very ill?" Monsieur de Mussy, already disquieted, evaded the question and replied; "And you, madame, how do you find yourself?"—"Not ill; I have often felt thus; I wish to repose."

Monsieur de Mussy retired to the adjoining room and wrote notes of intelligence to Claremont and Twickenham. During this time the silence was profound—so profound, that a friend remaining near the door was trembling with presentiment. "It seems to me that it is very silent here," said she to Monsieur de Mussy. He entered the princess' chamber cast a look at her, and raised his hands towards heaven. The passage from one life to another had been so sweet that the two women remaining near her bed, with their eyes fixed upon her, had seen no alteration in her features or change in her countenance; her visage had only assumed a more lurid paleness.

Her friends were still inclined to doubt it; on held her for some time in her arms, while another went for the princess. What can be said of these moments!

They watched four days by these dear remains. Many came from France to look upon them once more; they pressed into the chamber, praying and weeping over one who had so often given them welcome. She seemed to them still to smile, and those who saw her can never forget the peaceful, almost infantine expression upon her countenance. "That ardent exile" was at last at rest.

Upon Saturday, the 22d of May, she was borne from her dwelling, surrounded not by those come to pay her homage and respect, but by desolate friends. Sobs burst forth from every portion of that simple house in Richmond, and all the route over which the sad cortége passed, was hung with French colors, the cottage windows were closed as a sign of mourning, and showed what sympathy she had inspired in those around her.

Her remains were deposited at Weybridge, between the young and charming princess whom Claremont still weeps, and the king whom ou egrets have at length taught us to know. Without the noble intervention of the bishop of the diocese, this provisional place would have been denied her, and her poor body would have found neither an asylum in her adopted country nor in the one from which she had been exiled. This sainted priest thought that not less ought to be done for an exiled princess than for a queen of France. She rests there, near her friends.

If in these pages one thought, one word has wounded an opinion, or a person, let the blame fall upon the hand that wrote it ; and let not one bitter feeling arise towards one who ever wished to keep peace with all in her heart, and who, *not under the impression of her approaching end,* but in those years when an active life seemed still unfolding before her, pardoned all who had oppressed her, and besought those whom she had injured to forgive and forget.

If these eulogies bestowed upon the duchess of Orleans bear the impress of exaggeration, we will not try to defend them. We have painted her as she appears in our hearts. None can be judged but by his intentions. Thus we will not pretend to impartiality, if in order to attain it, we must cease for a moment to love her. We only ask that the duchess of Orleans' own words may be read with all sincerity of mind, and if we mistake not, the testament, drawn by herself, will justify what we have perhaps been able to say of the greatness of her soul and the infinite tenderness of her heart. God grant that tender thoughts of her may arise and rejoice her soul, in that harbor of peace, where all affection dwells, and from whence all suffering is banished.

W LL OF THE DUCHESS OF ORLEANS.

In the name of the Father, Son, and Holy Ghost.

I recommend my soul in dying to God, and implore his infinite mercy in the name of Jesus Christ, beseeching him to receive me in those eternal mansions, and reunite me with those for whom I have wept upon earth

I leave my maternal benedictions to my beloved sons, and pray God to guide them through life, to grant them prosperous days and accord them eternal felicity when they have nobly finished their destiny upon earth. To them, I address my last adieu, thanking them for the happiness they have cast over my existence.

I pray the queen to accept the last expression of my respectful gratitude. I bid adieu to my mother, to whom I owe so much, to my brothers and sisters for whom I hav always avowed a sincere affection, to my maternal family whose affectionate hospitality lessened the bitterness of our exile, to my friends and servants, whose fidelity in misfortune inspired me with grateful attachment, and inally to France that I have loved so much, and where the happiest years of my life rolled away.

I recommend my sons never to forget that the fear of God is the beginning of all wisdom, that it is a light in prosperity and a support in misfortune. May they remain faithful to the precepts of their childhood; may they also remain faithful to their political faith. May they serve Him, whether by constancy, in adversity or exile, or by valor and devoted patriotism when events shall recall them to their country, that constitutional France may count upon them to defend her honor, greatness, and interests, and that she may find in them the wisdom of their grandfather and chivalric qualities of their father. They will always remember the political principles that have made the glory of their house, and that their grandfather served upon the throne, and that their father adopted with ardor. His last directions have been the rule of their education.

In leaving the world, I recommend my sons to the queen. My beloved son, count de Paris, will be emancipated the moment my testament shall be enforced; nevertheless, I rely upon the moral influence of the queen and upon her respected authority to keep him near her; I equally count upon her maternal solicitude in praying that she will accept the tutelage of my beloved son, the duke de Chartres. She will not find these duties too burdensome, for I ask my brothers to aid the queen in the administration of their nephews' fortunes. I know the sentiments which animate them for the children of their deeply regretted brother, and I am sure that they will always testify a sincere affection for them.

I recommend my sons to remain always united, the indissoluble union of two brothers being the condition of their strength and mutual happiness. I desire my eldest son, as soon as he shall be legally permitted, to take part in the counsel of the family charged with watching over the interests of his younger brother.

I also desire that my faithful and tried friends who have surrounded my sons, and who were devoted friends of their father, not ceasing to manifest proofs of attachment in misfortune, should continue to remain near them.

My express will is that my possessions, all that is due to me legally, and all that I have a right to dispose of, be equally divided between my two sons; with this intention I divide as equally as possible between them the following objects I possess, leaving—

To the count de Paris:—My necklace, with four rows of pearl, which I hope he will some day bestow upon the countess de Paris, the six diamond pendants; the red album containing the beautiful collection of aquarelles, by French artists, having belonged to the duke of Orleans; all my furs and Scheffer's picture of the "Holy Women."

To the duke de Chartres:—My set of pearls composed of brooches, pins, earrings, bracelet and diadem. This set came to me from my godmother, my aunt Adelaide. My bracelet of rubies, willed to me by the queen of Belgium; two ruby knots; the sapphire ring and ruby ring; my beautiful lapis-lazuli cup; the Livre d'Heure, that his father had made; the necessary ensigns and my laces. I hope that the jewels and laces will serve the duchess de Chartres.

I leave beside these articles, some as souvenirs. To the count de Paris, the large portrait of his father by Ingres, the marble bust of his father by Jollet; the large picture of the "Portes-de-Fer," by Dauzats; the little picture from the "Col de Teniah," by Philippoteaux; all the manuscripts, papers, letters, little note books of his father's, and his father's letters addressed to me. I know that he will always regard these papers as a precious treasure, and I think that he may some day dispose of them in such a way as to make the world acquainted with one whom France lamented, though without having known all his merits. I leave to him the portraits of my two mothers; the aquarelle of Winterhalter, representing the queen with the two children of the duke de Nemours; the portrait in oil of the duke de Chartres by Winterhalter; the beautiful poignard made for the duke of Orleans by my sister-in-law, duchess of Wurtemburg; two of the albums containing his father's designs; the Psyche presented to me by the city of Paris upon the occasion of my marriage; the equestrian statue of his father in bronze, upon a pedestal of white marble; the great clock by Bégnet, which struck the hour of his birth, with the mantel ornaments accompanying it; the inlaid casket, containing his father's watch and several other souvenirs; the case containing the seal, and vermilion knives that I always used; half of the beautiful engravings from his father's portrait by Ingres; the little aquarelle of the duke of Orleans upon horseback, after H. Vernet's; one of my four beautiful fans; my wedding fan, in open work, which has already served the queen; my bracelet containing his father's portrait destined for his wife; my sculptured prayer-desk containing his father's cast; my papers, letters, little gift books which I left in England; his father's sword which he wore upon the day of his death; the palm that was given him by his division upon his return from the Portes-de-Fer.

I leave as souvenirs to the duke de Chartres:—The equestrian portrait of the duke of Orleans, by De Dreux; the small portrait of his father, by Ingres; the large picture from "the Col de Teniah," by H. Vernet; the head of his father in marble, after the monument of Triquetti; the aquarelle of the queen, by Winterhalter; my portrait, by Henriquel Dupont; my writing-table ornaments (vase porte-plume, vermilion ecritoire); the miniature of his godmother; my small watch; my memorandum-book in shell and gold, ornamented with family portraits; one of my beautifully painted fans; the bracelet adorned with his portrait and that of his brother, destined for the duchess de Chartres; the aquarelle, by Eugene Larny, representing a review of the Chasseurs of Orleans at the Tuileries (1840); the large portrait of the count de Paris when a child, by Winterhalter; two of the albums containing some designs by the duke of Orleans; the other of the engravings after the portrait of his father, by Ingres; the "Arc de triomphe de Dymilah," by Dauzats; my Alexandre organ; my wedding casket of jewels in Boule; a bronze equestrian statue of his father, with two bronze vases belonging to it.

I designate upon a special list, the souvenirs which I pray my family and my friends to accept as last testimonies of affection, and I ask my sons to divide the remaining objects between them, such as albums, bronzes, books, furniture, and trinkets. . . . .

Having at heart the prosperity of our House, I will, in case of improbable yet possible misfortunes, that is to say the pre-decease of my two sons, without leaving direct heirs, that I shall become proprietor of a part of their possessions, that the goods I leave be divided between the princes of the House of Orleans, and at their decease, between the princes their sons. . . .

Whatever may be the place of exile in which my days terminate, and wherever be my tomb, I ask my sons, and in case of their decease, my heirs, to bear my ashes to France, when our family shall be restored there, and to deposit them in the mausoleum of Dreux, near my husband's tomb.

I here terminate my last wishes, granting pardon to all those who have offended or afflicted me, and beseeching those to whom I may have given offence, no longer to retain the remembrance of it.

My last word is for my beloved sons—a prayer and benediction.

(Signed,) HÉLÈNE, DUCHESSE D'ORLÉANS.

EISENACH, January 1, 1855.

BIOGRAPHIC SOUVENIRS

OF

THE DUCHESS OF ORLEANS,

With Original Letters,

COLLECTED BY G. H. DE SCHUBERT.

I.

THE WAY OF LIFE.

"He is in the way of life that keepeth instruction."—Prov. x: 17.

The discipline, that leads and maintains the human heart upon the way of life, is both internal and external. Internally, it awakens the conscience to its natural relations with God, the author of life and being; it is the discipline of humility with the fear of God, that is the source of all wisdom and good in us. Externally, it makes us feel the hand of God in the midst of the vicissitudes of our terrestrial life.

The life of the noble woman, whose traits we here propose to describe, offers, in all its parts, the action of this double education. The mental discipline, with the fear and love of God, was already germinating in her filial and devoted attachment to her mother and governess ; she was early exercised in outward discipline by the painful severing of the dearest and firmest of ties. From this double education resulted the regular and ever progressive development of a life which has been blessed to so many souls.

What infant was ever held in the arms of a mother with a more devoted love than the princess Helen de Mecklenburg? She was within four days of her third birth-day when she lost her mother. January 20th, 1816, the anniversary of the young orphan's birth, became a day of mourning, not only to one house or one country, but to all the superior minds with whom she had a tie of relationship. Caroline Louise, the daughter of a nobly endowed prince, Charles Augustus, grand duke of Saxe-Weimar, had been brought up at the fireside of the sciences and arts ; though her mind was highly cultivated, the religious teachings of Herder had implanted a life far superior to science and human art. It was from elation with that life, that she changed the intellectual and animated circles of Weimar for the peaceful retreat of Ludwigslust, marrying Frederick Louis, grand duke of Mecklenburg-Schwerin, whose loneliness she sought to relieve by the gift of a sympathetic heart. Upon the 11th of February, 1812, the bride experienced the joys of maternity, by the birth of the prince Albert, a child endowed with rare faculties; then, two years after, by that of a lovely daughter, the princess Helen. Her soul then aspired to disengage itself from its terrestrial covering. The birth of a third child, who quickly passed from the cradle to the tomb, determined the crisis and put an end to her noble life.

The spirit of the mother had not fled; it mysteriously lived again in the souls of her children. Several months after the death of the duchess, I arrived at Ludwigslust, in obedience to the last wish of the duchess, and saw the young orphans. *I have elsewhere described my entrance into this new circle of activity, and the first impressions I received. I then chiefly spoke of the two young children of that august house, of prince Albert and his sister Helen. The latter, already in her third year, struck me with her infantile originality. I do not mention this as an individual souvenir, for this impression has remained in the memory of all who attentively observed the child, whose third year had not yet revolved. Even in the midst of her childish hilarity, happy in feeling and enjoying, Helen's expression was always impressed with a gravity which gave an air of grandeur to her posi-

* Third volume of Schubert's Autobiography

tions and movements; there was nothing studied; it was the seal which the mind impressed upon the body from its earliest awakening.

A friend to whom I am devotedly attached, Madame de Both, who accompanied the duchess Caroline Louise, as the friend of her childhood in her departure from Weimar to Ludwigslust, who remained with her till her death, and has surrounded her children with a devoted maternal affection, writes to me with regard to the princess Helen:

"From her earliest childhood, she had a nature peculiar to herself. One remarked something more than ordinary in her; it was as if no person could mistake the rank to which her birth and destiny called her. She ardently loved study, listened with a serious attention to all that others said, and early exhibited a certain poetic tendency. In one word, she was in every respect remarkable, and I was often struck with her resemblance to her mother, except that the latter was more calm and reserved, while Helen's mind was more lively and frank."

Helen loved above all things to hear those who knew her mother speak of her; she was never weary of hearing the slightest details concerning her;—what she had done and liked in her childhood, what she had said to Helen and Albert before her death, what had been her favorite places in the gardens and castle. She loved to find herself in the neighborhood of her mother's and young brother's tomb ; in short, the Eternal Country, for which the spirit of man was created, occupied the dreams of her childhood before it was trained for the study of the invisible world. It was by this discipline that the mind of the young princess was early led upon the road which leads to life. The permanent serious impression of eternity initiated her soul into ideas of a superior world, and impressed that dignity upon her whole bearing, which so early struck strangers.

I was in daily intercourse with prince Albert, and have often seen him with his sister Helen. Though I was not preceptor, in the strict sense of the word, I neglected no occasion of awakening first in the mind of the young prince, then in that of his sister when she joined us in the garden, the germs of knowledge, whose prompt action upon the mind has the same importance as the maternal milk upon the body of a child. Prince Albert, from preference, read and meditated with me upon Biblical histories, among which that of the prophet Daniel particularly interested him. Helen voluntarily remained with us and attentively listened. She frequently played with us in the midst of the flowers and listened to my stories and romantic narrations. The children also loved to hear me speak of subjects drawn from nature, trees, plants, stones, beautiful mountains; and, at the advanced age which I have reached, I still remember that the questions of those children, upon which their minds were revealed, more than once opened a new horizon to my view, upon the essence of things. It was not difficult for me to speak in language conformed to their age, for my soul was with their souls.

II.

THE ROOT OF THE VINE IN THE GARDEN.

THE fruit of the vine, more than that of any other plant, possesses the virtue of strengthening and rejoicing the heart. Thus the vine is specially cited among the productions of the promised land, and the Holy Scripture frequently mentions the care and pains bestowed upon its culture, the protecting walls with which the cultivator surrounded it, and the vigilance with which he watched each particular vine. The vine and the stock are more than once employed in Biblical language as an image for the chosen people or members of that people.

Among these, the force and action in the domain of spiritual life may be compared to the effects the blade of wheat converted into bread produces upon animal life. This action is beneficial, but as it is daily, it is less felt than the stimulating effects of a medicinal or spirituous drink. Thus like the vine, minds which ought to exercise a profound and salutary effect upon a people and upon an epoch, ought to be the object of special care and culture. It is not in the midst of flowery couches, nor in the luxuriant verdure of meadows, that the root of the vine germinates and grows, but the gardener transplants it to the rocky soil of those isolated mountains, to which the canticle of the prophet applies : "We have a strong city; salvation will God appoint for walls and bulwarks."

Helen, endowed with rare faculties and called to a high destiny, had need to be guarded in order to become what she did. She had lost the aid of her mother ; her father, who tenderly cherished her, was too much absorbed by government affairs to superintend the great task of her education. The young orphan had doubtless a guardian angel near her, under the guise of the lady of honor, or rather that of the intimate friend of her mother, Mademoiselle de Tann, who soon after married General de Both. Her attachment for the young Helen was beyond limit; it rendered her capable of all sacrifices. Still later, when her cares became less pressing, this faithful friend did not allow a day to pass without going to see the state of the young princess. She unremittingly sought to find traits in Helen resembling those of her mother, and when she marked a new one that recalled her, her heart thrilled with secret joy.

The whole nature of the child announced the germ of an intellectual independence which passed all ordinary bounds. One who closely observed her in childhood might have said: there is in this young girl the germ of a character whose development no external force will retard, and which will direct her with a firm step to her high destiny. Helen then needed a method of education, such as Kästner himself recognized and experienced:

"Als ich ein Knabe war, da trat *ein Mann* heran,
Da sah ich ihn und streckte mich, *und ward ein Mann.*"

In obedience to the dying request of his wife the prince de Mecklenburg sought the princess Augusta of Hesse Hamburg in marriage. She wished to decline this reiterated request for her hand, but a powerful voice within, which she was in the habit of consulting, replied affirmatively, and she submitted.

Thus had the young princess Helen a second mother, who exercised the most decisive influence upon her mental development and the direction of her entire life. A friend, who witnessed the results effected by the new duchess in the household of her husband and especially in the hearts of the children, thus writes:

"Humanly speaking, it is to the princess Augusta that the young duchess Helen owes her education, and I bless God that the world has been able to contemplate and appreciate in the duchess of Orleans, the fruits of the prayers and devotion of her second mother."

In the spring of 1819, I left Mecklenburg in order to renew my scientific studies. The eldest of the princesses, who later, under the name of the duchess Maria of Altenburg, was generally beloved and respected, had terminated her education, and my principal task was thus achieved. Providence had watched over the youngest children of the grand duke, Albert and Helen; beside the excellent governor of Brandenstein, prince Albert had a preceptor who possessed with the most profound seriousness a most affectionate disposition. The remembrance of this worthy man, so soon entered into rest, still moistens my eyelids, and the affection I professed for him can never waver in my heart. It was the theological candidate, Koch, son of the venerable pastor of Bellahn, who, after the example of the priest and king of Salem, led a holy and solitary life in the midst of his generation; extending his hand in prayer over a vast field in which his faith perceived the movement of the dry bones. (Ezekiel 37.)

The son had the fidelity and faith of his father; I do not know that I ever saw a man like him, who loved with all his heart and soul, combining the gentleness of St. Paul with the vehement zeal of St. Peter. The interest with which Helen took part in the religious lessons which he gave to prince Albert, has surely been blessed.

Besides the princess Augusta, who surrounded Helen with the protecting rampart of maternal love, the child was confided to the vigilant care of a Genevese, Mademoiselle Nancy Solomon, of whom I will speak in another chapter, several words gathered from the testimony of a faithful witness.

The end proposed by Eternal Wisdom in sustaining this delicate plant upon all sides, was soon revealed, by the approach of as torm which, breaking, proved the young vine even to the root. The noble grand duke, Frederick Louis, died upon the 29th of November, 1819, in the prime of life. By the side of his bed there were prayers and struggles that left a permanent impression upon the minds of the children. The letters which were then addressed tc me, enable me to witness that tried family and to follow the prince to his last resting place.

From my departure for Erlangen, I continually corresponded with my friends at Ludwigslust. The children had also written to me; prince Albert, dates from my departure from Mecklenburg in 1819; and as early as 1822, the princess Helen, added to her brother's letter the following words traced with a sure and correct hand, rare for a child of eight years: "Dear Professor, as my brother writes to you, I wish to tell you that I love to think of you."

I here quote several lines of the first letter properly so called, addressed to me by that dear child, at the age of nine years. It is dated, Ludwigslust, April 18th, 1823.

"Dear Professor! How I envy Madame de Bechtolzheim, who will have the pleasure of seeing you, as well as your dear family. I hope that she will tell how we speak of you and the beautiful stories you related to us. Our dear Mr. Koch also knows some pretty tales; he gives me lessons which give me great pleasure. Dream, I pray you, dear *pro.'** that I have not a single syllable from your hand, and that a little letter would rejoice me very

* Professor. Prince Albert, in his childhood, frequently employed this abbreviation, and his young sister imitated him —AUTHOR'S NOTE.

much. Adieu, dear Professor, do not forget your Helen. My Nancy cordially salutes you."

I granted this childish invitation with pleasure, and her correspondence has been to me, in the course of my life, a source of great delight.

III.

THE HAPPY INSPIRATION.

An ancient chronicler, relating the exploits and life of the great emperor Frederick I., the Saxon, says, he always seized the right hand of every thing.

These simple words are the best eulogy that could be bestowed upon the sentiments and actions of any man. The duchess of Orleans possessed this happy faculty from her childhood ; it was remarked in her thoughts and actions. Let me here present the testimony of a loyal witness, who daily saw the princess during the period of her youthful development. "The grand duchess distinguished the most vigorous germ of independence in her daughter's nature. Helen was in her eyes a new and often enigmatical study, which attracted all her attention. That which most astonished and often disquieted her mother, was the assurance and courage with which the young princess questioned, judged and decided, as if she had no need of reflection. This spontaneity had also its charm; it came to her as if by inspiration; it was the fresh effusion of a young heart, and a touching kindness made itself felt in all her words, judgments and actions.

"One would have thought that a certain presumption must be dissembled under a character so independent and a nature so decided. But it was not so. She had a delicate conscience that made its voice heard. With the aid of this good genius, she raised herself above her own nature. She early learned the secret of self-education; this secret consisted in being attentive, not to the remonstrances of men, but to the voice of conscience, which taught her her duty towards God and her neighbor. From her childhood she isolated herself to live with her secret thoughts, and revealed them oftener by her actions than by words. The more she felt the need of this inner life, the oftener she retired to her chamber, and when she withdrew from it one could read in her amiable, serious face, that she had been with the master and friend of her heart, that she had communed with God, and God with her."

Thus she preserved the strength that was the joy and consolation of her heart.

Dwelling upon the vicissitudes of the duchess of Orleans' outer life, it has often been said that it was an unhappy one. Her mother, who knew her as well as herself, judged of it otherwise. "Helen," said she, "has never been long unhappy. She always maintained her tranquillity in a manner that I do not myself understand. She has doubtless been deeply tried; after the death of her husband, she seemed to have lost all happiness and inward peace; for the duke was Helen's idéal as well as mine. For some time the sight of her children distressed her; she seemed only to feel the loss she had met with; but, arousing herself from this crisis, she found peace."

When she was in the flower of her youth, her happy disposition often manifested itself in outward demonstrations of hilarity, but above all when in company with the friend of her childhood, the countess Ida de Bassewitz, in every respect a graceful and amiable young girl. In her society, Helen willingly played for hours with dolls and toys, or bounded through the gardens and apartments. But her taste for dolls soon gave place to more elevated objects of art. She decked her chamber with choice plaster figures. Upon the right and left of her secretary were the figures of two children, one reading, the other writing. "How happy those children are!" exclaimed she; "they are never distracted, never rise, never turn their eyes from their work; O that I might read and write with such continued zeal."

IV.

FRIEDENSBURG.

THE moment arrived when the young princess was enabled to follow her decided taste for the study of the sciences. The grand duchess, who foresaw the happy fruits that a more vigorous impulse would have upon the development of her daughter's character, energetically applied herself to the accomplishment of the purpose.

Prince Albert, accompanied by the chamberlain of Brandenstein, and Koch, his faithful preceptor, had gone to pursue his studies at Zurich.

The grand ducal chateau, was then sufficiently large for the grand duchess and the princess Helen, upon whom she now lavished an undivided maternal solicitude. It also could offer a suitable apartment for the instructor who had been appointed to continue the education of Helen, then eleven years of age. Rennecke was predestined by God to this work, by a rare combination of intellectual and spiritual gifts. But the duchess decided upon a retreat where her activity might not be interrupted and where her daughter's powers might be developed in solitude ; in the autumn of 1825, she left the sumptuous apartments she occupied in a wing of the castle, and went to live in the retired palace which, at a later period, became the resort of her widowhood.

Then commenced a life, the original charm of which is described by a friend, in the following letter :—

" The dignity of the grand duchess' manners and all her eminent qualities led us implicitly to follow all her wishes. But when we sought to read them in her eyes, we soon realized that she had no other will than that of pleasing God, and contributing all in her power to the faithful accomplishment of her duties as mother, towards Helen. Thus we were all engaged in the same work, each according to the respective position held, and strength possessed. The organization of the palace, soon resembled that of a Christian household, in which from morning till evening, at table and elsewhere, the watchword is, " Do every thing that you do, in the name of the Lord Jesus Christ and as in his sight." Among the persons, who strictly speaking composed this humble household, each one's employment had some relation, more or less direct, with the work of the young princess Helen's education. Her preceptor Rennecke, commenced the day with reading the word of God, and then directed his intelligent pupil in the varied domains of human science. His teachings absorbed four or five hours daily, several other hours, beside, were employed in lessons with other masters and mistresses. At noon, the family dined together; then the young duchess in recreation and walks passed several hours; at eight o'clock in the evening, tea was taken in the garden under the shelter of an humble brick arbor, near the majestic poplar, or in the saloon of the palace. Two hours were passed in reading aloud and familiar converse; afterwards each one retired to her chamber to enjoy peace of conscience and bodily repose; sometimes however upon a starry night, the studious princess obliged her preceptor and several of her attendants to seek some other occupation than that of reading and conversing. She was not content with studying in her daily lessons of the empires of our terrestrial globe, she wished also to become acquainted with the principal stars and constellations as well as with the movements and laws of the solar system. This instruction had a great attraction for her, and in order to prove her gratitude to her master she designed an astronomical map upon blue paper, which she presented to him upon his birthday, adding that through him she had become acquainted with the celestial luminaries. She wished to express herself to greater advantage but could not continue."

The grand duchess did not desire to make the eminent faculties of the princess produce striking results, but to awaken her to perseverance, and love for application, and the acquirement of a taste for solid intellectual culture. This method entirely accorded with the character of the princess, who never wished to exhibit herself. Consequently, the most suitable mode of reading, seemed to be that of converting the hours for lessons into hours of work. Rennecke put this plan into execution with discernment and skill. Thus in the religious lessons under his direction, a Biblical book was read, he added the necessary explanations, then left the princess to note down for herself and to learn the passages that pleased her best, by heart. She naturally chose those which during the lesson, struck her as agreeing with the state of her soul. Thus her steps in Christian experience could be seen. Her progress was visible ; religious lessons were those which she preferred, because they introduced her into the kingdom of eternal truth. In short these lessons had not for an end simply dogmatic science, but an initiation into the true character of the kingdom of God upon the earth. The princess was never told that she *must* believe such and such a point, but that it might be admitted with certitude, and that it was always good to allow oneself to be governed by the spirit of faith.

All other lessons were in like manner made valuable. In studying the history of a people, a suitable work was read in connection with it. They designed a map to be filled little by little, which was to contain an index of the principal facts of the history of the country and its inhabitants. Rennecke and his scholar both drew their maps, and when the work was finished, it was not seldom that they made an exchange. In geographical lessons they also traced maps; and, in order to facilitate repetition, notes were made upon the margin of the most remarkable places. All this was but play for a princess whose zeal and conscience seconded her talents. Her mother assisted at the morning lessons, and took an active part in the afternoon instruction. Her spiritual observations debarred every thing trivial, and she frequently gave an unexpected interest to what had not fixed the princess' attention. She here unfolded all the simplicity and admirable resources of a discriminating judgment, which embraced without difficulty every thing within her sphere.

She was not contented with being with her daughter in the study-rooms; the promenades she often took with her in the forests and fields, became excellent means of study. She wished to share her exquisite delights in the beauties of Nature, whose depths she loved to sound. The natural sciences, in fact, were the favorite objects of the grand duchess' observation and meditation. The numerous writings of Dr. G. H. Schubert, former preceptor in that noble family, served as guides for that branch of science. They also made use of divers collections of natural history, and in the study of botany, of artificial plants of rare beauty.

From the fields and forests, where the afternoons passed so quickly, let us return to the evenings. Before dwelling upon them, I will sketch the portraits of some persons who passed some time with the grand duchess and her daughter.

When one dwells upon the career of the future duchess of Orleans, it must be incontestably admitted that Providence in a most special manner watched over her Christian education.

By a remarkable coincidence, three persons

maintaining different views of religious worship grouped around the princess. Her excellent governess, Mademoiselle Nancy Solomon of Geneva, who afterwards became the wife of colonel Bontems, belonged to the reformed religion. Having her heart open to the ancient faith in all its regenerating vigor, she inspired the respect of all who knew how to appreciate that serious Christianity which transfigures the whole man. Her black, piercing eyes were somewhat tempered by the expression of her mouth, which I shall call sympathetic, and which chiefly struck one when her glance rested complacently upon the princess. From the age of two years, her pupil had been confided to her care ; French thus became as a second maternal language to the princess, and she continued to make use of it in her conversations at Friedensburg. No person was more indifferent to all idea of personal merit than Mademoiselle Nancy Solomon ; she had a horror for every thing that might diminish the glory of God. She attributed the spiritual progress of the princess to God alone ; the grand duchess, playing upon her family name, was accustomed to say : " Nancy is a true daughter of Solomon." The mutual relations of both pupil and governess were most intimate and touching.

By the side of the governess, belonging to the

reformed persuasion, who watched over the princess, was Mademoiselle Gustarie de Sinclair, a Parisian by birth, and a zealous Catholic. She was maid of honor to the grand duchess and an intimate friend to Miss Solomon. Her good disposition and excellent qualities made her beloved, and the princess felt particularly attracted towards her. In general, Mademoiselle de Sinclair largely contributed to the life of the little society ; her cordiality and the ingenuousness of her observations rendered her company very agreeable to the princess. Let us mention another lady, Catholic at heart, with the faith of a child—Madame de Both, whose tender care for the princess Helen has been already signalized.

In face of these two influential elements, the princess' preceptor, Dr. Rennecke, represented the Lutheran persuasion. Scarcely could any other man so deeply feel the task of the education of so extraordinary a child, imposed upon him ; for he was animated by a spirit, whose flight is ever towards a height where the sun never sets. Let us follow him more closely in the work the Lord confided to him, for the good of many souls.

Through his various relations with the Lutherans of Silesia, particularly with Scheibel and Henri Steffens, he became a decided Lutheran. Despite his modesty and natural aversion to all religious pride, he felt it his right to spread the Lutheran banner over his function as the preceptor of a princess of Mecklenburg. But his zeal never pressed beyond the limits imposed upon him in the circle, to which the Providence of God had called him. It was his privilege to choose and read aloud edifying works at those evening reunions. Indeed, no evening passed without the grand duchess requesting the reading of an article that might strengthen her household in a living faith in the Son of God. Rennecke soon felt that the spirit of peace united all the members of that home circle. He endeavored to render the harmony always perfect.

They all wished to live, yet in such a manner as to be ever ready for the life eternal. Christ has sanctioned this view, by his precepts ; after those fundamental sources of our religious life, we have a stimulant in the example of that cloud of witnesses, whose lives have been glorified by being incorporated with Christ. To seek and hear those faithful witnesses who have confessed the name of Christ in their holy words and actions, is a noble task for those who love the Lord Jesus, and wish to live with God, through Him. The entire circle of the grand duchess' family sought this nearness to Christ, and passed with common consent from one mountain to another, upon which rested the feet of the messengers of peace.

That which they sought, they found in the principles and true representatives of the Catholic, Lutheran, and Reformed Religion, whose veracity could not be doubted. The Confessions of St. Augustine and other works chosen from the same author, were the vestibule through which they entered into the three naves of the Church. separated from one another by some barriers. As faithful witnesses of the life of Christ in the Catholic Church, figured alternately with the messengers of other branches—Fénelon, Fr. Léop, Stolberg, Sailer, Fenneberg, and Monsieur Boos. Among the Lutheran professors, they accepted above all, the testimony of Martin Luther, himself. They availed themselves of the book then widely spread through Ultsch, the Monument of the Reformed Church, which appeared for the jubilee of 1817. It comprises passages chosen from all the works of Luther, and arranged for all the work and fête days of the year. The book was also very convenient, because the dates limited the lesson.

What concerned the Reformed church, they found in the excellent little work, entitled the "Doctrine of Salvation," which is an extract from the ancient writings of the reformed theologians, mostly French. Outside the principal articles of the Church of the Low Countries and of the Reformed Church of France, they also sought acquaintance with those men who have been the pillars of their churches, such as Calvin, D'aniel Superville, whom the revocation of the edict of Nantes exiled into Holland, where he preached the gospel till his death; Jean Despagne, around whom the French refugees of London gathered in a body; Dallaeus, preceptor to the son of the celebrated Mornay; Mestrezat, whom cardinal Richelieu called the boldest pastor of France; and Pictet, author of melodious sacred songs. Besides these authors made known by the extracts from their books, they studied still further, Ezekiel Spanheim, first professor at Geneva, then ambassador of Frederick II. of Prussia, to the court of England. In his celebrated Academic discourses he made frequent allusion to Thomas, whom he loved to cite as a powerful witness to the divinity of Christ and the reconciliation achieved by his death. Several works of the Anglican church had their place in their soirées; among others, the edifying letters of John Newton, and the secret of sanctification by Marshal. The Moravian community were represented by biographies and other writings addressed to the heart.

We cannot here indicate all the elements of the

evening subjects; we only wish to prove that God can unite what men separate, and what separates men. He who opens *a* heaven to all who found their hopes upon the death of his Son, alone can effect a celestial communion upon earth.

The collections which have been sent to me upon the soirées of Friedensburg, contain a short lesson for the evening in which the princess Helen took a special delight, because the rules of spiritual life were concentrated under the form of questions and answers. Let me here introduce it.

"From whence comes all the evil in the world? From the thoughts of the human heart. What does God regard in man? The heart. What does God try in all its ways? The heart. What is the greatest spiritual good? Grace in the heart. What are we to watch most carefully? The heart. How will God teach us his ways? By putting his law in our hearts. What is the greatest of God's chastisements? Allowing the heart to become hardened. Where does God reveal his love? In our hearts, by faith. What is the effect of faith? The peace of God in our hearts, which is above all understanding, and which keeps the heart in Jesus Christ. What hearts does God love? He despiseth not the humble and contrite heart. What must be purified? The heart. What reward shall the pure in heart receive? They shall see God."

After having carefully designed the trunk and vigorous branches of the tree of life, which was the object of study in these evening reunions, let us cast a *coup d'œil* over its verdant foliage and fragrant flowers. Mingled with the grave or suppliant voices which formerly resounded through the temple one heard canticles and the sound of the timbrel and harp. In the visible world around us the sighs of the creature are also intermingled with accents of joy. Thus the grand duchess, whose solicitude extended over all, loved to introduce into the evening occupations, elements of another nature ; they were not direct rays of the eternal light, but they still reflected the animated wave of a fresh stream. They read, for example, innocent witty productions such as '*Wandsbecker Bote.*' They pleasantly occupied themselves with scientific works and travels when they were of an interesting and useful kind. The following letters which the princess Helen addressed to me, in her twelfth and fourteenth year, treat of these recreations :

Summer of 1825.

DEAR PROFESSOR,

I cordially thank you for your pleasant book and the letter you were so good as to write to me ; both gave me great pleasure.

How I pity poor Martelle,* who fell into the hands of the Turks, and was so cruelly treated by them ; but how I admire her great patience and energetic faith, which surely tempered her situation.

I much regret not having visited my dear professor (with Albert), who knew how to relate such beautiful stories to us, and not having traversed with him the beautiful environs of Erlangen : but I hope this delight is reserved for another occasion.

I beg you very cordially to salute your dear wife as well as Selma and Adeline. Adieu, dear professor : save a little affection for your

HELEN.

MY DEAR PROFESSOR,

You are very good to think of me and to send me such a pleasant little book. I cannot sufficiently thank you for the great delight that you have procured for us all. We read it every evening, and we have now accompanied you to Lyons. The description of the diligence amused us much, but it is a great pity you should have been so disturbed in your antechamber, by such a disagreeable travelling companion. I also took a lively interest in the beautiful history of the two good little children, who

* Allusion to a tale I published about this epoch at Erlangen

were saved in the Black Forest in such a remarkable manner.

Our Albert had a very great pleasure in seeing you last summer, dear *pro.* He has spoken of it so much to me, that I wish very much that I had been of the party, though I do not know that I should have had as much courage as your dear wife.

Next summer, if God permits, we shall make an excursion into Switzerland, to see our dear Albert. I was much rejoiced at the thought of seeing you again at Erlangen, but that was not to be. God grant that we may have this pleasure another time.

Mamma has probably already spoken to you of my preceptor, Monsieur Rennecke, who is extremely good ; I like him much and also his lessons. He already knows you, for we have often spoken of you, and he has a great desire to make your acquaintance.

Shall I dare pray you, my dear and good *pro,* to embrace your dear wife and daughters, and to think sometimes of your affectionate

HELEN.

Ludwigslust, May 26, 1827.

I am going to add a few words upon a portion of Prince Albert's youth, not only to render some passages of these two ingenuous letters clear, but also because what concerned the brother is in strict relation with the horizon of the princess Helen.

In the summer of 1825, he came to see me on his way to Erlangen, with his tutor, Monsieur de Brandenstein. I showed them the magnificent country and grottoes of Muggendorf; then I accompanied them to Nuremburg, to the house of my friend C. de Raumer, where they also made the acquaintance of Ranke, my future son-in-law. From Nuremburg, the two travellers next went directly to Switzerland, the end of their journey and desires. Prince Albert sojourned a short time at Zurich in order to extend the sphere of his acquaintances and observations by the study of the sciences and contemplation of the sublime works of nature.

At Erlangen, I charged them with salutations for my dear friend and brother David Spleiss, then professor at Schaffhouse, and also pastor at Buch. The acquaintance of this worthy servant of God was the first spiritual fruit that my dear prince Albert gained, upon setting his foot upon the soil of the great marvels of the Creator. He soon arrived at Zurich, the centre of Nature's magnificence. He was amicably welcomed in the house of Gessner, son-in-law to Lavater. The venerable Hess, then weighed down with years, received him with a paternal affection, and presented him with one of his spiritual writings, entitled, "Voyage to the Island of Hope." Dr. Hirzel, and Monsieur Jean Schlatter, became soon warm friends of the newly arrived guests, who also frequented the houses of the negociates Wichelhausen and Lochner, where they were as one of the family, as in the dwelling of Gessner.

In 1826, on my return from Italy, I made an engagement to meet prince Albert at Milan, where I found him in company with Monsieur de Brandenstein and his preceptor, Koch. I related in detail, in the last volume of my journey into the South of France, the excursion we made together to Brigue, in Valais, by Lake Majeur and the Simplon. Prince Albert described the course of his journey to me on his return to Zurich, in a letter of the 17th of October, 1826.

In a later letter, of the 31st of October, 1827, he spoke freely of the happiness that a visit from his mother and sister Helen had given him. That interview in Switzerland, and above all at Zurich, was a source of mutual joy to the brother and sister, such as they had never experienced. In taking leave of them, the venerable Hess blessed and prayed for them, laying his trembling hand upon the head of the princess Helen and her brother, and

I do not know but the words pronounced by that faithful pastor, remained graven upon their hearts.

It seems appropriate that I should mention, that shortly after their joyful meeting at Zurich, they were called to a tomb to meditate upon their own end. It was first the prince's turn ; and the experience of his heart, is revealed in the last letter he wrote to me from Zurich, dated 13th of April, 1828.

"Our travelling party has lost one of its members faithful Puls,* after an illness of fifteen days ; he died of tumor of the lungs. I need not tell you that his loss is deeply felt by me. The view of suffering, then that of the corpse, leave an inefface-able impression. When I saw him for the last time, he was seated ; his eyes were fixed, his countenance livid and distorted ; his sufferings had reached their height. When I saw the corpse, the impression was different. Suffering had disappeared, the mortal envelop was there under my eyes, but the mouth was closed for ever ; the soul had fled. Death ! said a voice in my heart. I saw him for the last time in his open coffin, with a bouquet of flowers upon his bosom and a smile about his mouth ; then I believed him at rest, and felt that he was happy.

* The name of one of the prince's loyal servitors, who journeyed with us the preceding year to Milan.—*Authors Note.*

Ah! yes, God will reunite us near his throne, where there is no more mourning, weeping or suffering!

I again place at the end of the chapter, a short poem written by the princess Helen, at the age of 14 years, upon her return from her journey in Switzerland (1827). As its contents indicate, it was composed at Dobberan, upon the shores of the country, and in view of the sea that she came again to visit.

Seyd mir gegrüsst ihr lachenden Hügel
Herrlich gekrönt mit grünendem Laub:
Mild unweht von Zephyrs Flügel
Werdet ihr keines Sturmes Raub.

Sey mir gegrüsst, o ruhiges Meer,
Brandende Wogen am eisenam Strand,
Spiegel dem nächtlichen Sternenheer,
Sey mir gegrüsst mein Jugendland.

Theure Bilder verflossener Freuden,
Verschwunden sind sie nach kurzem Spiel,
Möge der Schmerz vom irdischen Scheiden
Wenden das Auge zum seligen Zeil.

V.

AFFLICTION AND JOY.

THE death of a friend of the princess Helen's soon after, made a deeper impression upon her heart than that which affected her brother.

I have already mentioned the young and amiable countess Ida de Bassewitz. From her third year, she had been educated with Helen as a sister ; growing up together, the two friends had but one heart and one soul. Ida was somewhat older than the princess, and her tender affection for her adopted sister led her voluntarily to place herself in the second rank. The slightest desire, the faintest wish that she could divine in Ida's look, became as a law to Helen's heart, which she immediately obeyed. One might say that the bond of affection between these two children resembled the perfect happiness of a conjugal union ; Helen's relations with Ida were those of a spouse who has no will but the will of her husband. They had, it is true, ceased to live near each other, because count de Bassewitz had returned Ida to her mother, but they made frequent visits and their friendship expanded itself in intimate correspondence. Several weeks after hei confirmation, Ida suddenly died upon the 6th of September,1829. The grief of the young princess was far greater than one would have expected from her age and the natural liveliness of her character; it was preparing her for another and heart-rending grief awaiting her, thirteen years later, the death of her husband. They could not dissuade her from taking a journey to the tomb of her friend ; the agitation of her soul produced the germ of a nervous fever which burst forth on her return and put her life in danger. The vigor of her youth arose above it ; she recovered, but notwithstanding the return of her habitual serenity, a serious tendency was remarked in her, which confirmed the truth of the French proverb ; "Sadness is in the heart ; gaiety in the mind." Still later, at the epoch of her life when she was smitten with the most overwhelming of blows, this tendency became habitual, though the cheerfulness of her mind mastered it.

This trial, which joy and grief commingled,

and eternity much occupied her thoughts, had a special bearing upon the princess at this time. The image of her friend was incessantly before her eyes; but she did not attract it earthwards as formerly; it seemed to her, she said, that her friend from the home of the blessed, was blessing her and filling her soul with the rays of an imperishable love. It was a solemn and serious moment to her, when on the 30th of May, 1830, she made the following profession of her faith, which she had written with her own hand, in the church at Ludwigslust.

"After God, in his grace and mercy, has received me by baptism into the alliance of reconciliation through Jesus Christ, after he has made me acquainted with his Word, and through it, of my sin and corruption, after he has drawn my soul to Him by continual appeals and exhortations, I here publicly make a profession of the faith, which by the action of the Holy Spirit, has become the sure foundation of my temporal and eternal life, as well as of my hopes.

"I believe in God the Father, creator of the heaven and the earth, who so loved the world that he gave his only Son, that all who believe in Him might not perish, but have everlasting life. He has thus had compassion upon me, pardoned my sins as his child reconciled through the merits of his Son. It is upon faith in the only Son of the Father, that I build the salvation of my soul, and satisfy the justice of God ; for Jesus Christ, by his humanity, his bitter sufferings and death, did for me what I cannot do for myself ; and by faith in his inexhaustible love and grace, renders meparticipant of his salvation. After having opened to me the gate of heaven by His resurrection and ascension, he intercedes for me with the celestial Father, so that I may not die in my sins, but that I may live.

"I surrender myself entirely by faith in Him who has saved and redeemed me. Regarding each circumstance of my life as a dispensation of his love, I pray him, who is the chief object of my faith, to preserve me from all evil by His Holy Spirit, and to preserve me in close communion with Him, that I may pass my life constantly looking to Him, and that I may be found faithful. Amen !"

NOTE—Professor Schubert here mentions the princess choice of the canticle, and introduces a poem by her, which will be found at the end of the volume.

VI.

A NEW SCHOOL OF LIFE.

THE princess having attained the age of seventeen (1831), Monsieur Rennecke, her faithful preceptor and spiritual guide had finished his task in the ducal mansion ; he went to fill an office to which he had been called by an unforeseen direction and by the spontaneous wish of many friends. He first made a voyage into the South of Europe, passed by Munich, and came to see us with his companion, whose mind, like his heart, was assimilated to his own. His arrival was announced to me by a letter from princess Helen, who was equally dear to us both :

DEAR PROFESSOR :

I have for a long time desired to write to you, to express the gratitude your interesting works awakened in my heart. I have always been arrested by the fear of robbing you of precious time, and I contented myself, while reading your writings, with sending you in thought, a cordial acknowledgment. But since a favorable occasion now presents itself, I joyfully make use of it, to recall myself to your remembrance and to pray you kindly to accept a small gift, which I hazard sending you under the patronage of my mother, and which perhaps will recall our dear North Sea to you.*

Our good Monsieur Rennecke, doubtless, will have arrived at Munich, and will have satisfied the desire he has for a long time cherished, of forming a nearer aquaintance with you. The reading of your books which I accomplished under his direction, and the frequent conversations of which you have been the subject, have been the commencement of liaison which he will now have the happiness of forming. I have an inexpressible desire to witness it, but must await his return, and now enjoy the anticipation of all that he will have to tell us of the *pro.*

Last year, in reading, "The Primitive World and the Fixed Stars," I was eager to study the heavens and its planets ; I admired the incomprehensible calculations of the learned, and thought of

* It was an excellent design of a site from the shore, near Dobberan.

you, in resorting to our old globe. This year, a new world, but an animated world, has been opened to my view, in your "History of the Soul," which I have found very attractive. Unhappily the departure of Monsieur Rennecke, did not allow me to finish the reading with him ; but I finished it with my dear mother, who has opened the eyes of my understanding to the obscure passages, and placed them upon my level, when my simple mind could not reach them.

But now, dear Professor, it would be indiscreet for me to turn you longer from your important occupations; I then hasten to conclude, once more praying you to keep me in your remembrance.

HELEN.

The departure of the worthy and active preceptor of the princess did not arrest the development of her education, for she knew how to procure in instructive books what she felt the need of. The inner school of the heart, in joy as well as in grief, remained what it had been ; the invisible preceptor, under the superintendence and discipline of which she found herself, remained faithful to her. With these two means of the development of the soul and mind, was also associated the school of the world, developed by social relations, observations, experiences, sufferings, and heart trials.

9

At this period, the hand of a friend will direct me and frequently accompany me through varied events, by which the princess Helen was prepared for her destiny. It is a friend, whose pious and loving heart frequently sustained that of the princess, and whose spiritual life was in such harmony with that of Helen, that it was as a mirror. The lady of whom I speak, is the same who, in a well known house of mourning, has been a faithful spiritual support to broken hearts, and has witnessed the powerful consolations of the gospel, beside the dying bed of a loyal and sincere prince, whom the princess Helen loved and respected. Several passages in the course of this work, marked with a special sign, have been taken from letters addressed to that friend.

Upon returning from her excursion in Switzerland and a great part of Southern Germany, the duchess Helen, under her mother's faithful escort, yielded to the reiterated invitations to visit the new residence of her sister Maria, in beautiful Thuringia. One of these journeys she made in the course of 1831. She passed through Berlin, where duke Albert then was. The princess went to see, in his company, the master-pieces of the Royal Museum, which made a profound impression upon her young imagination.

At Weimar, the family of the grand duke and

the entire people loaded them with proofs of the faithful and deep affection which had transmitted itself from the defunct duchess Caroline, to her children, and above all, to Helen. She describes with transport, the circle of the reunited family at the house of her beloved sister Maria, in quiet, pleasant Eisenberg. She found in her sister's husband, duke George of Altenburg, whom she surnames, "the lever of all noble aspiration," a faithful brother, even till death ; her eyes and her heart rejoiced in the sight of the infantine caresses of the three young princes, pledges of that happy union. At Rudolstadt, two sisters of the grand duchess welcomed the travellers with open arms.

These family delights were soon disturbed by the terrible news that the cholera had invaded Helen's country. It was necessary to return without delay to Mecklenburg, if they would escape the ennui of a quarantine. The duchess Maria and the princess of Rudolstadt, besought the grand duchess to prolong her sojourn with them, until the scourge should rage with less vigor. But the young princess, seconded by her mother, represented with all the eloquence of her heart, that in such a time of distress, the faithful citizen ought to be in the place assigned in his country, where he would be under the sure guidance of God. It was then, "with an unutterable joy," as she wrote, when towards the end of September, 1831, she again saw the soil of her native country.

The fears that the cholera had inspired were not so soon dissipated; nevertheless, she had the joy, in the summer of 1832, of finding herself surrounded by her own dear ones at Dobberan, which she called "the Eden of her childhood." In short, prince Albert, and the duchess *Maria*, with her husband and children, there took up their abode. The presence of several guests, not less distinguished by intellectual gifts than by princely éclat, became a new source of delight to the young princess, then eighteen years of age.

I here transcribe, almost at length, four letters written by her hand during this period of her development. They will serve to complete my observations.

DEAR AND HONORED PROFESSOR:

Having written to you a short time since, I shall perhaps appear importunate, but it is impossible for me to allow a letter of mother's to be sent to your address, without obeying the impulse of my heart, or without expressing my profound gratitude for your goodness. A few days since, I received the little package which I opened with an ineffable joy, because I recognized your handwriting, always dear and welcome; my delight was still more augmented by the reading of your friendly letter, and by the sight of the instructive books which accompanied it. My thanks, doubtless, arrive rather long after the departure of your gift, from having been delayed, by a journey into beautiful Saxony, to visit my dear sister and some relations, which prevented us from finding M. de Oettl at Dobberan. We saw him only a few moments at Altenburg, when he could not remit your gifts to mother, and promised to send them to Mecklenburg. During the short sojourn of the queen of Bavaria at Altenburg, I had the delight of hearing your name mentioned by prince Otto, with affection and respect; I made his acquaintance with much more pleasure, from mother's having received your favorable opinion of him. I envy the prince the happiness of being at your side, and receiving lessons which you alone can give!

It would be indiscreet longer to abuse your patience by my wearisome words; I confine myself to entreating that you will sometimes think, in your prayers, of your Helen, who reveres you and is entirely devoted to you.

EISENBERG, August 18, 1831.

The second letter expresses the tendencies of the princess in the first months of the year 1832:

MUCH HONORED PROFESSOR:

I would not permit myself to trouble you in your occupations, if your goodness, already tested, was not a guarantee of your indulgence. To express to you my sincere gratitude is a necessity of my heart, for I experienced ineffable joy in receiving your beautiful letter, and your very interesting little book. My insignificant work did not merit the welcome which you gave it; it will be a happiness to have it sometimes used by you, not the least, in having provoked such an excellent letter, in which you happily hold up the swan, as the symbol of the spirit of life.

You mention in your letter the great triangle of the stars in the heavens, in which you see the image of the Trinity in unity. I was greatly delighted, for this thought had previously struck me when reading it in your '*History of the Soul;*' I love, on starry nights, to discover this great symbol, in the midst of other luminous worlds.

The biography of the venerable Oberlin has greatly interested me; I have read it with great pleasure; and in order that you may know, dear professor, that we occupy ourselves with your writings, I will again tell you, that to procure innocent pleasure we follow you in your journey in Italy, that with you, we admire that magnificent country, and the heroism of your dear wife. We are now at

Genoa, where I listen with great interest to what you have to say of the productions of ancient art; after your suggestion, I hastened to read the sequel which promised still more instruction upon that subject.

My dear Monsieur Rennecke, who has given an account of his sojourn with you, has apprised me that the princess Matilda takes lessons of you. I will sincerely avow that envy glided into my heart upon learning it; for, since M. Rennecke is established at Dargun, I am reduced to the *means* which he left me for continuing my studies; the spirit which gives life, absolutely fails me; hence, would I love to share the happiness of one who finds occasion for development in the domain of science. Oh! that I might from time to time be present at your instructions!

My letter may become too long, and I should be injudicious if I further tested your patience. I then hasten to conclude, presenting the compliments of my Nancy, whom you have doubtless not forgotten, and praying you, dear professor, sometimes o think of your devoted

HELEN.

LUDWIGSLUST, Feb. 13, 1832.

The third letter, written the same year as the

preceding one, has a special importance in the short series of letters of this period, which reveal the spiritual progress of a heart subjected to discipline.

DOBBERAN, Aug. 12, 1832.

DEAR AND HONORED PROFESSOR,

Behold yourself again forced to read a few words of lively gratitude, written by a well-known young hand, which counts anew upon your entire indulgence and patience. Your friendly lines and pages, of which the contents are so interesting, were remitted to me by your friend the ecclesiastical counsellor Oettl, a man who awakens the confidence of the heart, and the most profound respect ; the affection which he bears towards you, was from the first instant, his best recommendation. Accept my heartfelt thanks for the remembrance of which your letter has assured me. The persuasion of not being entirely out of your memory and your thoughts, is very sweet to me. I will even say that it strengthens the mind and the heart ; and ought to exercise a happy influence upon the life.

Prince Otto has often interested me, in speaking of you and the lessons which you have given him. He appears to be an amiable young man ; I find that he already awakens interest by his career and by a certain naïveté, which, with him, is so attractive

Though I have wished it, I have never succeeded in efforts to converse with him upon the most serious subjects ; nevertheless, I am convinced that they would have more charm for him than the fugitive questions of this life. But what obstacles in the accomplishment of our wishes ! how often useless verbiage takes the place of worthy conversation.

Until this time God has protected our happy family reunion ; but now we must all flee from this smiling Dobberan, from this beloved sea, for these shores are infested by the miasma of the cholera. The moment of separation is at hand ; every one follows the example of the noble and gracious queen.* She departs with all her court, but leaves a durable remembrance in the hearts of all who have known her. The same is the case with the dear Bavarians who accompany her. They have all gained my heart by their amiable and cordial manners. Oh ! if all the inhabitants of Bavaria resemble them, it must be a magnificent and delightful country.

Dear professor, pardon I pray you my *babillage* ; for this separation afflicts me much ! I would also go to Munich, and hear once more from your lips those beautiful words which come written to me.

* Queen Theresa of Bavaria, sister of the duke of Altenburg

Do not think ill of my praying you to accept amicably a little souvenir, which I hope you will find use for.

HELEN.

The fourth letter from the princess, was written shortly after an event which exercised a decisive influence upon her life. The experiences and adventures of her sojourn at Dobberan, during the preceding summer, still form a portion of the subject of this letter.

LUDWIGSLUST, April 26, 1833.

DEAR PROFESSOR,

To-day it is impossible for me to resist the desire I have long had to write to you. The date of this day will be my excuse, if I rob you of a moment of your very precious time. It is a day very dear to the hearts of all those to whom you have done so much good, by your words and writings, in awakening in their souls a voice which is not of the earth, but which is an echo of heaven. Such a day authorizes me in congratulating all those who, like me, know and revere you, and in expressing my most ardent wishes for the year you are about to commence.

My gratitude for the ineffable benefits that you alone are able to produce by your writings, would express itself otherwise than by a dead letter, the feebleness of which I deeply feel, when, my eyes pause upon that dear little blue book,* which speaks so eloquently to the soul, and breathes a spirit which you alone could animate. It is also that spirit which forms the bond of our circle this evening as we are engaged upon your beautiful work ; it sheds a peace over us which renders the remembrance of you still more dear. There are always some real transports of joy, when there comes to us a new jet from that abundant fountain; each one of us there seeks with avidity for acquaintance with the truth, and becomes strengthened by it. But this is also the only consolation for so long a separation, which seems to me like an eternity ; for, since your departure from Mecklenburg, a whole existence for me has rolled by, in which I have little by little set aside the dreams of childhood, in order finally to grasp the true signification of life. Sometimes still, I renew my taste for childish fables, in which repose the undeveloped germ of life. It is several years, for example, since, in that old city of Nuremburg, I found myself under the mysterious arches of the St. Lawrence church, where the stained glass broke

* Allusion is here made to my "Communications upon the times of the Empire," to be found in my work entitled "Ancient and Modern."—*Author's Note.*

the rays of the setting sun ; since at St. Sebald, the majestic sounds of the organ filled the nave, and identified the past with the present ; how gravely the four apostles of the ancient castle looked down upon me ; how the entire city, symbol of ancient probity, awakened before me at the sound of the bell, and how the fields exhaled their evening perfume, when I seemed to hear from all sides enchanting voices, and lived again in the region of childish dreams. And you, who awakened those beautiful visions in my imagination, and who embellished them with your tales, you were not there; your absence was so sensible to all, that if I had had any power of the magician in my nature I would have made you come from Chemintz. I then thought much of your beloved daughters. I knew that they lived in the same country, but unhappily I was ignorant of the place of their sojourn. Do me the kindness to transmit to them my friendly salutations. I was rejoiced to find their names in the little blue book.

The long period of time which has rolled away since your last letter, has abounded in political events and in intellectual progress for our nation. Bavaria and Greece have, in a manner, commingled their history ; all hearts have palpitated with enthusiasm and sympathy. A lively interest accompanies the heroic expedition into the beautiful country of the Hellenes, whose soil it must be delightful to tread ; this unfortunate region will surely bloom again under the protection of a wise government, and will find in obedience to the laws, the true liberty which it vainly sought in anarchy. The touching and solemn reception which it has given to its king, may justify the liveliest hopes. This young king ought to be happy in thus knowing himself to be surrounded by so many prayers raised to God for him, for his happiness, and for that of his people. You, also, dear professor, you surely have not without emotion seen your pupil borne away to fill such weighty engagements ; his departure must have deeply affected the heart of his excellent preceptor, M. de Oettl.

Shall I dare pray you to recall me to his remembrance ? My interviews with him the past summer have been faithfully retained in my memory. Your goodness has so often crowned my wishes, that I dare address you still another prayer ; if your thoughts some day flow toward Ludwigslust, recommend me some reading which you judge instructive in every respect. The present moment must offer many interesting publications, and yet it is rare that they reach our northern regions. Many hearts here beat for animating, intellectual productions, and ardently desire an unadulterated source.

I must at last cease to chatter ; I close, recommending myself with all my heart to your remembrance and prayers.

I remain, dear professor, with the highest consideration, your grateful

HELEN.

P. S.—My Nancy and all your friends here present their affectionate regards. My brother, this summer, will visit the rectory of Gastein, and will surely not go thither without seeing you. I should be jealous if I loved him less.

VII.

LIGHTS AND SHADOWS.

AMONG all the friends and relations at Friedensburg, none dared hope for the restoration of the grand duchess, who had reached the crisis of a malady, which threatened her life. The skill of physicians seemed of no further use than to determine, with apparent precision, the number of hours her sufferings would continue ; friends of both sexes who approached the dying bed, had no further need of controlling their emotion, for the invalid neither saw nor heard any thing. Among all the persons who visited the grand duchess, Helen only, then nineteen years of age, clung hopefully to her mother, in whom was wrapped up the happiness of her life. No discouragement nor hopeless grief was revealed in her countenance, which reflected only the serenity of a soul in constant communion with God. She had the full assurance that God would not take her cherished mother from her. Calm and self-possessed, she watched night and day according to her strength. Her hopes were not disappointed ; the grand duchess was restored to her kindred.

The danger passed, the young princess, whose faith alone had sustained her, then realized the severity of the blow which had threatened to fall upon her. She thus expresses herself in a letter dated from the baths at Toeplitz, addressed to her intimate friend.

" He who graciously received me, gave me the courage of a child, that is to say, blind courage, and now raises the veil which he had himself drawn over my eyes. Now all lives again, within and without me ; my mountains, my dear and beautiful mountains, awaken within me a song of mirth. They also infinitely rejoice my dear mother, who to-day has already rode out twice. She is happy in being convalescent, and finds a new charm in every object ; she scarcely remembers her illness and sufferings, everything appears to her smiling and serene."

Frederick William, according to his custom, passed several weeks at Toeplitz, in the summer of 1833. The princess Helen already interested him.

because of her possession of qualities rarely united; goodness of heart, high intellectual culture, amiable simplicity, and serious modest mien; but she was besides, the sister-in-law of his daughter, wife of the young grand duke Paul Frederic, of Mecklenburg-Schwerin. He often went to see her, and was forcibly struck with the exquisite tact with which she received and entertained him, which was always directed by the judiciousness of her mind, and perfectly accorded with the faculties of her soul. This impression was not a fleeting one, it was still living in the affectionate heart of the noble king, when his counsels, at a later period, directed the choice of the duke of Orleans towards the princess Helen of Mecklenburg.

From Toeplitz the two princesses went to Dresden, where they passed several days. In that beautiful city, art and nature simultaneously impressed the princess's mind, but the works of art chiefly transported her imagination. Her taste and judgment were so fine, that she soon recognized what was truly worthy of admiration, and distinguished them from those which excite the delight and astonishment of the curious multitude. "In art, as in life, there is an eternal truth under the outward form," wrote she to her young friend. "It is truth which touches the heart, at the first *coup d'œil* cast upon a work of art ; the form is only a vestment, which some exterior motives modify. But false enthusiasm is passionate for the form, which it changes, and takes for the truth."

After passing the winter at Jena, in the immediate neighborhood of the celebrated doctor and intimate counsellor, Starke, the grand duchess Augusta returned to one of the bath establishments in Hungary. With her return of strength, she experienced the reawakening of her intellectual life, which naturally sought aquaintance with all that is worth knowing. She soon formed around her, a choice circle of *savants* and professors of the University of Jena, and under their direction set about sounding all the depths of science. After her example, the mobile mind of the princess Helen, easily bent to the task of gathering varied information. These intellectual labors afforded the princess ineffable happiness. "Our life," wrote she to her friend, "is at once calm and agitated, outwardly uniform, but inwardly rich in delights. The professors are very communicative ; it is a delightful life, which to me has an infinite attraction."

The charm of a sojourn in that city devoted to the worship of the muses, was augmented in the eyes of the princess by the neighborhood of Eisenberg, which often permitted her to see her sister.

and by the still greater nearness of Weimar, the residence of her mother's relations.

"Surrounded by souvenirs of my mother's life," wrote she, "I passed delicious days in the circle of my kindred. I also became acquainted with many good and interesting things in that ancient German Athens."

Thus terminated the year 1833, during which the young princess had much enjoyment; she also commences the year 1834 with a grateful remembrance.

"I am always astonished," writes she to her friend at the end of that year, "I am astonished at the joys God grants me, as if he would console me for the past and future. His paternal love powerfully attracts me towards Him; how can I but offer Him my life, a sacrifice for merciful acts. Since the re-establishment of my mother's health, this year has been happy in every respect. Provided only, that joy be not without consistence, and flees not like the shades of evening, leaving no trace. In that case, I should desire affliction to establish my heart and mind. For what are the delights of this world, if they do not elevate the soul toward heaven, the primary source of all felicity?"

This desire for a call which should elevate her heart to God, even though it might be through tears, was only too soon satisfied, in 1834. Prince Albert, upon whose future his sister and mother founded their dearest terrestrial hopes, in a grand military parade had a fall from his horse, which subsequently caused violent headaches; this tendency, I am told, was again aggravated by another fall from the top of a high wall of the castle of Cobeda, near Jena. When he made me a second visit, at Munich, in 1833, upon his return from the baths of Gastein, I found him very different from what he had been in 1828. In his interviews with his friends, though he had ever the same vivacity of mind, his gayety had given place to a sombre mood, which often painted itself upon the features of his countenance, even in the midst of animated conversation. "If you knew," said he to my wife, "what continual pain I have in my head, you would comprehend the morbid silence which I continually keep with friends."

This disposition did not entirely proceed from his physical suffering; it also had its source in a profound agitation of the soul, which he described to me in a letter dated from Gastein, from whence he expressed his intention of coming to see me.

WILDBALD-GASTEIN, January 23, 1833.

MY BELOVED MASTER:

Upon my departure from Berlin, I received

from my mother the good news that you would permit me to visit you upon my return, and to pass several days with you as formerly. I cannot express the great joy I experienced at the thought of seeing you again, and of telling you that after the lapse of so many years and divers events, I have the same filial and cordial affection for you that I had in my childhood. I am very impatient to see you, to open my heart to you, and to ask your counsels and benediction.

Since we have met, some very trying days have passed over me ; my soul has been in great danger of shipwreck, because the evil germs of my nature commenced to take root. But in the midst of these storms, I have always heard a voice unceasingly exhorting me, which seemed to be a cherished echo of my boyhood ; then came that indefinable *malaise*, which reminded me that I ought to set at liberty a noble slave enchained in my heart. In the midst of the insipid life of the world or upon the sick couch, the Spirit moved within me, and I finally experienced a profound disgust for all that is mere nothingness. God has granted me strength to master my passions, and with a good conscience, has returned the delight in life, which I had lost. To say all this to you verbally, dear professor, and to hear again from your lips the old language of the heart, is a permission for which I cannot sufficiently thank you, for it is already a welcome balm to my soul.

In leaving Gastein, I leave a place in which I have finally found the happiness which had for a long time fled from me. The remembrance of Ber lin is painful to me.

I was happy then, in leaving for the dear countries of the South. I felt another spirit within me ; I was calm, serious, joyful. I could again observe with attention, and collect and arrange my impressions so as to render them profitable. I first proceeded to Dresden, where I tarried long enough to visit the gallery leisurely and to traverse Saxon-Switzerland. From there, I went by Tœplitz to Prague, that ancient city with its tombs of saints and kings, archives of the history of Bohemia and Germany, more instructive than all the scribbling of our modern protoculs. At Linz, I again saw the snowy Alps, to which my eyes had not for a long time been habituated. I crossed the lake to visit Ischl ; then, down lake St. Wolfgang to Salzburg, which is a charming city. There, I thought much of you and my dear Oettl. I visited the Kœnigsee ; I clambered over the Watzman glaciers, and after having cleared the passages at the Lueg and Klamm, found myself here. I have been living here tranquilly nearly a month, 3,000 feet above the sea and even in the bosom of the lofty Alps. When leaping over the rocky abysses, when contemplating the play of the sunlight upon the snow, what a world of plants I see living around me where the silence is alone interrupted by the uniform noise of a cascade, which comes to my ear like the pulsation of the life of Nature ; then as I recoil within myself, all the dear, good thoughts of my childhood awaken a slight feeling of pain ; my joy changes itself into a mute prayer, and I renew my engagement to remain faithful to the God of my youth and manhood. I live here in company with persons dear to me, and with whom I am at ease. We have here the arch-duke John and his wife ; this noble prince is the image of a German of the old stamp. When questioned at hazard, he has a reply for every one ; in the Tyrol, he is acquainted with each valley, and village, and with most of the families in the mansions and cottages. His noble face, à la Hapsburg, bears the impress of perfect goodness. With all this, he dresses like a peasant, and, in all his manners, is simple, thoughtful, and amiable.

Without being able to fix the day, I shall leave Gastein in the beginning of August, and think I shall proceed directly to Munich, passing through Innspruck. Since I know it will give you pleasure, I shall seek your hospitality without ceremony I thrill with joy at the thought of seeing you again with the affection of former times, and of presenting myself to you, not as a stranger, but as a devoted, thoughtful son.

How delighted I shall be to see all my dear friends in Munich! In the meanwhile very cordially salute your dear wife, my good Oettl, and Dr. R.

Once more, dear professor, I thank you from the depths of my heart for your permission, and I wait for the moment in which I shall be able to say so, directly, with impatience.

Your affectionate, constant, and respectful pupil,
ALBERT, duke of Mecklenburg.

Upon the prince's return into his country, the pain in his head increased in an alarming manner. As the physicians presumed, and as the autopsy later verified, a tumor pressing upon the brain often occasioned convulsions, followed by violent pain. A sojourn at Franzensbad, in the spring of 1834, had produced no good effect; the dying prince was brought to Ludwigslust. His sufferings assumed a character which lacerated the hearts of all who witnessed them. Notwithstanding the sinking of his body, his mind was always collected, and unfolded itself in touching expressions of love and serious self-abnegation. Finally, upon the 18th of

October, 1854, that painful contest ended; they laid the corpse of this young prince, which seemed to sleep sweetly after the fatigues of a laborious journey, beside his parents.

Whoever saw the princess Helen during the period when his mortal sufferings diminished all chance of life, could scarcely recognize a trace of her natural gaiety of mind. She was not altogether overwhelmed.

"The trials of life contain the germ of my eternal happiness," wrote she to her friend, after the death of her brother.

She then delivered herself with still more ardor to the task of "strengthening and purifying the bonds which united her to those who remained upon the earth." Upon her part there were only words of love and acts of devotion, first for her kindred, then for all those who interested her and had need of her. She knew, in the Christian sense of the word, that *that* only was profound mourning. Then, and still more at a later period, sensibility to her own griefs awakened within her a delicate sympathy for the griefs of others, and a power of consoling, the magnetic virtue of which the afflicted experienced. This was her principal occupation during the first portion of the winter of 1834.

She wrote me from Ludwigslust, upon the 14th

of January, 1834, the following letter, which is the expression of the tendency of her soul at this epoch :

DEAR PROFESSOR,

You loved him with us, you wept for him with us, and you rejoice with him in the eternal felicity accorded to his soul, as indemnity for all the sufferings of a short, but agitated life ; you rejoice with him in that celestial peace which his impatient desires sought for, upon earth, and of which his faith gave him happy presentiments. In the midst of indescribable sufferings, a soul like his could only be led to patience and docility by the power of God; in the touching outpourings of the last period of his life, the powerful succor of the Most High was manifested in a most consoling manner, rendering him so calm and thoughtful, and preparing him for the contemplation of the eternal light, by a filial submission to the will of God. The happy conviction that he is now in possession of an incorruptible inheritance, was a solace at the hour of his death to our afflicted hearts, and it remains a possession which neither the poignancy of doubt, nor the pain of a now isolated life, can ravish; the firm persuasion that he is happy and that we shall rejoin him, will accompany us through the rest of our career, and will direct our eyes towards heaven like the finger of an angel; it will be the sure pledge of our eternity and the sacred bond which unites him to our world of sorrow.

In the midst of the most agonizing grief, man feels that such hours in life, are hours of purification; he learns to kiss the hand that smites, whose powerful aid alone can save him from despair. You recall the divine consolations, in such a touching manner, in your letter, dear professor; permit me to express how profoundly grateful I am for all that you have done for us. Alas! dare the sister form an adieu for you, in behalf of the brother so sensible to the affection you manifested for him during his life, so happy in the benedictions which he owed to your prayers and his veneration for yourself?

But no, eternal recompense is found in the affection and intercession itself; you aspire to no other reward than the answer to your prayers.

I dare not speak of myself, for I blush to complain, knowing that my brother is in the mansions of eternal happiness; I am nevertheless too weak to withdraw my thoughts from my loneliness and to surmount sadness. How shall I again attain the happiness of my childhood, when he who was the *glory*, the *joy*, and the *pride* of my life sleeps in death; when my hopes resemble unbalanced scales which rise and fall from one side to another. But no, I will not speak at random, only in heaven shall I again find all who formerly attracted me by bonds of love; yes, in that promised land where ardent desires are appeased, where tears are dried. Yes, affliction is good!

I am very grateful, dear professor, for your kind intention of sending me a souvenir, which was destined for my Albert; be persuaded that any gift coming from you has great value, and that beautiful present, which will remind me of a favorite name,* will be of double worth. Your eyes have complacently rested upon those features which reveal the sublime genius of the poet; your kindness destined that emblem of divine force for my brother, and now you wish that I should adorn my little apartment with it; what could be dearer to me than an object recalling such remembrances?

In concluding, I again transmit the compliments of my relatives; first those of my mother, who thinks of writing to you soon, then those of my sister and the prince. General de Both, my Nancy, and the good L———, desire to be remembered to you; your faithful friend B——— now addresses you from a better country than that of Mecklenburg.

* Dante.

Still another request before taking leave of you ; your benevolence and affection for my brother will insure its acceptance. The thought of your having in your hands a souvenir of his possessions would be very precious to me, for I might hope that it would sometimes set the image of my brother before your eyes. Shall I forward it by the next courier ? I believe I hear a very kind yes, and confidently hazard the execution of my design. Your sympathy encourages me ; may it be a legacy left by the deceased to his poor and unworthy sister, and a source of benediction all her life.

I remain, dear professor, with the most profound respect, your entirely devoted

HELEN.

A friendly salutation to your dear wife ; if you see M. Oettl, remember me to him. He was infinitely dear to my brother, and merits all our regard. I have taken a lively interest in making the acquaintance of your friend Schom ; he is an addition to Weimar.

This letter was followed by another, dated Feb. 20th, 1835 :

DEAR PROFESSOR,

Without awaiting an affirmative reply to my petition, I have courage to give it success, counting upon the remembrance which you surely retain of my dear brother, and upon the affection of which you gave him so many proofs.

I have thought that the telescope which always accompanied him in his travels in Switzerland, in the valleys of Silesia, in the magnificent plains of Lombardy, and in the steppes of la Marche, might be also useful to you in the course of the long journey you contemplate into the classic plains of Greece and to the sources of the Nile ; the plan of which voyage transported my brother, who intended to take part in it. If you find this object of service, make use of it from time to time, and think affectionately of one who is no more, and who wished for your sympathy.

Accept, etc.,

HELEN.

My reply to the first of the preceding letters, and my thanks upon the occasion of her sending the beautiful Dollond, and which accompanied the second letter, reached their destination more happily than the plaster bust of Dante, for, after a long delay, it came broken into the hands of her for whom it was destined. Nevertheless, in the letter which she wrote after the arrival of the case, she expressed her gratitude for the expression of my good will, and dwelt upon the genius of Dante, and the impression which his "Divina Commedia," "chant of eternity," had produced, and still continued to produce upon her soul, but of the bust she spoke not. I regret that this letter has been unhappily lost or mislaid among my papers. All of its contents are not entirely effaced from my memory. At the time I received it I was incessantly occupied with labors which must be finished before my departure for the East. Besides, from the autumn of 1835 to that of 1836, when I commenced my journey, a portion of my time and strength was absorbed by university duties. It is probable that the last letter, addressed to me from Ludwigslust by the young princess, disappeared in the midst of papers that I have not had leisure to examine.

VIII.

LIFE, A DREAM.

To souls which have received the gift of a lively and lofty hope, life here below, with all its vicissitudes, is a perpetual prophetic dream, which is only realized when, after the dissolution of the earthly tenement, a new existence commences for the soul. This is expressed in the following passage by an apostle, who by his words and acts, testified that he felt the importance and signification of terrestrial life, as the embryo of life eternal. "But we know," says he, "that if our earthly house of this tabernacle were dissolved, we have a building of God, an house not made with hands, eternal in the heavens." (2 Cor. v. 1.)

This promise to man is indeed not accomplished till the soul leaves its earthly tent; but is often manifested symbolically in life, when man sees the crumbling of an edifice, which in his dreams he has elevated as a sure shelter. This human work, the feeble vessel in which one has confided his happiness for the present and future, is submerged by the tempest ; he sees himself alone, floating at venture upon a wreck, in the midst of fogs and darkness. But the invisible hand of eternal mercy has directed the winds and the waves ; dawn appears, and the shipwrecked one who believed himself lost, nears the isle of deliverance, where open arms receive him with affection, and where peace and joy re-enter the soul.

The foundation of the edifice of dreams of the future and of terrestrial happiness, which the loving heart of the princess had erected, was the hope of passing her life near her brother Albert. This hope vanished, she found herself in the same situation as the bird whose home is in the branches of a tree, which is suddenly struck by lightning. Fatigued with flying, it seeks its daily shelter, and beholds it calcinated upon the earth ; but the bird is full of life, the first rays of the sun awakens it as before, and it makes its morning song heard.

In the month of April, 1835, the princess' grandfather, Frederick-Francis, entered upon the 50th year of his government. The general jubilee which accompanied the fêtes of that anniversary, had an echo in the heart of the princess, who, for the first time since her brother's death, found serenity of mind. She wrote to her friend that the surrounding joy not only had not made her shudder, but had even communicated a certain gayety to her. She loved to render herself useful to those of the most humble condition; during the winter of 1836, she occupied herself in extending and ameliorating the Caroline Institution, which was founded by her deceased mother, and which was designed for the education of those destined for domestics. She did not dream of one day leaving her country, when from the height of the ancient castle of Schwerin, situated in the midst of a lake, her eye complacently rested upon the snow and glacier, which in winter surrounded the isle and the castle like a rampart. What an abyss between this peaceful dwelling which satisfied her heart, and the vast horizon which the design of God was secretly opening, about this epoch.*

About the time of the princes' departure from Berlin, the first part of the apostle's words, which

* Prof. Schubert here makes mention of the visit of the French princes in Berlin, and the king's counsels with regard to union with the princess Helen. Since the substance is the same as that in the previous memoir, it is not necessary here to quote him.

pertain to the dissolution of the earthly tabernacle, seemed about to be realized with regard to the princess Helen. At Eisenberg (where she was visiting her relatives) she was attacked with hepatitis in so severe a manner, that she even believed her end approaching. The rumor, indiscreetly spread, that the heir to the throne of France had a view to her hand in marriage, painfully affected her, for her thoughts were now rather directed towards the hope of which the second part of the apostle's text guarantees the certitude.

Nature remained victorious; the thought of death gave place to the hope of a terrestrial happiness, prepared by the marvellous counsels of God, and not by the foresight or efforts of men. Soon after the re-establishment of the princess' health, the family were apprised of the truth of the rumor, and in the beginning of the year 1837, the news spread from Mecklenburg, throughout all Germany and Europe.*

She was, with regard to these disquietudes, in

* Prof. Schubert, here also mentions the death of the grand-duke, and Paul Frederick's opposition to the princess' union with the duke of Orleans, and adds, "But, according to her habit, she followed the inspiration of her heart and remained firm, for she felt that she was directed ever by the hand of God."

the same courageous state of mind in which she was when she wrote four years before, to her friend, when she had yet no dream of her future destiny: "My imagination," wrote she, "easily leads me, and often touches my whole being with its magic ring; but when it is necessary, exultation and golden dreams vanish; I bow to the iron rod of destiny, and, whatever may be my repugnance, I humble myself, seeking the finger of God in the course of events; His ways are not always those of the heart and desire of youth, but they are always those of our true happiness."

In this circumstance, the way in which she was directed was not difficult to follow, for all that she had learned of the duke was so conformed to her wishes that she had given him her heart, even before she had seen him. He was, in every respect, the man whom she would desire to guide her life. Her attachment for the husband of her choice, was then, and always remained, purified by the fire of divine love.

The Easter fêtes of 1837, arrived in the midst of the contests produced by this project of marriage. The Thursday before Easter, the princess received the communion, and obtained, to use her own expression, "a new life through the gracious gift, the power of which passes all conception."

"At this solemn moment," wrote she to her friend, "I deeply felt that all is nothingness beside this grace, and that all feeling which flows not from the love of God, and which is not sanctified by his Spirit, is neither pure nor durable. Ah! if we could only always build our edifice upon Him, in prosperity as well as in trial; and if, in all our life, we could have the firm persuasion that He loves us, and that His love produces precious fruit in us!" *

The best letters brought by M. Bresson from the royal family, were those by the duke himself. The princess opened a correspondence with him, through which she became as well acquainted with the heart and mind of her betrothed as if she had been personally acquainted with him for years.

The joy which seemed to fill France upon her arrival, contrasted strongly with her departure from Mecklenburg; the latter seemed like a funeral train, of which the former was a veritable ovation. This striking contrast forcibly reminds me of an ancient canticle, the words of which faithfully reproduce the inward impressions of the princess, and the

* Prof. Schubert's remarks concerning the princess' departure for France, and her reception along the route, so entirely accords with those of the marquess de H—— that they may be omitted without detriment to the work.

experiences that there were before her, in the future.

"Ich traue denien Wunderwegen,
Sie enden sich in Lieb und Segen;
Geung, wennich Dich bei mi hab!
Ich weiss, wen Du willst herrlich zieren,
Und über Mond und Sterne führen,
Den führest Du zuvor hinab."

IX.

THE ARRIVAL.

A MORE solemn moment than those of these outward distinctions awaited the young betrothed at Châlons-sur-Marne. She did not yet know her future husband by sight, who had come there in advance of her. He also, was very impatient to see one who was to be the companion of his life. It was known that the princess was endowed with great loveliness and high intellectual faculties, but at the same time less favorable rumors had been spread with regard to her personal appearance. A French lady who had seen her in Germany, wished to rectify this opinion, but the queen forbade it, charging her to say nothing to her son, in order that he might have a sweet surprise. The likeness which the prince had received of her, did not render the life and grace which particularly marked Helen's physiognomy ; hence was he struck with it. He entered with an almost timid air, but his eyes, at first cast down, became radiant with joy and emotion, when, in the course of an animated interview, the delicate features of his betrothed became so transfigured that they composed an *ensemble* of ideal beauty, while her noble bearing and the *spirituelle* dignity of her whole person awakened an indefinable sentiment of respect. The impression which the duke made upon the princess was not less favorable. In short, in the judgment of a shrewd observer, the young and handsome duke of Orleans, was the most accomplished and distinguished man of his time, by the union of physical advantages and intellectual and spiritual gifts.

The prince, who now bore the image of the princess in his heart, hastened to Fontainbleau, where the royal family received the duchess with such affection, that she soon no longer dreamed of being in a foreign court. Upon the 30th of May, the day fixed for the marriage, the ceremony commenced according to French custom, by the civil marriage in the gallery of Henry II. At half past eight o'clock, the king appeared, giving his arm to the princess Helen, and was followed by all the royal family, as well as the numerous cortége of the officers of the palace. The ministers, marshals, deputies, municipal corps, with the generals and many invited guests, were there assembled. The princess' witnesses were, M. de Rantzau, marshal of the grand duchess' court, M. de Bresson, French minister to Berlin, who had conducted the marriage negotiations, and the duke de Choiseul. The chancellor, Duke Decazes, read the civil act in a solemn voice and in the midst of profound silence; then he asked the duke of Orleans if he was resolved to take as his wife, Helen Louise-Elizabeth of Mecklenburg. The prince turned respectfully towards the king, and, upon an affirmative signal from his majesty, he replied to the chancellor in a firm voice: "Yes, Monsieur." The same question being put to the affianced princess, she turned towards her mother, the grand duchess, and after another sign of assent, said in a trembling voice: "Yes, Monsieur." The signatures were finally affixed according to the prescribed ceremonial; after which, the civil marriage was at an end.

It is not without a motive that we have recalled all the circumstances of this act, the solemnity of which was further enhanced by the lively interest manifested by the great personages of rank. A witness, placed somewhat behind the scenes, was more chilled than edified. "I have never been," said he, "the friend of these theatrical representations, which have the effect of exposing sacred things to the view of a curious multitude. This spectacle left me absolutely unmoved, though I was so easily affected by a simple canticle sung in a village church."

When, in 1804, Napoleon drew Pope Pius VII. to Paris for his coronation, it was desired that some church music, of extraordinary power, should relieve the éclat of that solemnity. Twenty-four harps composed the orchestra ; one may easily believe that such a harmony would have a powerful effect upon the minds of the spectators. The ceremony commenced ; the twenty-four harps struck their accords ; the multitude expressed their delight by gestures and low exclamations. The pope then approached the altar. To the harpists succeeded the choir of the Sistine chapel, which sang the ancient church canticle, *Tu es Petrus.* Here the acclamations of transport from the multitude gave place to a mute surprise, which awakened in many hearts a truly religious feeling.

The meditation of the princess did not depend upon external circumstances. The feeling of the sacredness and indissolubility of the marriage filled her heart ; for she felt that it was decided, not by the will of man, but by the favor and counsel of

God. Her union was decreed in heaven, and her mouth, as well as her heart, gave the high and public testimony before God and man.

From the gallery of Henry II., where the civil act was achieved, the great assembly withdrew to Henry IV.'s chapel. The bishop of Meaux, dressed in pontifical robes, made a touching address, followed by the marriage benediction. The names of the two affianced were finally inscribed in the church register.

Then followed a new act according to the usage of the court of France. The assistants proceeded toward the Louis Philippe saloon. Here, was an altar covered with red velvet ; a crucifix was placed between four lighted tapers and before an open Bible ; the curate Cuvier, dear to many among us, was ready in a black robe before the altar, to bless the married couple, in his turn, according to the Lutheran rite. In a gentle, but firm voice, he made an exhortation, the power of which proceeded from the word of God. The sight of this couple, possessing such rare qualities and evidently directed by the Spirit of God, gave to his voice, the eloquence of his heart. After having put the same questions to them as the chancellor, and having heard their affirmative response, blessed them by laying on his hands, and finished the solemnity, saying, "What God has joined together, let no man put asunder." The duke, the duchess, and witnesses inscribed their names in the register.

The young duchess of Orleans from that time regularly attended worship in the Lutheran church in Paris. The impression made by her first appearance in that church, was reproduced upon every occasion of her public appearance ; a lady who was an eye-witness, thus makes mention of her :

"Being in Paris in 1848," wrote a friend to me, "I happened to be at the house of the pastor Verney; (the same, who died at Strasburg, several years since;) conversation turned to the arrival of the duchess of Orleans and to her first appearance in the Protestant church. Madame V——, with her habitual vivacity, said : "I heard much of the impression the duchess of Orleans produced upon every one. But we French, do not make much of princes and princesses, and I thought people had erred in extolling her so much. I then went to the church with the intention of not allowing myself to be ensnared. When she entered, as she advanced down the aisle with her slight figure, as she bowed to the right and left with her fascinating and serious grace which suited the sanctity of the place, I was also smitten and my eyes were moist, as were those of all present. My intention to see nothing [illegible] that of an ordinary lady, and to do nothing but praise or criticise her toilet, had entirely disappeared. I was asked in the city, 'Did you see her bow to the right and to the left? Did you remark that during the chant, she did not raise her eyes from her hymn book, etc?' Then I understood the preoccupied thoughts of those who found themselves in her path."

We will not here recall the *fêtes* given in Paris in honor of the princess' arrival, for it is easy to form an idea of them. The entire city and environs took an active part in them, and employed all their ingenuity to afford the princess an agreeable surprise. At the ball given at the Hôtel-de-Ville, upon entering, she saw panellings ornamented with pictures representing views of her own country. There were views of Ludwigslust, Schwerin, and Dobberan, drawn by the pencil of a skilful artist. What we may still add, is, that neither the agitation of all these fêtes, nor inward emotion, nor the magnificence of the royal apartments, nor the interview with persons of the highest distinction, could for a single moment disturb the calm which was so natural to her; she accepted those inevitable honors without being distracted or fatigued; it could be seen that she was touched and rejoiced; one admired her manner of salutation, of observing everything, of understanding all, as well as of listening and speaking ; one was astonished at the sound of her gentle, pleasant voice, and her pure French accent.*

* The grand duchess relates a trait characteristic of her perfect calm and habitual dignity. They conducted the princess as in triumph to her apartments, where she found displayed all that Paris could offer in the shape of trinkets, pearls, apparel, and other objects for the toilette. They expected transports of surprise, or a burst of joy. But she passed them in review with an unalterable *sang froid*, as distant from disdain as from admiration ; it was a perfect tranquility which revealed a legitimate gratitude. "Oh ! it was magnificent to see" adds her noble mother with emotion.

AUTHOR'S NOTE.

A frenchman of rank, wrote about this epoch to a frrend in Germany : "The papers will have long since informed you of all the particulars of the journey and of the arrival of the duchess of Orleans, also of her marriage and the fêtes which followed. But what no gazette relates and what I should endeavor in vain to describe, is the grace of that young princess, whom we have now the happiness of possessing. Praise to her education, intellect and lofty reason, has long since been accorded ; but what no person among us expected, and the prince less than others, is the indescribable charm spread over all her person and delicate features. Of all the conquests we have made in France, this is the most precious, and God be praised ! she will remain to us. She possesses all the qualities which are indispensable among us for a princess, and which are of greater price than the greatest beauty. It is impossible to associate so much truly royal dignity with more presence of mind, reason, grace and modesty. Dream that I have daily under my eyes the model of all those qualities in the person of your adorable queen (Amelia); but I ought nevertheless to say, that the duchess possesses all that I can represent to myself of what is noble and attractive.

The princess had then a share in the happiness which springs from affection, a happiness for which the human heart would wish an eternal duration. Yet she then recalled the fragility of earthly possessions, as she separated from one very dear to her. Her faithful governess, Miss Nancy Solomon, who had educated her with such perseverance, affection, and success, took leave of her former pupil, and affected with contrasting emotions returned to Geneva, the place of her birth.

X.

LOUIS PHILIPPE IN THE FAMILY CIRCLE.

CONTEMPORARIES have drawn a portrait of the character and acts of Louis Philippe, which according to the different points of view, present the original in a more or less favorable light. They have succeeded as a painter would, commissioned to portray the face of a celebrated man, who has never sat for him, and who at the most has only seen him pass in the street. Wind, rain, or any contrariety whatever, would sensibly alter the lineaments and even modify the habitual bearing of the model. A friend who had daily been able to study the natural expression of his countenance, would not consider the portrait sketched upon a public place, a perfect one, and would regret that his friend had never been able to sit for the artist.

Whoever could have seen Louis Philippe in the midst of his family, in the evening, after the fatigues of the day, would have been touched with the affection borne by all the members of it to this good father, and which united them to one another. One could there contemplate the happiness of this care-laden king, when found in his natural element ; a cordial and sincere affection was there realized in the just medium which he in vain sought to establish among contending parties. In public life, if one is forced to render justice to his perfect probity and to the benevolence of his character, sometimes one might be contemned, sometimes another, sometimes both ; but, in the family circle, he was what all desired—a devoted father, who desired but the happiness of his children.

This need of affection, and outpouring of the heart ought to have been one of the dominant traits depicted in the character of the king of the French. The faithful friend, whose intimacy was not confined to entering the apartments, but also constantly sounded the depths of the heart, takes care that in the midst of the dangers with which Louis Philippe was threatened, this dominant trait should be preserved and even enforced. The period of the birth of Louis Philippe (1773) was not favorable to the growth of such good germs. The salutary influence that might have been exercised over him by the artillery officer, Bonard, the preceptor of his childhood, was certainly not developed by Madame de Genlis, under whose direction the young prince was placed at the age of nine years ; the warm atmosphere of a conservatory may well produce the leaves and flowers of the palmy zone, but not savory or aromatic fruits. At a later period, the young duke de Chartres, by his prudence and valor in the revolutionary army was indeed applauded in the Jacobin Club, which he entered at the age of seventeen years, (1790) following the example of his father ; but this was not the standard ; a sentence of exile and four months of danger in the midst of mountains was necessary to develop the best germs in his heart. Those good principles were still further strengthened during his sojourn at Reichenau, where under the name of Chabaud Latour, he occupied the place of professor of geography and mathematics. He there gained the affection and esteem of his pupils, as well as the regard of the inhabitants of the country. The news of his father's execution, forced him to quit this place of repose. His resources would not permit his prosecuting his plan of going by the way of Hamburg to America ; they sufficed for a voyage to Denmark, Sweden, and Norway, as far as the North Cape ; this voyage developed his knowledge in more than one direction.*

"In the provisory government formed after the forfeiture of Charles X., Lafitte proposed that the duke of Orleans should be appointed lieutenant-general of the kingdom. Every one, weary of the contest, and desirous of order and tranquility, rejoiced when the duke, esteemed by both parties, accepted his election. Becoming king of the French, he took the reins of government in hand, with the chimerical hope of reuniting the most diverse pretentions in a just medium.

It is useless to speak words of peace in ears deafened by the storm of passions ; whoever seeks to act as mediator in contests between people insensible to reason, risks drawing the explosion of their fury upon him. The hatred of the revolutionary party burst forth on the 28th of July, 1835, in the horrible attempt of Fieschi against the life of Louis Philippe, during a review. Twenty-one persons were mutilated in the immediate neighborhood of the king, who returned uninjured to the pious Amelia, whose prayers seemed to be his guardian angel. The following year, on the 25th of July, 1836,

* The sketch of Louis Philippe's life at this period is in substance the same as that given in a note in the work of the marquess de H——.

Alibaud sought to assassinate the king, but failed in his purpose ; and, in the month of December in the same year, the pistol of a workman again spared the life of Louis Philippe. The remembrance of these murderous attempts, were yet recent, when the princess Helen arrived in Paris to marry the duke of Orleans. She could see serious indications of the instability of a throne built upon so fragile a basis ; a less courageous soul would have been easily alarmed for the future.

But while without in the political world, always ill at ease, contests between life and death continued unremittingly, the same peace reigned in Louis Philippe's home circle. The good and pious Amelia, above all, contributed to sustain the heart of her husband, and those about him. If the king, wearied with the cares of the throne, found at home an asylum of repose, joy, and affection ; her soul was constantly at peace. The king besides felt, that the hand of the Lord would protect and guard him until he had finished the laborious task of guiding the helm upon an incessantly agitated sea.

We have still to mention some essential members of this family circle, who assembled twice a day around the king's table. Louis Philippe's sister, Adelaide, had a right to equal respect with the queen, by the analogy of intellectual and spiritual gifts, as well as by the rank which she occupied in the family. If the queen felt the most tender maternal affection for her son's young wife, the princess Adelaide, recognized her as a messenger of good, "an angel sent from heaven to the royal family."

The eldest son of the house, Duke Ferdinand Philippe of Orleans, whose place was beside his mother, not only attracted the attention of the stranger by the regularity of his features, but by the energy depicted upon his noble physiognomy. It awakened confidence and sympathy rather than fear, and when animated, became irresistible. At the age of twenty-one (1831), he arrested the terrible outbreak at Lyons solely by his personal influence, without the use of threat or of the armed force commanded by marshal Soult. He confidently advanced into the midst of that unfortunate working class, distributed all in his power to ameliorate the misery that the insurrection had still more augmented, and became the instrument of Providence for these unfortunates. The poor of Paris afterwards also learned to know and love the young duke of Orleans, when, during the terrible invasion of the cholera, he visited the sick at the peril of his life, in the Hôtel-Dieu, and other hospitals in Paris. Louis Philippe also loved his people; but that sympathetic power was enfeebled and neutralized with him by prudence; whileh is son forgot himself in dreaming only of the happiness of the nation, and thus gained the general affection.

The duke of Orleans was in his twenty-seventh year at the time of his marriage. He was born on the 3d of September, at Palermo, the ancient residence of the sovereigns of Sicily. In his fourth year, he accompanied his mother to Paris, but soon left the Palais-Royal, to seek refuge with his parents in the village of Twickenham, near London. That exile was not long, and when his father found himself free possessor of his appanages, he confided the education of his eldest son to the public schools, a step which the Bourbon family highly censured, and which was received with great favor by the people. At nine years of age, Ferdinand entered the Henry IV. college. He cheerfully submitted to all the tasks of his companions, and shared their punishments and rewards. After having followed the course of the Polytechnic School, he honorably passed the examination of that celebrated institution; he then devoted himself to the study of the modern languages and military tactics, and became colonel of the first regiment of hussars. At the siege of Anvers, he commanded a division of the army; three years after, he shared the dangers and fatigues of the French army in a campaign in Algeria and in the taking of Makara.

Duke Louis de Nemours, worthy of emulating his eldest brother, also attracted attention by his noble chivalric bearing. He was the younger by four years, but he had had the same education. By the side of them at the royal table, might be seen Duke Henri d'Aumale, aged fifteen years, Duke François de Joinville, aged nineteen, and the duke Antoine de Montpensier, who was only thirteen years of age. The princesses Louise, Marie, and Clementine, were attracted to their new sister, at the very first sight. Louise, who was the eldest, soon after married king Leopold whom she accompanied to Belgium; Princess Marie, married the duke Alexander of Wurtemberg, and found in Germany, quiet, domestic happiness, but it was followed by a premature death. Clementine, the youngest of the king's daughters, adorned the life of Duke Augustus-Louis of Saxe-Coburg.

If Louis Philippe's horizon was often o'erclouded, the members of his family were like so many stars whose friendly light reminded him, that, above the region of clouds, there was still a world of light, and that beyond the contest of passions and parties, there was a horizon of peace and unalterable love

XI.

THE NEW LIFE OF THE FAMILY.

We here give, at the dictation of an exactly informed friend, a description of the days which the duchess Helen of Orleans, justly called the happiest of her life.

In summer all the royal family ordinarily removed to the pleasant Neuilly Château, where Louis Philippe, before his accession to the throne, loved to retire during the finest portion of the year, in order to enjoy the beauties of nature and to flee from the noise of the Capital. "Here at Neuilly, France might have contemplated a model of simple and domestic virtues if the prejudices of the great world had permitted the appreciation of manners so patriarchal. And nevertheless it was these domestic virtues which survived the splendor of the throne;

for when Louis Philippe let the sceptre, which he had too promptly seized, fall too easily from his hand, domestic happiness still remained to him ; the bond of affection which united the noble members of his family to him.

At Neuilly, where the young couple retired shortly after their marriage, the king and the queen lived in the same castle with their unmarried children and the princess Adelaide. At fifteen minutes' distance, in the centre of the park, is the little Château of Villiers, which the duke and duchess of Orleans occupied ; they had assigned to the grand-duchess Augusta, and her suite a pleasant row of almost contiguous lodgings. That *spirituelle* princess, who became soon the object of the royal family's respect and affection, had received the pressing invitation to remain near her daughter, until she should be well familiarized with the new existence of the duchess, and should have had leisure to enjoy all that might interest her in Paris. Even at Neuilly, persons who held the first rank in the great world of the capital, might be seen at the king's table.

Upon Sunday. the duchess of Orleans accompanied by the grand-duchess, her mother, frequented the Lutheran Church of Paris, in which some ecclesiastics of rare merit alternately preached in

French and German, the doctrine of salvation through Christ. Beautiful evenings were consecrated to excursions, even as far as Saint Cloud; the borders of the Seine, were then bordered with curious gazers. Sometimes the young princes amused themselves with making bonfires; and, when their royal father remarked that the lawn and fields had not been properly tended, they replied that they had wished to gratify their sister Helen, and the king accepted the excuse, for he was indulgent to his daughter-in-law.

The duchess who had given all her heart to her husband, rendered him as happy as it is possible for one to be on earth; she was, one might say, the better half of his soul. He watched for the happiness of his wife with the greatest solicitude, who on her part, submitted to all his views, finding in him an aid and model, and asked God in all humility to render her more worthy of being the companion of such a husband. The duke manifested the most delicate attentions in the slightest details; he superintended the régime of his wife, and proud of her beauty, controlled her toilet and went himself to gather the flowers in the Villiers garden with which he wished her to be adorned. When she walked out, leaning upon his arm, and when the multitude pressed to see the princess, he would say, smiling with pride, " Yes, my friends, this is my wife."

This sentiment of happiness was not less lively, when the duchess seeking information in her interviews with the most erudite men, put questions to them which forced them to turn their meditations upon new subjects. She had early been habituated to serious thought, to listen and observe with attention, and to meditate upon good books ; endowed with a good memory and an active intellect, she often made a surprising but always just use of what she had learned. Yet, she remained humble and modest. When one praised her scientific progress, she replied : " Yes, what I know best is, that I know nothing, or at least nothing complete." One day while visiting the royal library, she heard some one express astonishment at her erudition, and replied, smiling: " Yes, I am a *savante* who does not even comprehend the rudiments of science, Greek or Latin.

This humility of her heart, showed itself to the best advantage and most habitually in her relations with the duke of Orleans. She wished to receive culture of mind and heart from him ; and nevertheless it was he who felt elevated by her influence. The eminent faculties of the duke seem to have taken a more noble direction after his marriage. The duchess was his right arm even in the minutest details; she was, especially, his treasury for works of beneficence, and in the accomplishment of these offices, she calculated the extent of misery rather than that of her resources; for her purse was opened so largely for contribution that she sometimes found herself in a veritable embarrassment for money.

XII.

A LETTER WRITTEN IN A GARDEN.

I HAVE already said, that about the epoch in which the life of the princess Helen took an unexpected direction, I effected my voyage to the East. Before setting out on my journey, the vague rumor of an approaching marriage had reached my ear, but I paid no attention to it. It was not until the month of January, 1837, during my sojourn in Egypt, that I read in the Augsburg Gazette, the rejoicing confirmation of this report ; and from that time, during all my journey across the desert and the Holy Land, I did not cease, so to speak, to address my thoughts and benedictions to my dear pupil. For a long time I was unable to write, and until I reached Athens, did not even know where to send a letter. While in quarantine at the lazaretto of St. Leopold, an opportunity presented itself of sending a winged harbinger, and shortly after, a letter dated from my prison.

I have related in detail, the event to which I make allusion, in the third part of my journey in the East. An ill-humored lieutenant, who then acted as commandant of the lazaretto, absolutely wished to strangle and cast into the water two charming *bull-bulls*, or Oriental Nightingales, for fear of their propagating the cholera. I gave one to a young French officer who had accompanied us in a long-boat, from the steamer to the entrance of the lazaretto, and in exchange for this present, which gave him great pleasure, I begged him to remit the other to my friend, the physician of the vessel, Fosse, with the request that he would forward it to the duchess of Orleans. My commission was loyally fulfilled; shortly after my return to Munich, I received the following letter from the princess, the contents of which proved, to my great joy, that she had not forgotten her former professor of Mecklenburg.

OCTOBER 7, 1837.

You have greatly rejoiced me, dear professor, by sending your pretty *bull-bull*, and by your friendly letter. Accept my best thanks; permit me also to add that every word coming from you is blessed to my soul, and that each testimony of your good remembrance has great value in my eyes. The ideas you have expressed upon the subject of my marriage, in a letter addressed from Cairo, to my mother, have always done me inexpressible good. The letter, post-marked from the lazaretto, which is lying near me in the garden redolent with the perfume of autumn flowers, develops the same subject and touches me deeply, for you approve the direction my life has taken, you see in it a special benediction from God, and you double my joy by making mention of the high esteem, with which the noble family to which I now belong, inspire you.

While you were making your pilgrimage in the beautiful Oriental countries, and while you were seeking to discover in the dreams of those dormant lands some sound of the language of the past, I also took my pilgrim's staff, tore myself from my country with its cherished tombs and sweet souvenirs of my childhood, and directed my steps towards the West where the voice of my heart and the destiny of my life called me ; where the benediction and counsel of my mother directed me, and where I now realize the dreams of my early years. Here my inward life receives new strength, and finds new aliment in the political contests ; I have a high mission in perspective, which exhorts me to prayer and serious activity. I should be very happy some day to see you here, in my new country, so beautiful and so active; I would show you that the remembrance of you has faithfully accompanied me from my earliest childhood, and the graceful bird, whose song often relates the marvels of his distant country to me, would also salute his old master.

Several extracts from your letters, which have appeared in the Augsburg Gazette, have warmly interested me, and have given me more vivacity in hoping that the oriental traveller, formerly known under the name of "Rist,"* will, without delay, communicate the fruits of his pilgrimage to friends who already owe him so much.

My compliments to Madame de Schubert, and to you, the assurance of my highest consideration.

HELEN,
Duchess of Orleans,
née, H. de Mecklenburg.

* As in my childhood I was accustomed to say that I would one day compose as beautiful poetry as Rist, my sister surnamed me "little Rist and great dreamer."—AUTHOR'S NOTE.

XIII.

THE VOICE OF FILIAL GRATITUDE.

The young duchess, who had been the object of so many varied proofs of affection, after her entrance into the royal family and into the choice circles of Paris, was especially happy in the general respect paid to her dear mother. She was more grateful to the preferences paid to the grand duchess, than for those paid to herself. She was indeed sufficiently acquainted with her mother's tastes to appreciate the sacrifice which she had made in changing her tranquil retreat of Friedensburg or Rudolstadt, for the great world of Paris. But here, and chiefly at Court, was recognized the maternal devotion and clear views which the grand duchess had evinced in the education of her daughter; thus was her return to Germany about the end of 1837, deeply regretted

She left tranquilly and happily, for she had witnessed Helen's happiness. She wrote on the 15th of January, 1838 :

"I might have sought in vain throughout entir Europe for a family circle where Helen would be as well cared for and as happy as in the one which I have learned to know. Ought I not to sing praises to my God, and testify my gratitude to Him ? For I see in all things how good *He* is towards me."

With regard to these words impressed with faith and gratitude, let us here place some letters by the duchess, for the first time since her seventh year, separated from her mother; a mother whose devotion surpassed the limits of human strength. The passages that I here transcribe are textually imprinted in the original letters I have under my eyes.

ST. CLOUD, October 3d, 1837, Evening.

The first day of our separation is now passed, my dear and beloved mother. I am rejoiced, not only for myself, but also for you, for I know by what I have suffered to-day, that our adieus have not been less painful to one than to the other, and I greatly fear lest your health be affected by it.

Permit me again to say from the depths of my soul, how grateful I am for all that you have done for me since my childhood ; grateful for your love, which made you indulgent, patient, thoughtful—which has accompanied me *each* moment of my life—which has shared every thing with me, and which has diligently watched over me, with a prayerful spirit. Dear mother, it was not possible for me to express my feelings of love and gratitude, without weakening my strength, without paralyzing the courage which I wished to keep for your sake and the duke's at the last moment.

But now, let me unfold my heart and tell you that my gratitude is profound, and that the remembrance of the time when I was still under your wing will constantly accompany me and be my guardian-angel for the future. But I do not know why I speak thus ; for how can a child thank a mother for what she has done from maternal tenderness? Your love directed you in every thing, and mine understood it, or at least *felt* it, when I was blind and did not know your intentions. It will eternally live in the depths of my soul and will be my holy safeguard. Oh! dear mother, in thought I kiss your cherished hands, pray you to give me a benediction this evening, and to kiss me upon my forehead.

P. S.—Though I have not much tact for writing, I cannot let this letter of our dear Helen's depart, without telling you that your place remains vacant among your devoted children. F. O.

October 4, in the Morning after Breakfast.

I was interrupted last evening by my dear duke, who begged me to stop, because I was full of emotion. He wrote with his own hand the preceding words, and I to-day send the continuation of my letter.

The queen, who has come to see what the orphan is doing, charges me to write that she thinks much of you, that she regrets your absence and counts upon your promise. She has told me that she can never take your place, but that she will do her best, and that you may count upon her maternal affection. It is very true that no one can replace you, but I am happy in finding in the duke's mother, one who inspires me with such a firm confidence, and towards whom I feel so warmly attracted.

I regret that I must close, for we are to be present at the king's breakfast. We go to-morrow to the solitude of Trianon.

Ah! dear, dear mother, how impossible is it for a letter to take the place of a life passed under the same roof! God grant that I may soon receive good news from your hand. Adieu, dear mother; always your daughter

HELEN.

P. S.—After breakfast.

The king and court have been very good to me, the king manifested much cordiality and sympathy.

TRIANON, October 6, 1837.

MY DEAR AND BELOVED MOTHER,

Returning an hour since from a long promenade with the duke, who spoke much of you and finally left me to go to the chase, I found two words from the queen, who received your telegram at Paris and sent it to me, adding that I ought in my turn to forward a few lines before night, which would again reach you. I need not say how much I have been touched with your attention, and how much I should like to respond at length, and according to the promptings of my heart. This method of communication brings us near one another, but it is so laconic! After my calculation, you quitted French soil to-day at noon, my dear mother. You experienced a pang, I am persuaded; for I deeply feel the pain this thought has caused me. I cannot tell to what extent I miss you, for you would believe me ungrateful to my good duke, who does every thing to lighten this painful separation. Your presence tranquillized us; what you did for us, appeared much when you were here. Now it seems to us that we ought to be much more upon our guard, for no eye accompanies us or watches over us like yours. Ah! dear mother! I should write entire volumes, if I would reproduce all the reflections that your departure has suggested to me, and the mourning this void causes me ; but I do not wish to sadden you, neither do I wish to make myself more melancholy than I am already ; it would afflict my dear duke instead of diverting him, as it is my duty to do. We are, in short, in our little hermitage at Trianon, and we live entirely alone. I here propose to do for him all that is in my power, and to render this abode where he will have no other resource than my society as agreeable as possible to him.

The royal family, who accompanied us from St. Cloud, and who send you their love, went to walk with us in the little wood, the rare vegetation of which you admired ; then they returned to Versailles. To-day we rode in the carriage to St. Cloud to congratulate the king upon the occasion of his anniversary. I was touched to see the good and excellent king in the arms of his sons, and to remark the joy which their congratulations seemed to give him. I now eat strawberries every day, "in memory of you." Ah ! my good mother, how we miss you ! Adieu, my guardian angel, pray for your child, and often think of the affection she bears you.

HELEN.

I do not reproduce a letter of the 11th of October, expressing the same affectionate regrets for her mother's absence, and the happiness of having received a letter from her; it also contains some details upon the African expedition. The following contains several passages from a letter of the 20th of October :

"But now, before all things, I kiss your dear hand for your excellent letter, which was a journal of your life. At each word I thought to hear your voice ; I saw you before me and was happy in being near you. My joy is a little disturbed, because I cannot share it with my duke, who awaited as impatiently as myself for news of you, and who will not return from the chase until this evening. Without him, I only half enjoy it ; he so affectionately shares my sentiments, and so faithfully my grief! He again fully proved this to me, on the 18th of October, a day* in which our thoughts certainly met upon one tomb. He well understood my grief, for, from all I communicated of my dear Albert, he learned to love him also. It was a consolation to me. That day was passed in complete retirement, although on the preceding one we had celebrated the marriage of Marie, which quickly recalled to our memory, the 30th of May and Fontainebleau."

I do not make any use of several posterior let-

* It was the anniversary of Prince Albert's death.

ters, also addressed to the grand duchess. They contain some news of the African campaign, up to the taking of Constantine ; the duchess Helen here takes as lively a part as if the most ardent Frenc blood flowed in her veins.

The duke of Orleans, like the entire royal fami ly, was animated with the same sentiments. All the princes and princesses were occupied with their mother in writing joyous messages to their distant friends, even as the duchess did to her mother. It would be pleasant to hear her describe the taking of ports, the brilliant fêtes at Paris, and the joy of the people at the victory of the army. The enthusiasm of the princess for the glory and prosperity of the nation which had become her country, gives a particular attraction to the description. But there are other fêtes than those of which the echo ceased so quickly, other songs than those which filled the churches of the capital, where the grave tones of the organ, sometimes alternated with operatic airs. We have here in view, "those songs of triumph and deliverance which reverberated in the tabernacles of the just to celebrate the victories that guard the right of the eternal." In the following passages of a letter written in 1837, during the Christmas festivals, there are questions of inward joy, the success, glory, and honor of which exist eternally :

MY DEARLY BELOVED MOTHER:

To-day, our thoughts perhaps oftener meet than ordinarily. You have always marked it by many testimonials of love; it has always been a fête day for your children, and my heart swells at the thought of the dispersion of all the inhabitants of Friedensburg, who were a year ago assembled around the Christmas-tree, and happy in examining the beautiful presents offered by the hand of affection. I am also grateful to-day, but grateful in another point of view from that of a year ago. When I dreamed of France under the Christmas-boughs, and tried to paint what my future would be, I did not dare hope that God would grant me such a rich, noble destiny. Oh! if you might only be here to-day, and to-morrow, dear mother; for to-morrow, at the beautiful Christmas services, I shall take the communion; my heart feels the need of kindling itself by the fireside of light and truth, and of strengthening itself against my lukewarm nature, which would extinguish the spark of faith, if not preserved from the vain frivolities and seductions of the world. Without you, without some one affected in a like manner with myself, who understands me and to whom I love to reveal myself, my task is difficult. I have hitherto been somewhat spoiled; in some respects it is better for me to be alone, that I may turn entirely towards the Lord and wait for the action of his Spirit upon my heart; for the rest, is one alone when one has Him for a friend, and when one dare ask every thing of Him? I am rejoiced that Christmas is also thought much of in this kingdom. The Queen and Clementine are gone to prepare for the communion to-morrow.

Ah! my mother, how far am I yet from the model that our Saviour has given us! Perhaps I have never felt so culpable as now; for my lukewarmness seems more inexcusable now that I am in the midst of prosperity; though I recognize a thousand calls from the Lord, in my present position, in the affection which surrounds me and in the duties which are incumbent upon me, I am guilty in having so little heart to respond. In a word, I am much humiliated on account of my indolence and feebleness of faith, yet I am far from feeling sufficiently humble for the measure of my faults. When I am in this state of mind, I feel an inexpressible need of conversing with you; for, near you, I should be better, more faithful, more childlike, more firm. What a great blessing to have such a pious and faithful mother! I cannot duly bless God for having given you to me, in order that I might receive warmth under your maternal wing.

CHIRSTMAS MORNING.

Yesterday, my dear mother, after returning from church, I could not find a moment to write to you, and I regretted it very much, for it was a day when the holy communion was rendered very precious to me! I warmly and deeply felt the nearness of the Saviour at the moment of communion. I took the "Imitation of Christ" with me, and I could read it with delight. Cuvier had marked a short sermon upon confession; I examined myself upon each point, and I was chiefly humbled in considering what is said of indolence and lukewarmness. I approached the altar, and was strengthened in my faith and love for the Saviour, who alone has power to keep one faithful in the right way.

On Christmas-eve, the good queen had prepared a surprise for me, by secrectly furnishing a beautiful tree, which was placed in my *salon blanc*, in order that I might be reminded of Germany. She is so ingenious in preparing pleasant surprises, that in seeing her, I often dream of you.

Another letter, written at the end of the year, expresses sentiments analogous to many letters of the first month of the year 1838.

XIV.

DOMESTIC PROSPERITY AND INWARD HAPPINESS.

The duchess' ardent desire to see her mother again, was gratified in 1838, when she had the hope of giving the duke an heir. The state of her health obliged her to live in absolute retirement, where she communed only with God, her husband and herself. At this epoch she had still another source of delight. Mademoiselle Nancy Solomon, of Geneva, who had watched over her from her infancy and who shared all her joys and sorrows, passed several weeks with her, and seconded the duke in the attention which the situation of the princess required. The duchess addressed me a letter about this time, of which the following is a copy:

Dear Professor:

Accept my sincere thanks for the interesting

letter and oriental parcel which you forwarded to me in the beginning of spring by young Schmidt. I was then suffering and living in entire solitude. Your words, the rose of Jericho in the marvellous progress of its unfolding and development, and finally the manna of the desert, which was given to you by the monks of the St. Catherine Convent, upon Sinai, with the leaves which surrounded these little treasures, all these souvenirs truly rejoiced me; and, if I am late in expressing my gratitude, it is not less sincere.

Let not your wishes cease to accompany our king, his children, and his subjects, for you can bring down to us from heaven true benediction, that benediction we have need of every hour, in our situation in life, and which is necessary above all to the king in his position. When the fatigues, burden, and responsibility of every decision are so great, the hand of our God alone can strengthen us; it alone can direct us in the right way. I also, in my more restrained sphere, implore His assistance, and you will understand, that I expect the precious effects of it most specially at this moment and in a future which is opening under such happy auspices.

You will certainly learn, with interest, that I am expecting my mother, who is to pass the [illegible] mer and autumn with us. She is nowhere so beloved as in my own family, and she will never be able to find a son more faithful than the duke, after the loss of one who was so tenderly attached to her.

As you have always known how to appreciate the eminent character of Miss Nancy Solomon, you will doubtless be rejoiced to learn of her marriage with Colonel Bontems, of Geneva, known by his interesting travels, and an excellent man. After a life checkered with trials, it seems as if a happy and peaceful fate ought to be now in reserve for him.

Tell Mrs. Schubert that her salutations gave me great pleasure, and that her promised visit gives me one not less. Yes, come and see for yourself all that is good, grand, and noble, here.

I am, with the highest consideration, your old pupil,

HELEN.

NEUILLY, June 17, 1838.

About the time when the preceding letter was written, the duchess had the long wished for happiness of seeing her mother. Upon setting her foot upon the French soil, the grand duchess already found a letter of welcome ; and, even after her arrival, the tête-à-tête did not suffice always for the duchess, who employed her pen to outpour her heart, when she had been prevented from seeing her mother. The following, among others, is a note written one evening :

"Again a cordial good-night, my very dear mother. Unhappily *by writing*, since it has not been possible for you to come to me. As we could not have an evening reading, I here copy a stanza,* and hope that you will awake early on the morrow and in good health. Your child."

On the 24th of August, the birth of the count de Paris was a happy event for France. The grand duchess remained with her daughter until the end of the autumn, and then their correspondence again took its course.

I extract only one passage from a letter of the 17th of November, 1838 :

"Last evening, I made the acquaintance of our great German painter, Cornelius ; he explained to us the designs of his Last Judgment, which he is painting in the choir of the Ludwigskirche. He told me that he meditated upon this creation for

* Here is found in the original, a stanza of an evening hymn, by Paul Gerhardt.

twenty years, and that he had particularly studied Dante, after which he has reproduced the seven successive infernal regions of the damned. I find this plan incomparably more beautiful than that of Rubens, which I saw at Dresden; I like the idea of placing the personified conscience in the centre of the picture, the book open upon the breast, and the eye raised towards the Judge, who with one hand banishes the wicked, and with the other, calls to Him his own."

A few days after, the duchess thus spoke to me, in the following letter, of our great master, Cornelius:

PARIS, Nov. 19, 1838.

I have, for a long time, dear professor, had the intention of thanking you for the letter you sent me by Madame Zech; I have been prevented until now by joyous events, which doubtless will justify me in your eyes, and in which your heart will surely take part. The birth of my dear child, the indispensable cares which followed it, and then, the last delights of my mother's sojourn, made me suspend all correspondence; I only commence to re-unite the ties which attach me to my own country. The hand of your friend,* will remit these lines to you, and I hope that this circumstance will procure a

* Cornelius.

good welcome A short interview which I had with him, leaves me with the regret that he does not make a longer sojourn in Paris, that we might be better able to appreciate so eminent an artist and man. The simple words which he expressed upon the subject of art, from their truth, found an echo in my soul, and I wish that our artists were animated with as serious a mind as his. In this respect also, the bonds between France and Germany are precious to me, for it is evident to my view that the two nations would gain by uniting them.

I remember with great pleasure the first days of my childhood, in which you filled my young heart with joy by your tales full of life and variety; I find myself also wishing that my child may also have, from his earliest age, such an amiable *pro*, who may successfully influence his heart. His happiness, his future, his development, already occupy me more than I can tell; you, without doubt, understand me. The first impressions, of which the subsequent direction always bears the impress, appears very important to me, and a mother ought to watch them from the earliest days: but for this wisdom, strength, and courage are necessary from on High. May Heaven grant them to me! Pray for me, that the will of God may be accomplished in us.

You perhaps already know that my mother wishes again to leave me, and to pass the sad winter in the solitude, now desert, of Ludwigslust. We have had very sweet interviews during these happy days, and her loving heart has been warmly attracted towards her grandson.

I conclude, etc.,

HELEN.

P. S.—To my great regret, the pretty little bull-bull died this summer; I am accorded the melancholy consolation of having it stuffed to serve as a play-thing for my young son. Children ought to learn to like such things; this pet merits a special liking.

"In my last journey to Paris," wrote the grand duchess after her return, "I lived much more alone with Helen, because she remained from necessity at home. The dreaded moment passed so happily, that I have been humiliated on account of my fears. I have rarely seen so sweet a little babe as that."

The grand duchess had other ideas than those of her daughter, as to the effect produced upon the state of her mind by the solitude of Ludwigslust. She wrote upon the subject: "I accommodated myself as much as possible to the life at Paris; but

I well see that it is difficult to live in the great world, though the grace of God renders that constraint less painful. I find myself altogether at ease in my solitude, which I would sometimes render still more profound."

The happiness of the duchess of Orleans' family had now attained its height. Louis Philippe, already disposed by nature to affection, had become the father of a still more tender family since the birth of his first grandchild. He often paused beside the cradle of the sleeping infant, which he contemplated with an audible satisfaction; and, still later, when the child, with his precocious intellect, comprehended the affection of his grandfather, extending his hands not less affectionately to him, the king experienced a delight above all others.

In 1839, the duchess Helen had the grief of being separated for several months from the duke. With his chivalric disposition, he could no longer resist the desire of taking part in a second campaign to Algiers; he made his arrangements, and, accompanied by the duchess, set out, through the south of France and the Pyrenees. I possess a letter which she wrote to me in the course of that year so important to her and many persons; but as this letter contains only things which concern myself, I substitute another addressed to her mother, in order to give insight into the plan and direction of the voyage.

PARIS, August 2, 1839.

I write to-day in the midst of a great preoccupation, which I shall doubtless retain for some days, and which always precedes a journey. Though I can fearlessly confide my child to the queen, I cannot separate from him without a pang. We shall set out on the 9th, from to-day the 8th ; business still indispensable, the preliminary studies, the desire of approaching the table of the Lord, in order to receive strength and blessing, all this occupies me and keeps me from doing any thing with calmness. You are acquainted with this feeling, and doubtless pity me a little. You will surely follow us in thought, in our pilgrimage ; and your benediction, dear mother, will not fail us. Upon the 17th we shall arrive at Bordeaux ; our plan is to remain there six days, then go by the departments of the south, to visit the beautiful Pyrenees and to go through Toulouse and Perpignan. The 9th of September the duke embarks at Port-Vendre for Algiers ; I depart in all haste, arrive on the 14th at Randon where I am to find my aunt ; and, after having passed several days with her, return to Paris, to take my child again under my care.

During my absence, the family go tc Eu, where

they will doubtless take the child. Such are the vast projects which sometimes appear problematical to me, because here, the slightest thing overthrows plans for the future. You know well, dear mother, that your remembrance will accompany me, during all the journey. Provided nothing happens to the child ! that thought always agitates my poor heart, and I can only assuage it by the following prayer:

> "Breit' aus die Flügel beide
> Und nimm dein Küchlein ein !
> Will Satan es verschlingen
> So lass die Englein singen,
> Dies Kind soll uverletzet seyn."

Is it not this, dear mother, that you also will ask of God for him ?

Arrived at Port-Vendre, the department of the oriental Pyrenees, the duke took leave of his wife. This separation did not cost him less than it did her. He could not withdraw (he wrote in his journal) his eyes from the window where the duchess continued her adieus, by waving her handkerchief; but finally, distance put an end to that touching scene. After her return to Paris, the duchess consecrated herself entirely to her child. The king permitted her to live in retirement during the absence of the duke. Even when her husband was not the centre of her domestic life, she could only live in spirit with him and near him. The duke himself neglected no occasion of writing to her from Algiers ; and when the public journals sounded his praise, she was altogether happy. The royal family often came to see her at the hour when the little count de Paris slept, for that tender mother would leave him only then. When she received visits from the youngest members of her family, they read or sang in French. When seated beside her child's couch, she often occupied herself with rewriting a journal of her journey into the beautiful countries of the South-west of France; this journal, illustrated with drawings, was destined to divert her cherished mother in her solitude of Ludwigslust.

But I have still to mention another advantage which her excursion into the south of France and the Pyrenees produced, if one may so speak, for thousands of persons. The marriage of the duchess of Orleans, but still more her passage through the departments of the South, where the reformation counts many proselytes, had awakened legitimate hopes among the Protestants. Several friends, and among others, Heimpel Boissiers, who visited me at that time, have painted to me the joy and emotion which the presence of the duchess by the side of her noble husband excited among their co-religionists.

Upon this occasion, I ought specially to reveal the influence, more or less recognized, which the professed religious belief of the duchess of Orleans exercised upon the French nation. Though she carefully guarded against publicity with regard to her principles and life, the nation learned enough of them to esteem itself most happy in having such a mother to educate the heir to the crown and to inculcate firm principles, noble sentiments, and love for his future subjects. If the Protestants had not been then tolerated, the people would have been forced to respect a faith which a princess of such distinguished merit professed. Without claiming the least privileges for her profession, the duchess, by the fruits of her faith, gained the public esteem for her cause. Louis Philippe, the first, expressed himself in the following manner: "I desire my grandson to be a Catholic, but I will never suffer the religion of my daughter-in-law to be the object of diplomatic negotiation. That is an affair between her and God, and she shall never hear a word upon that subject, not provoked by herself." The confidence which the king and queen had in her was so great in this respect, that finally, she ventured herself to compose the first short pages for her children. While she frequented her modest, old Lutheran church in "la rue des Billettes," her young son, led by his grandfather, went to hear mass, and afterward read the infantine prayers which his mother had written for him in large French characters.

It was not only at Paris, but also in all France, from the Rhine to the Ocean, from the Pyrenees to la Mancha, that the coreligionists of the duchess Helen saw in her a friend of the Lord, who was also a devoted friend to them, and if necessary, a protectress ready to intercede in their behalf.

In 1840, the duke de Nemours married a German princess, who had her place in the circle of the royal family of France. In her, the duchess of Orleans acquired a sister with whom she shared all the remembrances of their common country, which thus lived again for both in the midst of France and the court.

The duke of Orleans returned to Paris, and found, with his Helen and his young son, domestic joys which he ranked above all others. When they were seated at tea round the queen's table the duchess was always at his side; but when his military duties called him elsewhere, "she was accustomed to gain permission to remain in her room;" she then placed little Count Paris in his cradle, and amused herself with his sweet childish babble, until he had closed his eyes under the influence of her songs. Then she absorbed herself in the study of

Beethoven, whose admirable music she called the purest and noblest language; or she consecrated her short leisure moments to writing to her relations and friends in Germany, whom she often desired to have more near her. She thus expresses herself in a letter to her friend:

"When the soul outpours itself in a confidential letter, it seems that in that interview so full of charms, we feel still more deeply the happiness of affection, the grief of absence, and the impatient desire to be eternally reunited. I speak of a reunion in eternity, which alone is uninterrupted, for that here below, which I doubtless love much, is ever but for a time."

Sometimes, but less often than in the first year, that peaceful domestic life was interrupted by excursions made with all the family, either to St. Cloud, to the château d'Eu, in the neighborhood of the sea, and interesting Tréport.

The following letter from the duchess, raises a corner of the curtain which unveils to view her calm, sweet domestic life:

NEUILLY, July 7, 1840.

Behold a salutation coming from France to your address, dear professor, and to that of Madame

Schubert, by the means of the amiable little lady de Zech, who returns to Germany to remain there. I would rest upon each word destined to recall me to your memory, for it seems to me that years, far from enfeebling the impressions of my early years, increases my attachment and respect for you. It is as if your image presented itself always lively and fresh to my mind. I nevertheless desire with all my heart to see it animated with the reality, and from one year to another I count upon the visit you have promised me.

Your bust adorns the chamber of my child, who calls it grandpapa ; his may also have its place in your cabinet, that in glancing at it, you may address a thought of paternal affection and benediction to my son. I confide it then with this prayer to Madame de Zech, and join with it another little souvenir for your wife, which, from its quadruple utility, will perhaps be agreeable to her. Beg her to use it in remembrance of me, and to see in the casket the image of supreme affection—wisdom and grace—life, light, and love.

I end with the assurance of my old and constant attachment, I no longer dare call it filial, for that age is long since passed.

HELEN.

I have under my eyes still another letter, anterior to the preceding; there is always the same spiritual harmony, but the accord is still more elevated in this; the more restrained circle of a mother's tender cares for her child makes room for that of an ardent affection for her new country, whose fate warmly interests her:

TUILERIES, March 4, 1840.

The expression of my profound gratitude, very dear professor, has long since advanced this letter by the medium of the countess Giech, who has spoken much of you. I cannot, however, longer delay addressing my most lively thanks directly to you, and to tell you the pleasure that the reading of your interesting work, in which posterity will gather the fruits of your long labors, perseverance, and fatigue, gives me. I have not yet gone with you to the Holy Land; I am exclusively occupied with Egypt, that land which has caused such grand questions in the modern world, after having guarded with its deposits of antiquity, that of immortality, the greatest of all. The altogether modern civilization grafted upon the old trunk of the votaries of the Koran, would be a study of very great interest.

If the spirit of Christianity in modern civilization was more sound, more lively, and more animated by the powerful breath which enkindles the flame of faith in souls and reverses incredulity and superstition! But it is not thus! We ought not, nevertheless, to doubt that the good seed, destined one day to fertilize the soil, will be thus propagated.

Your wishes, your prayers for our country, and our house, which, according to your just expression, is placed in the fire of the bivouac of Europe, are always a great consolation to me, for I have faith in their efficacy, and I feel that we have need of them. Ah! let us ask that faithful souls may not cease to pray with us and for us; that the Lord, in the midst of so many tares, may let the wheat grow; that in the contest the right may triumph; that in the whirl of frivolity, His word may not be forgotten; that in the general interest, the salvation of all may gain victory over the malign passions. We live in a checkered world, where images the most revolting and the most noble arise, where faith and impiety come in collision. Pray, pray, is the watch-word; pray that His kingdom may come, that His will may be done.

My young son, of whom you speak, is a dear child, gay and happy; he has my features and his father's eyes; he is gentle, yet nevertheless has his own will; he is very sensible, yet independent enough; may God guide him! He only can; I wish to place my whole confidence in Him.

Salute the good Oettl and your daughters, Selma and Adeline, whose features present themselves confusedly to my mind, as a dream of my childhood. I do not forget your dear wife, whose perseverance in that distant voyage, I have often admired.

And now, adieu, think of me and pray for me, as a father.

HELEN.

When I cast my eyes upon the terrestrial happiness which the princess, called to such a high mission for time and eternity, enjoyed at this time, I feel pressed to recall once more the epigraph of a preceding chapter: "Life is a dream."

Upon the 9th of November, 1840, the happy mother had a second son, Robert, duke de Chartres. A short time before, she, with the count de Paris, had been attacked with the measles, and for a moment her life was despaired of. But the danger was passed; and, independently of the duke, two loving and devoted hearts took a lively part in the maternal joys which followed her deliverance, these were the grand duchess Augusta of Mecklenburg, and Madame de Bontems (Nancy Solomon) of Geneva, who passed the winter in Paris. Care of her health obliged the duchess to live in almost absolute retirement; she could then more frequently and uninterruptedly enjoy the charms of a little circle, composed of the duke, her two children, with her mother and her friend. The following letter, which she addressed me as a wish for a happy New Year, proves how she appreciated this happiness, how grateful she was, and how her inward joy must outpour itself:

TUILERIES, January 3, 1840.

The message which I owe to your bounty, dear professor, gave me pleasure. You spoke of the accomplishment of my most ardent wishes, and my heart might well wish to accept the desires as prophetic, which sometimes change into mute prayers, as you yourself express it. Can the heart of a mother form a wish more profoundly felt, than that of seeing her child, her children grow up for the glory of God—that she may be a faithful instrument in his hand, of leading their young hearts to Him, and of one day seeing them upon the way of life! You join in this prayer of my heart; let me thank you for it, dear professor, your prayer is an aid to mine, I might say, a wing which gives it more easy access to the Lord.

The interesting tales written by you as recreation after more serious labors, also merit special thanks. They often enlivened my mother and myself, in those hours of repose which followed the birth of my little Robert, and which we were so happy in passing together. The day will come when it shall also serve as instruction for my children, one of whom, even now, often asks for little stories. Would I had your gift for narrating ! its charm exercised such a powerful influence over children who surrounded you.

I still remember the happiness I felt in my fourth year, when you assembled us around you, and when the most pleasing objects crossed my imagination. The tales have vanished, but the taste for listening attentively, and attachment for the dear narrator, still remain to me ; and like the bee, I still draw a sweet and strengthening honey from the calyx of my first remembrance.

The old year has now fled ; it has abounded in blessings for me ; but it has failed in one ; shall it be received in the course of the new year ?—your visit, so long a time promised, shall it be realized ? I await like a child who counts upon a promise, and I shall continue to hope even until you are here.

HELEN.

The pleasure which the indulgent duchess expressed to have received from the reading of the first portion of my tales, emboldened me to pay her the homage of the second, which I sent to her with a letter. The reader can divine the contents of her response, because the sentiments of the princess, so humble and so faithful to the impressions of her childhood, are well known.

I am forced to extend a mourning veil over the portrait I endeavor to sketch.

XV.

ENIGMA OF THE PRESENT LIFE.

In the tropical regions where the ardent solar rays fall upon the heights, night surprises and astonishes the traveller coming from the North. He cannot here count upon a long twilight, which insensibly prepares the passage of the glory of the day to the obscurity of night. The sun sinks from the horizon, and the stars, arising from their incalculable depths, quickly shine from every direction; a new world seems to unfold itself to the solitary traveller.

Such is the image of the unforeseen event, which awaited the life of the duchess of Orleans in 1842; it burst upon her by a dispensation, the depth of which no eye can measure, the bearing of which no intellect can fathom. Nevertheless, when the loving heart of the princess found itself suddenly enveloped in darkness, the stars shone out in the midst of the night.

From the beginning of the year 1842, thoughts of death traversed the mind of the princess, who wrote to me in the month of March, in reply to a letter of mine :

"She has attained her destination and her end ; the peaceful solitude of an afflicted woman—such was the destiny ; the attainment of good—such was the end ; two-fold mercy ; your words so profound and serious, so impressed with faith, have done me inexpressible good. Burning tears have erased those lines," etc.

The grief with which her heart was then affected, though profound, was not yet the thunder-stroke of the 13th of July, which broke a heart already wounded.

In the midst of the happiness which she was enjoying in France, her remembrances recalled her to Mecklenburg. When she conversed with the duke, the manner in which she spoke of her relatives in Germany, made him love them. The sojourn that the grand duchess had made in Paris established the most intimate relations between the court of France and that of Mecklenburg. In such circumstances, the death of the grand duke Frederick-Paul (on the 7th of March, 1842), deeply moved the heart of the princess and was not without its influence upon the derangement of her health.

[Professor Schubert here speaks of her departure to Plombières, and introduces the following letter to her mother:]

PLOMBIÈRES, July 14, 1842.

MY DEARLY BELOVED MOTHER:

Behold me in a peaceful and solitary valley of the Vosges district, where I often think of you, and where I, to-day, write this letter. Since you have heard tidings of me, we have happily made the journey, but by short stages, for my good duke cares for me like a new-born child. We crossed "la Champagne," passing through Vitry and Toul, where is an ancient and very beautiful church. We saw Nancy, where the remembrance of the good Sanislas is still living; from there we reached Plombières, through Epinal. The Vosges district, in the midst of which I live, reminds me, forcibly, of the forests of Thuringia, the fresh and verdant valleys of Eisenach, and sometimes of the valley of the Schwarzbourg. The population is good, tranquil, peaceable, brave, faithful, and very monarchical. It is in the Vosges department, that Wallach is, the community of Oberlin; I count upon going there, and shall think much of you, if possible, I shall go to see his tomb. Last Sunday, I received a visit from the minister Jaudt, who officiates at Raschau, in filial communion with the good Oberlin.

For eight day sI have been alone here. I have frequent moments of melancholy at the thought of being thus separated from the duke, my children, and all those that I love; but this retired life, in which I find repose, has also its charms. I pray God to bless this sojourn to my soul.

I believe that the baths will have a happy effect upon my disordered stomach. Do you know what I have eaten since the month of May? Three milk porridges a day; all other nourishment distresses me; with that I do well. But since I could not live upon that all my life, and should become enfeebled, they have sent me here to habituate me insensibly to another régime. The baths are very agreeable, but they sometimes try me. Think of me, dear mother, on the 25th of this month; that day I shall reach Strasburg, and shall remain there a week with the duke. This excursion, it is true, will interrupt my cure; but it will be very agreeable to me. Without knowing it, Alsatia has always been dear to me, for the population is both French and German; there are such excellent people here, that I am happy in studying this portion of France. I experience a feeling peculiar to the idea of being near that good Germany.

Nevertheless, the painful presentiments which had agitated the duchess in taking leave of her husband, were only too well founded. It was a separation not for a few weeks, but for all her life. I here allude to an event which soon happened, the news of which traversed Europe, and the remembrance of which is still present to the minds of many.

On the 13th of July, the duke went to Neuilly.*

At the time of the catastrophe the grand duchess was at the waters of Marienbad; receiving intelligence of it through a courier, she hastened to join her daughter at Paris. She was providentially prepared for the mission she had to fulfil. In a word, before her departure from Mecklenburg, she was anxious to see Prince Albert's old instructor again, the pious pastor Koch. I have already spoken of that worthy ecclesiastic, whose memory will always be dear to me, though I had no further intercourse with him than that from Milan through the valley of the Rhone, in company with prince Albert.

* Here again, is an account given, of the accident which happened to the duke of Orleans, substantially the same as those previously given in former portions of this volume

He had been dangerously ill since the month of November, and seemed to be in a state of convalescence. "In that hope," wrote the grand duchess, "I dared to ask for an interview with him before my departure, and gained permission. I found him still feeble, but amicable and rejoiced to see all three of us; that is to say, Miss Sinclair, L. Lützow, and myself. I passed several happy hours in the house of this dear pastor. His aged mother appeared to me dying. She had been bed-ridden for some time; I found her with clasped hands, awaiting the hour of her deliverance. I thought to say a last adieu to him, though my heart was pained at then taking leave of him. Two days after, he enterèd into the joy of his Lord. Oh! what a new and painful vacancy in our circle!"

Strengthened by the last benediction of a faithful disciple of the Saviour, who was now in that happy country, where his soul through hope had been, as it were, in advance of its release, the mother and duchess reached Paris and her daughter. She was not astonished to find in her a resignation which seemed incomprehensible to others after such a trial, for she knew from whence she drew this resignation. The lines which the duchess had written to her mother on the 6th of July, already bore the impress of it.

DEAR AND TENDER MOTHER,

The most frightful blow has fallen upon me; you are already acquainted with it, through the queen's letter. O God! thou art severe and mysterious in thy decrees, but nevertheless, I have faith in thy compassion!

Dear mother! my heart is lacerated. You share my grief, for you loved him so much, and he had so much affection for you. I can only write of my misfortune, for my head is weak, my eyes burn, my hands tremble, and my heart is ready to break. Alas! very dear mother, what a journey for you! at your age again to have such bitter grief! Oh! come, come, that we may weep and pray together!

P. S. I arrived to-day from Plombières, and am well; my children also, God be praised! the king even, but in what a state! no words can describe it.

The duchess was ordinarily calm and silent, but she refused no obligation imposed upon her by the rank she occupied. Some hesitated to admit a few persons of her house, who desired to express their sympathy, but she replied: "Make them enter; I wish to welcome as soon as possible all testimonials of others' grief, that I may be able sooner to be delivered entirely from mine."

The children did not understand their irreparable loss, nor the cause of their mother's tears, which redoubled their tenderness to her. In the first days which followed the death of the duke of Orleans, the count de Paris often asked for his "petit papa," and was astonished to see his mother's tears flow more abundantly at these words.

The tender affection of the grand duchess assuaged the deep grief of her daughter. Never perhaps had the duchess offered more hearty thanks for having such a mother preserved to her. She committed her entirely to God, awaited every thing from Him, who had found it good to lay such a sore trial upon her. He had applied a balm to her wound; He had indicated the route which she ought to follow, in a life now lonely and clouded. She had the assurance that He would never forsake her, that He would reattach her, if necessary, to that life which in her eyes was no longer precious.

In the midst of her profound grief, the queen also aroused herself; she could not contemplate her daughter, who had met with such a great loss, without emotion and admiration; the duchess, on her part, redoubled her affection and respect for the mother of her husband, for she knew what he had been to the queen.

The young widow, in the height of her grief,

gratefully recognized the inestimable price of the happiness which she had enjoyed. "I would not have given my five years of felicity," said she to her maternal friend, Madame de Both, "if I thus might have escaped the sufferings which have latterly been my heritage." She expressed the same sentiment with still more energy, when she said to another friend, that "the sacrifice of a moment of her preceding happiness, would more than have ransomed her years of affliction." "Her felicity," she added, "had been too great to be durable. She then could but render thanks to God for the past, and seek to forget her grief by only speaking of causes for gratitude." When the hours of anguish and bitterness came upon her, she besought God that these moments might bear fruit for eternal life. Sometimes, doubtless, the desire of departing was so strong within her heart, that she was tempted to ask deliverance of the Lord; but the spirit of peace and resignation soon led her to quell her impatience.

We still perceive, in these inward struggles, that human consolations are impotent, from the letter addressed to me two weeks after the duke's death. I only transcribe a few passages.

CHÂTEAU D'EU, Sept. 12, 1842.

In the midst of the darkness which surrounds me, dear professor, your letter has for a moment unveiled the eternal kingdom of truth to my view; and my stricken soul has been for a moment cheered and strengthened. Such was surely your desire: it is fulfilled. Now I, in turn, express the wish of my heart; when you think of me, in my great misfortune, in the severe tests that the Lord allots me, do not address me words of consolation, but words of truth, which in time, will give me heavenly consolation. Always write to me what the Word of God reveals upon eternity. Faith has surely the privilege of entering the kingdom of the blessed, in advance; but mine is still too disquieted to cast an assured glance thitherward. The sufferings of a broken heart, of a broken life—the grief into which the thought of my children, my country, and the future plunges me, is still poignant; its voice speaks too loud for me to hear the voice of the Lord. At times it seems to me well to hear a word of the kingdom of the dead, or rather of the kingdom of the living; a word descends from the cross into my wounded heart; but it is soon silenced by the lamentations of life. In the contests of my soul, I have however kept the unalterable conviction that the most mysterious and painful of

God's dispensations are always an effect of His love; when I can no longer even pray, I have yet daily to offer Him, the sacrifice of my ineffable grief, saying: "Lord! I resign him; Thou hast willed it, so let it be!" Pray for me, pray for my poor children; ask of the Father of orphans that he will have pity upon them.

HELEN.

XVI.

DAY DAWNS.

THESE words recall a well-known passage of the Psalmist: "Light is made for the just, and joy for the upright in heart." (Ps. xcvii. 11.) The duchess inwardly experienced the truth of these words of the prophet-king.

Insensibly she found a new life in her love for her children, angels of peace whom God had left her, in taking him away whom she had loved so much. She recovered all her energy, and always serenely regarded her high mission of educating her young sons in the fear of God, and love of their fellows. It was feared that that long struggle would prove injurious to her health; but contrary to all expectation, she gained more strength than before. She showed more enjoyment in her relations with her family; she had such love for others and such desire to render them happy, that she soon learned to bear her sorrow alone ; she tried to smile, that the serenity of others around her might not be disturbed. Nothing was more touching than the sight of such a resigned affliction. Her passing gaiety resembled a sunbeam glancing through a dark cloud ; her inward grief sometimes reappeared, chiefly at certain dates which recalled old remembrances. We remark this in the letters addressed to her mother.

She wrote upon the 2d of June, 1843 :

"On the 29th (May), the sixth anniversary of our arrival at Fontainebleau, our thoughts doubtless flowed together ; and the 30th, you surely read with emotion that beautiful passage in our choice of sacred texts : "What I do, thou knowest not now, but thou shalt know hereafter." I have been struck with the mysterious hope implied in that consoling passage."

DREUX, July 14, 1843.

We have passed two days in this asylum of peace and eternal repose, from whence I wish to write before my departure, my dear and beloved mother. Here, where I have felt peace and hope enter my soul, by the tomb of my husband and in the midst of the most painful remembrances, here even, I pray you, have no more disquietude about me, when you know I am at Dreux, and no longer repeat to me, "do not go thither." The Lord has bestowed grace and peace upon the prayers I addressed to him in this sacred place of repose ; I have found such consolation in the assurance of an eternal reunion, in my meditations upon the mercy and love of God, that I go away cheered and strengthened, I who came here crushed and despondent. It is as if I had breathed the pure air of eternity, from whence a ray of light penetrated into my heart, from whence an accord of celestial harmony fell upon my ear. Yes, yes, the Lord is with us at the tomb of our beloved ones, when we ask Him with confidence and from the depths of the heart. He, the friend and physician of the soul, He remains faithful to us, and makes us see the country where all tears will be dried, where there will be no more grief, nor crying. Dear mother, I also prayed ardently for you yesterday, the 13th of July, when I *felt* your prayer, when I knew that you were near me. We arrived in the evening to pass the 13th together. A high and solemn mass of requiem was performed in the newly-built church. There was something of exaltation in the chanting of the psalms, and of the *dies iræ dies illa,*—but neither solemnity, nor sermon, nor human word can equal what the Lord says to the soul from the silence of the tomb ; no language can express the feeling it made me experience. Cold, dead, and languishing as I was, I had not latterly wished to approach the sacred table ; to-day, I leave with the pressing desire to receive the communion at Neuilly day after to-morrow, and I hope that communion with my Saviour will increase my love for Him and strengthen my faith and hope.

I embrace you, in thought, my dear and beloved mother ; now, since I have so frankly spoken of all that has passed within me, you will no longer apprehend any thing when I go to my dear tomb. Your

HELEN.

I quote only one passage from a letter of Christmas, 1843 :

"I communed yesterday in the church of Redemption, after a very edifying preparatory service, conducted by the pastor Verny. Last evening he delivered an excellent discourse upon fidelity, and we have conversed together for a long time upon that subject. 'Ah ! if only the heart was *firm* and not always rendered culpable by so many little infidelities.' He particularly insisted upon the necessity of keeping the soul constantly under the eye of the Saviour. When a distraction comes, we ought to receive it praying; 'Lord, abide with me.' In a word, one ought to live in the presence of the Lord, under his eye, like children under the eye of a mother. That is very difficult for me, for my default is losing myself in vagueness and then forgetting daily life with its hourly dangers. May God aid me to open my eyes upon my state and give me strength to labor for myself."

The duchess continues, in the course of the year 1844, to describe the experiences of her heart to her mother, at the period which most specially reminded her of the death of her husband. We confine ourselves to abstracting a few passages.

Letter of the 2d of July, 1844:

"I cannot tell you, dear mother, in what state I am since the fatal month has commenced. It is two years to-day since we departed for Plombières; during all the journey, he loaded me with attention and testimonials of his affection. Each hour, alas! has its sweet remembrance, and each hour brings me nearer the terrible day, on which I lost so much. How falsely men judge, when they think time will heal wounds! Grief is no longer so devouring, but it is not less intense; the more the wound seems to heal upon the surface, the deeper also becomes the suffering. May God only sanctify my affliction, and preserve my soul from being consumed! This fear is now so habitual and painful to me;—it is frightful to feel the approach of spiritual death. May God preserve me from it."

Letter of the 14th of July, 1844:

"Though the modern transformation of the sepulchre at Dreux, at first somewhat disturbed me, God again received my prayers and granted me very happy hours, in which the certainty of a reunion consoled me. After having prayed by the tomb, during the night I extracted the following passage, which comforted me, from my little collection of verses: "I have loved thee with an everlasting love; therefore with loving-kindness have I drawn thee." (Jeremiah xxxi.: 3.) I passed the terrible 13th of July, in praying, reading, and conversing affectionately with Louise, who becomes more dear to me, and edifies me by her exalted religious views. We left at seven o'clock in the evening and arrived at two o'clock in the morning. This morning, my dear little Paris appeared to me like a sun beam. He was so happy to see me, that it made me feel well. He had copied a beautiful verse for me and sent it to me."

On the 24th of January, 1845, her birth-day, she wrote to her mother :

" Such days, which have no higher significance than to cause us to cast a glance over the past and to elevate our hearts to God, one specially feels the rapidity of the flight of time, and the many things that have affected our hearts. Oh ! if our inner life could only advance each year by the blessing of the Lord, towards our eternal destination ! How long-suffering the Lord is towards us, when he observes our slow progress, and often our culpable immobility. How forcibly we feel that this patience is an attribute of his divinity, for we are not capable of possessing it.

" Since I wrote to you, dear mother, the brilliant Parisian court, has again taken its course. Balls, concerts, and dramatic representations succeed each other at the Tuileries. As for me, I live tranquilly in my cell, and when I hear the music below me, at the home of the Nemours, I feel that, in the midst of my grief and solitude, God has given me the good part, and that separated from him for whom I bitterly weep, I live more with him through the communion of prayer and the spirit, than if we were both in the whirl of the world. Those are happy moments, in which I experience the peace of heaven; but they do not last, and the bitterness of life always comes to tear them from me."

Upon the recurrence of Easter, 1845, she wrote:

"To-day is the beautiful Easter service; I hope that it may be blessed to you, dear mother, and with you I enjoy the holy signification of the day. How miserable our lives would be without hope, without the conviction of the resurrection which this service gives us, without the seal of the great work of redemption! how bitter our tears would be, in thinking of those whom we have lost, if we did not already see them in all the glory of a new life."

Nevertheless, when she contrasted the sufferings of her long mourning with the joys which had preceded them, she always concluded as in this passage from a letter to her mother:

"You have passed our frontiers; this new barrier afflicts me.* How many times, in the transit, you must have thought of our journey in 1837!

* The grand duchess' return to Ludwigslust, May 10, 1843

How different and how beautiful every thing then was! For some time my hopes were not disappointed; they have often been more than surpassed by the reality. And though they are now engulfed in a tomb, I would not exchange my lot for any other."

XVII.

PROGRESS OF OUTWARD EVENTS.

Admiration and affection for the duchess of Orleans, arose almost to enthusiasm. "In her we have a great support," said a Frenchman, "for the love that she inspires, exalts the nation. This sentiment will bear its fruits for her children, and then she will again find happiness."

Days and months followed each other without modifying her course of life. She wrote as often as formerly to her mother, but less often to her relatives. She fled, she said, from revealing the sufferings hidden within her soul, to distant persons who could not offer a word of encouragement or sympathy at the moment.

Already in 1843, she succeeded in procuring a preceptor for the count de Paris, who responded to all the wishes and exigencies of her maternal love.

"Among thousands of men," she wrote, "I could not have found one more competent to direct my little Paris with wisdom and affection. The little one, progresses very well; his heart, mind, and health develop themselves in a cheering manner."

I place with the number of the happy remembrances of my old age, the pleasure which I had in a passing personal acquaintance with that young preceptor, M. Regnier, who remained faithful to the duchess in the first painful years of her exile.

In the same letter addressed to her mother, she says with regard to the duke de Chartres: "Though pale and thin, Robert is no longer ill; but is full of vivacity and mischief."

She obtained a German governess for her youngest son, that he might learn her native language; she frequently procured little German books written for children, for him, among others those by Pocci.

She had the consolation of having with her, during a portion of the summer, 1843, Madame de Bontems, whose affection, wisdom, and experience never failed to exercise a blessed influence upon her former pupil. Until the middle of autumn, the duchess sojourned with the royal family either at

Neuilly or at the Château d'Eu, situated near the sea, the air of which strengthened her; she still passed the month of November at St. Cloud.

Persons who were habitually with her, and even her less intimate friends, soon remarked that her sympathy for all that concerned them, was even more lively than in former times. She had learned in the school of her own sufferings to apply the true balm to wounded hearts, which those are rarely acquainted with who have constantly lived in prosperity. She directed their reflections to the merciful ways of the Lord, who could work for good, in every affliction.

"But," she wrote, "our eyes are often too blinded to recognize them; our hearts too cold to feel them. Yes, the principal cause of our sufferings is in ourselves. If we were, as we should be, in true communion with God, every thing would be presented otherwise to our minds, and the most bitter stream would have its sweetness. We must then pray that the Lord would draw our hearts to Him, that he would enlighten us and make us deeply feel the price of his favor; for life will then receive new value in our eyes, and every thing will appear to us in its true light."

The following letter which she addressed to me, in the month of March, of the following year, again testifies with what gratitude she welcomed the slightest proof of respect and affection, even when offered by the most humble of her old friends.

TUILERIES, March 16, 1844.

If I would tell you to what extent your last gift rejoiced me, dear professor, (for I cannot exchange that title so dear to me for thirty years, for any other,) I should be obliged to show you the joyous look of my child, when he listens to the tales I relate to him of Moffat.* Your work has provided me with a daily spiritual aliment; and in the evening, with my two children, I have followed that faithful servant of Christ in his heroic pilgrimage. Accept my most hearty thanks for all the contents of that little volume, and for your friendly letter, which has deeply touched me.

I have conversed much of you, with M. de B—— who bears this letter to you. I seize every occasion with joy which offers itself to revive the remembrance of you, in others; as for myself, I have no need to be reminded of it, for I very often think of the faithful and dear preceptor of my childhood, and I desire again to hear his voice in this world, if God wills it.

HELEN.

* Allusion is here made to the life of Moffat, grandfather of Livingston, missionary to the south of Africa.

About the time in which this letter was written, the duchess had the pleasure of forming a personal acquaintance with a native of Steinthal, Daniel Legrand, whom she loved and esteemed several years after. He had several times sent her good books at the Christmas festivals; but chiefly, at the most painful period of her life, she had received a letter from him impressed with a Christian sympathy which deeply touched her. It will be seen from these letters that in him she recognized a man possessing the faith of a child and a touching piety, "an Israelite indeed, in whom there was no guile;" she calls him a faithful servant of God, of the good school of Oberlin.

At this epoch, she sought with preference the society of persons animated and penetrated with that Spirit of Christ, which is the principal of all truth. Hence she found great pleasure in making the acquaintance of Madame de Staël, who resided in Paris, during the winter of 1844, with the younger son of the duke de Broglie.

"She sometimes comes to see me," wrote the duchess, "and always does me good by her presence. She imposes one by her holy dignity, or rather by the reflection of the presence of God, which from her soul, radiates her whole person, to such an extent that one can but have good thoughts while near her. She is deeply sincere, and no person has ever made so great an impression upon me; all that she says, all that she feels appears as purified by truth. She has been a widow for seventeen years; this long, long period of trial has purified and strengthened her. She has not only been deprived of her chief happiness, but in losing an only son at an early age, she has not even had in perspective that mission of maternal love which suffices to fill life, and which has remained to me. Since that day, she has not been able to shed tears. She passed several years in isolation, and it seemed natural to her to tear herself away from every thing, that she might live only for *Him*. But her sister-in-law, the duchess of Broglie, died, and her husband remitted his child, at the age of five years, to her for education. '*Why is this?*' she asked of the Lord; 'ought I again to form a new tie?' This question was not solved in her heart, but she surrounded the child with the most maternal and affectionate care, till she came to Paris to give him up to his father. Sometimes the duke de Broglie wishes him still to be under her guidance. They live in two different houses, and the child lives alternately with his father and his aunt."

The duchess wrote the following to me, on the 15th of February, 1844:

"How much I thought of you, yesterday, while I was engaged with Madame de Staël in an animated conversation, in which her faith and confidence in God spoke to my heart, and enkindled it. Hers is a very rare nature, upon which suffering, and above all grace, have had a powerful effect. One feels that she has had great conflicts, that her heart has loved and suffered much; one feels that she has gained the victory and acquired peace of soul; what attracts me most towards her, is the impress of entire truthfulness. Such a plenitude of spiritual life could not be associated with more simplicity, calmness, and absence of all pretension. What attractions she would have for you!"

When the duchess met with such persons, she did not disquiet herself with differences of worship, provided their faith manifested itself in love for the Saviour and his ransomed ones. At the period of the inauguration of the new Lutheran chapel, she did not approve of all the ideas expressed by a highly esteemed preacher, upon the disagreements of the Roman and the Lutheran Church, but she was deeply edified with the sweet and conciliating spirit, breathed in the prayer of M. Vallette at the end of the service.

The attention which she accorded to the events of this world was small in comparison with the sympathy awakened within her by events of a superior order. Hence she took a lively interest in the vocation of Mademoiselle Marriana de Rantzau, the friend of her childhood, who became directress of the new institution of deaconesses in Berlin. Before entering upon her duties, this lady visited the most celebrated hospitals of Germany, England, and France, and upon this occasion had the happiness of seeing the duchess again, who wrote soon after:

"Her visit gave me very great pleasure, and her serious and holy resolution touched as well as edified me. May God bless her resolution and lighten the burden of that great administration. She will have to contend against many difficulties which oppress her and often disquiet me for her sake; but the Lord, who has led her to this decision and has given her the firm conviction that she is following his will, will remain at her side to support and guide her."

Nearly six years later, she thus judged her noble friend: "She is in every respect independent of all odious party prejudices, religious as well as political; she is beloved by all; throughout her whole nature there is a clearness of view, decision, and government over herself, which one must admire; but one also happily feels that she remains loving and devoted to all her former affections."

Mademoiselle de Rantzau could only consecrate a few years to her noble vocation; she was one of the numerous friends of the duchess who preceded her into eternity.

A letter written to me by the duchess Helen on the 29th of June, 1846, of which I here quote a few passages, procured me the privilege of also making the personal acquaintance of Mademoiselle Rantzau. I do not make special mention of the letters that I received the preceding year; they were chiefly with regard to procuring a German valet de chambre for the young duke de Chartres, through my mediation and that of a friend of the duchess who then resided at Munich. The letter of the 9th of June announces the arrival of our protégé:

He arrived yesterday, Friday, in the morning, and commenced his services to-day. He seems to possess a good disposition, but it is necessary to see his work before judging of it. Once again receive the expression of my sincere gratitude for your cooperation in a circumstance which might have seemed insignificant, if, like me, you did not think nothing unimportant that concerns the associations of a child, and that all who approach him have their influence upon him. We have a visit from our prince royal in expectation. After so long a time, after twelve years, I am rejoiced at the thoughts of seeing him again, and hear so much said of him that his arrival will give me double pleasure. I doubtless wish that his wife, my dear Maria, might accompany him to Paris; but one cannot count upon this journey in the midst of her absorbing affliction.* What a loss her death is to my dear aunt! All Prussia feels it deeply.

I promised to speak to you of one of the friends of my youth, and to recommend her to your good-will, paternal counsels, and guidance. I refer to Mademoiselle Rantzau, niece of the excellent Madame de Rantzau, whom you knew in Mecklenburg. She is a lady of great piety, who loves the Lord, and is entirely devoted to his service. Her independent position suggested the thought of consecrating herself to the care and direction of children in Fliedner's establishment of Deaconesses, near the Rhine. She several months since occupied this

* Allusion is here made to the death of the princess Wilhelmina of Prussia, sister to the grand duchess Augusta of Mecklenburg.

important and difficult office, when she was called to the post of directress of the new house of Deaconesses in Berlin, which the king of Prussia wished to found. She has not accepted it without great contests, but she believes that she sees the call of God in it, and declares herself ready to undertake it. For the interests of the work, the king of Prussia desires that she should visit the principal establishments, where the sisters of charity labor, in several places, and among others at Munich. She desires that you should take her under your protection. I know I am making a request which will be agreeable to you, for you never refuse your assistance and good counsel, and to a child of God less than any other person. I here enclose a few lines to the address of Mademoiselle de Rantzau, begging you to remit them to her with your own hand, and I once again recommend my friend to your affectionate interest.

Receive, dear Professor, etc.,

HELEN.

Thus unremittingly did the noble activity of the duchess display itself; she only found herself happy and at peace when the Lord offered some new devotion to her loving heart. But the first necessity of her heart, and the first duty of her life was always the education of her children for the glory of God, then devotion to her neighbors, and particularly to her country. By the fidelity, love, conscientiousness, and judgment which constantly marked her maternal duties, the duchess of Orleans has rendered herself worthy of being an example for all mothers. We are going to introduce a few fragments of letters addressed to the grand duchess; they refer to the early development of her two sons, which will give us an idea of the care she bestowed from the earliest moment upon their education. At the time these fragments commence, the count de Paris is nearly six years old; the duke de Chartres is in his third year.

M. Regnier, to whom allusion is made, entered upon his duties the 1st of June, 1843. The duchess writes to her mother on the 1st of June:

"The relations between M. R. and the little one are excellent. You would be rejoiced to see with what gentleness and yet with what firmness he manages the child. Paris is attached to him, and dares no more disobey him than myself and Madame H. I anticipate excellent results from these new relations. As to Robert, he is very unhappy at being separated from his brother. He asks for him every moment, for he sees him but seldom, and loves him much. He has need of being with other children more than Paris; he grows weary when he plays alone. Paris is contented by himself, but he is nevertheless happy in being able to play with Robert two hours daily."

JUNE 18.

Every morning Paris reads Robinson with M. R., who leads him to many instructive conversations. I previously give him a short lesson in sacred history, which commences with a prayer. I cannot say that he is always attentive, but he nevertheless likes these narrations very much.

OCTOBER 15, 1843.

I now also go from time to time to Versailles with Paris, in order to show him the historical pictures, and thus early to impress the history of the country upon him. He takes an interest in all, and sees nothing superficially.

DAY BEFORE CHRISTMAS, 1843.

To-morrow will be a trying day; it is the opening of the chambers. I asked the king's permission to lead Paris to the queen's tribune. In doing so, I knew what task I was taking upon myself; but it is good, I believe, for the members to see the little one, without his timidity being called in play, and without his being called into action, which could scarcely be expected of a child of five years I shall go then, and take my seat opposite the throne, which will always appear vacant to *me*.

JANUARY 1, 1844.

We, as formerly, ended the year at the king's, under the lighted tree. The children received great delight from their presents ; Paris above all, at the sight of a small cabinet of objects according to his taste. I returned with him, soon after, for it was late ; upon reaching his chamber, he quietly took a book, seated himself, and began to read without any appearance of distraction or excitement. His play-things arrived ; he did not cast a glance upon them, and said he wished to finish his history. That pleased me ; it is a good sign.

MARCH 6, 1844.

My children are well and are developing very happily. Paris is always well employed ; but as he is very nervous and subject to headaches, his studies are not yet very heavy. Robert now studies nothing, for since his sickness at St. Cloud, we have omitted all study, and I do not yet permit him to begin again. He loves me very much, and in a very touching manner ; I believe, that notwithstanding his affection for his nurse, he prefers me above all the world ; he wishes to be always at my side. Paris has a passion for drawing; he also writes many riddles, and takes great delight in dissecting each word in order to make a rebus. Geography, mathematics, history, and stories, all equally captivate his attention.

From a rather later date.

Paris at the table relates his tales to me with delight and an ever new zeal. Cyrus, Alexander, etc., play a great role in his narrations ; Robert daily becomes more lively, more comical, and more original. His passion for design has rather surpassed that of Paris, since we played some English, German, and French pieces upon a little theatre that his father had given him, and which we have discovered. Robert also now learns English, for he complained much of not being able to understand the English piece. His German is not bad.

April 14, 1844.

I measure time by the development of my children ; they advance, particularly Paris. He is truly an amiable boy, tall, rosy, graceful, and above all, very studious and brave ; he has a good heart, with frankness and well-balanced ardor. He has been twice with me to the exhibition ; you can imagine what resolution it required of me. I should never have done it, if so much had not been said of the seclusion in which I retain the child. It had an enormous success; the people almost suffocated him with joy; and, as for him, he was neither foolish nor timid, but natural and busy, that is to say, full of interest for his dear machines, which he has a passion for. Happily, praise and admiration do not at all dispose him to vanity; he does not set value upon it. Little Robert, who examined the people more than the machines, and was in the back-ground, was very happy that the people also took notice of him. There was nothing on his part but sallies, good humor, and vivacity; sometimes I do not know how to put an end to these little impertinences; he is too amusing; but, notwithstanding his good heart which is in his favor, it is necessary to be severe with him.

JULY 5, 1844.

Paris and Robert have their little conversations together, in which the character of each is displayed in a strong light; one full of reason and depth; the other, of intelligence and vivacity.

JANUARY 2, 1845.

What will you say, dear mother, upon learning that I was present at a reception party, yesterday? The king wished Paris to be present. The child made a good appearance ; he was tranquil, polite, natural, and awakened sympathy. In a word, he gave me great pleasure that day ; in the morning he brought me a letter which he had composed and written entirely alone ; he was besides cordial and happy, and clearly proved his affection for me. The poor child had many letters to write for the new year ; but yours and mine, without aid from any one whatever. He wrote them *in love.*

JANUARY 13, 1845.

The differences of the two characters, happily for their mutual relations, add to the difficulty of their education, for it is necessary to lead and direct them differently, without appearing unjust. If I punish one, and confine myself to giving a lesson in a playful tone to the other, it appears partial, and nevertheless one can often reach the same end only by different roads. God will surely lead them.

TUILERIES, July 24, 1845.

My children are well and rejoice me by their progress. Paris becomes more frank towards me ; what he formerly possessed in the depths of his soul without the power to express, now pervades his whole nature.

Upon returning lately from the opening of the

chambers, he wished to dictate the discourse of the king, which he had listened too with great attention, to M. R. He acquires a great facility of analysis, which will be very useful to him.

You ought to see *the joy* of my children, their happiness in *giving*. They have worked a long time, to their surprise. Paris printed a geography* of Mecklenburg for me, with a map designed by his hand; a copy is destined for you which will soon be sent. Robert has learned to read in German, has recited something in English, and made good progress. It was pleasant to see their delight, which lasted all day. We are reunited at Neuilly.

JUNE 8, 1845.

To-morrow I shall accompany my little Paris to a concert of a thousand young singers from all the schools of the city, who sing justly and without instruments. They come from Sunday schools which unite in the Champs-Elysées. I had been besought to take Paris there, that he might encourage the efforts of his less-favored cotemporaries by his presence.

EASTER, 1845.

Robert went to-day to mass for the first time.

* With a little printing-press, a present from his grand father.

He went alone with his brother and the king The latter was very content with his conduct, and the little one well satisfied with himself. His regard for the holiness of the place will arise little by little ; the Lord will always expand this feeling in the souls of children ; we only ought to pray faithfully for them.

These passages give us sufficient insight to the maternal occupations of a princess who had herself been educated with a view to the contests of life and the peace of eternity. To end this subject, I here insert another letter addressed to me.

TUILERIES, Jan. 3, 1846.

A voice, which is the echo of the country, the echo of childhood, profoundly moves the heart. But when that voice is that of an old master and friend, whose accents, always harmonious, never resound in vain, then the emotion becomes joyous and responds to the expectation of one who provoked it.

If you knew to what extent each word coming from you is precious to me, you would feel all the depth of my gratitude.

To-day, it is still more lively, for the heart of a

mother is more touched by the goodness manifested to her children than by that of which she is the object. I have at this moment to express to you the joy of my son, whose face became radiant when I remitted him your beautiful present, and found that he could there fluently read interesting and instructive things. He loves, as well as a child of seven years can love, science, and all that is grave and profound. He likes to see a *savant;* he has your name in great veneration, not only from that motive, but for all that his mother has related to him of the faithful preceptor of her childhood. The book which you sent him will become more and more dear to him, in proportion as his young intellect comprehends its depths ; your teachings which ascend always to the Creator, as the primary source of all that we find beautiful and marvellous, will diffuse that freshness and candor in his heart, which dry dead science often destroys.

His preceptor faithfully aids me in keeping him in this way, for he combines heart and character with a superior degree of intellect.

The agitation which manifests itself in Germany is without doubt serious, and also much occupies me. God grant that the true German spirit may come out victorious from all these embarrassments, and that the nation may enter in possession of the indispensable liberties in the progress of the human mind and the truth. May all this disquietude terminate peacefully!

My cordial salutations to Madame de Schubert and your dear Selina.

HELEN.

The grand-duchess Augusta wrote in 1847, after her return from Paris:

"The hand of God guides Helen and her children; what have I to fear? He has permitted me to pass some time with her; I have more and more recognized with admiration that she is at the height of her difficult mission, and I have felt how small I am beside her."

The conduct of the duchess during the course of the following year (1848) well justified the unwavering confidence which the princess Augusta placed in her daughter's high faculties. After having once more fulfilled the duty of protecting the rights of her children, and contended in favor of the maintenance of order and happiness in her dear adopted country, the duchess of Orleans passed through all the perils of that year with a pure conscience and inexhaustible courage. She had doubtless long had the feeling of the instability of a throne which could not be strengthened by attempts to conciliate hostile and heterogeneous parties.

Coming to an end of an important period of the life of the duchess of Orleans, I will here recite the judgment pronounced upon her by one of the best German papers.

"Whatever may be the design of Providence with regard to the moment in which the king shall be called to resign the task of his life, all concurs to prepare the count de Paris worthily for his future and important mission. The prince receives an education in every respect distinguished, under the superintendence of the king himself and the duchess of Orleans. One is moved to see with what indefatigable solicitude and with what maternal love the duchess watches over her children; she is, in this respect, the model of women and mothers, and has conquered the esteem of all the nation. A princess in France has rarely enjoyed a parallel popularity among all classes of the people, and without distinction of party; wherever she presents herself, she receives testimonials of it. Her benevolence, to whom no unfortunate appeals in vain, has contributed, not less than her piety, to gain all hearts. One may see, twice a week, a simple carriage issuing without escort from the Tuileries, and taking the direction of the Protestant chapel. It contains the duchess of Orleans, on her way to attend worship at her church.

XVIII.

THE REVOLUTION OF FEBRUARY AND ITS CONSEQUENCES.

For the first time since the death of her husband, the duchess wrote that "her birthday had been a fête, which the most tender testimonials of the affection of her children had rendered dear." On the 5th of February, scarcely three weeks before the event which the world called a great misfortune for her and her sons, she still speaks in a letter of her inward happiness and attachment to that beautiful France, her country, where she was anticipating a visit from the friend whom she was then addressing.

This peace at the approach of misfortune, is a somewhat prophetical manifestation of the eternal joy which is to follow the light afflictions of this world. According to the testimony of the Book of Revelation, the celestial army already hear the shouts of triumph, when ruin and distress mutter like the storm, and outpour themselves upon the powers of the earth.

In her letters to a few influential friends, and to her relations in Germany, the duchess of Orleans had a good right to contradict the rumor, spread by several public pamphlets, that her relations with the royal family were altered since the death of the duke; she had never ceased, said she in her maternal language, "to be borne in the arms of love." If the situation of the duchess remained the same in the family circle, Louis Philippe nevertheless in the loss of his son had lost a pledge for the future, and a counsellor, who, seconded by the duchess, opened the eyes of his royal father to the consequences of an inopportune resistance, and moderated excited measures, by a spontaneous prudence or foreign influence. We are not here to describe the past events of the revolution of February; that task belongs to political history; for no witness can embrace the whole, and each judges differently, according to his point of view. Nevertheless the most divergent witnesses agree in rendering homage to the presence of mind and courage manifested by the duchess of Orleans. An account of her conduct during the days of February, is essential to her biography.*

Mademoiselle Sinclair accompanied the grand duchess to meet her daughter at Ems, and in a letter describes the meeting of the two princesses. We quote the following passage, which vividly depicts the inward disposition and outward desolation of the noble exiled duchess.

"I still see her, as she appeared upon her arrival at Ems, on the 18th of March; she was at the foot of the front steps, pale, but full of energy and confidence in God. I see her fold her mother, whose arrival she had awaited so impatiently, to her heart. How touching and sublime she was! Whenever my memory recalls the peaceful weeks at Ems, it seems to me as if a little sanctuary opened before me. She was almost destitute of necessaries, but the dear princess was grand in the midst of all these privations. She still wished to simplify every thing, and to renounce every thing not indispensably necessary. I shall never forget what she said to me one evening, in a playful tone, 'Clara, we will indulge ourselves in a little fête to day; we will drink some tea;' (the domestic reg-

* Prof. Schubert's account fully accords with the one previously given, and is essentially the same.]

ulation forbid tea.) I hastened to order it; the good duchess, always amiable and naive, first tasted it, then insisted that M. Regnier should also come and drink it with his colleague. She begged me to invite them; but delicacy led them to refuse; she went herself, and they obeyed. Oh! those were hours which no words can describe, and which one must treasure in the depths of one's heart."

Even then "she was not unhappy;" this assertion of her august mother is assuredly a great truth.

A loving heart never sympathizes more deeply with the trials of others than when itself stricken by misfortune. This the duchess experienced, and it led her to write me a letter from Ems full of solicitude for the young man of Munich, who, upon my recommendation, had entered into the service of the duke de Chartres.

Ems, April, 1848.

Dear Professor:

Since the storms which it has pleased the Lord to send upon my dear France, I have had the feeling that your prayers and thoughts were accompanying me. I also believed I shall one day receive some word of faithful remembrance from you. I hope for it now, for I will never doubt your sympathy. Mine is always with you, and I have more than once been saddened in thinking of the cares you have had in these latter days.* May God calm these disquietudes!—this hope is well founded, since your king seems to take the great task to heart, which has fallen to him in these difficult times. My prayers and wishes accompany him and the queen.

Yesterday, dear professor, I wrote to you with regard to the excellent young man, who in happier days, you recommended to the office of valet-de-chambre to my youngest son. At the moment of the revolution, when I was obliged to leave that dear city of Paris, he was separated from me, and returned to his own country several days after; for it was unhappily impossible for me to retain him in my service, notwithstanding the zeal, fidelity, and intelligence, which he had constantly manifested. I promised him that I would have recourse to your benevolence to procure another position, if possible. If you say one word, in my name, to the countess Grawenreuth, and perhaps to queen Maria, they will doubtless offer him a place. During the years which he devoted to my child, he gave proofs of integrity, capacity, and rare intelligence; I infinitely

* She alludes to the troubles of Munich and to the accession of Maximillian II.

regret no longer having him with my son. In the midst of the immeasurable disaster which has fallen upon our family, one of my most bitter cares, is the disability hereafter to recognize the services of so many faithful servitors. That affects me most, after the thoughts of my sons' future. But God, who has dispensed to us so great affliction, will still be our support and guide.

If you can send me a reply, I pray you to address me under cover of my mother's name, who is also at Ems, where we shall live in absolute retirement until the bathers drive us away. We are at the England Hotel. Adieu, dear professor, I recommend all who are dear to me to your remembrance and prayers.

HELEN.

The republic appeared to consolidate itself, and rendered the perspective of a return to France impossible. On the other hand, Ems ceased to be a retreat; it filled with bathers, and at the same time with curious intruders. Among various asylums offered the princess, she chose Eisenach. She retired there with her suite, increased in number by the preceptor of the duke de Chartres, M. Courgean, and a few domestics. Persons of high rank, who previously composed her retinue, came by turns to

Eisenach, during periods of time more or less long, and served her as formerly at the Tuileries, Neuilly, and Eu. The marquis de Vins, reader to the duchess, and M. Boisimlon, former preceptor to the duke of Orleans, who now aided her by his counsels in the education of her sons, never left the duchess till her death. Thus a veritable French colony was formed at Eisenach ; they there scrupulously observed the French customs, for the duchess still believed that the crisis would soon pass, and she wished the young princes to remain in every respect faithful to their country. If, in the education of the count de Paris, she did not lose sight of the high mission to which he might be called, she at the same time did not undervalue the advantages to be obtained for her sons by their exile. Brought in closer contract with ordinary life, they learned to become better acquainted with it ; they found themselves in social relation with the most varied classes, and studied the customs and occupations of the peasants with interest. The duchess invited M. Regnier, his wife and two sons, to Eisenach ; the nearness of their ages to that of the two princes, and their intellectual development, made them suitable companions for them. The exiled princess herself gained new strength and life at Eisenach ; the beauty and salubrity of the country, the artistic interest which the renovation and decoration of Wartburg offered her, the neighborhood of Weimar, the residence of her family, the society which sufficed to exclude all feeling of solitude without being a burden, all these advantages made this place of abode peculiarly attractive. Eisenach, besides, possessed a Catholic church, under the charge of a pious and worthy ecclesiastic ; this circumstance the duchess particularly valued for the sake of her two sons.

Those who had formerly seen the duchess at Paris, surrounded by all the *éclat* of the rank which she occupied, could not help sharing the general admiration due to her elevation of mind. This sentiment became still more lively, when they saw her at Eisenach, deprived of all external pomp, and despoiled of all the natural resources of her high and active intellect. The noble falcon of Schah Béhéram Gour, the great hunter, was magnificent to see, when adorned with the golden ring, it proudly rested upon the silver-mailed hand of his master, seated upon his elegant courser ; but the eye of the hunter admired the beautiful bird much more, when, released from its golden chaperon, rings, and bells, it soared rapidly through the air or majestically hovered over the castle battlements.

XIX.

INFORMATION DERIVED FROM THE BEST SOURCE.

MUCH information is derived from the letters of the duchess addressed to me from various stations of her exile; this may be perceived from the first line of the following:

EISENACH, June 10, 1848.

DEAR PROFESSOR:

I wrote to you from Eisenach that the German Synod had been very clamorous; from Eisenach, the asylum of the holy Elizabeth and of Luther, where your letter with its friendly counsel reached me. If I have not sooner thanked you, it has been because my time was occupied by my correspondence, though I do not like in this manner to open the wounds of my heart and the agitation of my mind; on the other hand, it is difficult for me to resolve to converse with you only upon accessory things when the great questions of the time exclusively occupy both one and the other. This motive however ought not longer to allow me to appear ungrateful. Permit me to say how much I am touched with your words, and how grateful I am for your counsel to seek an asylum in Bavaria. That was also my first thought; I had an idea of Wartburg, of Bamburg, of Nuremburg; but in the midst of my hesitation, I received from my uncle the kind and paternal invitation to come here, and accepted his offer. I have then provisionally pitched my tent under his direction and feel as happy as one can feel in exile; I find the country as beautiful as it can appear to eyes blinded with tears, and I am the object of an affection as welcome as is possible to a broken heart, which sighs after its country. My mother's presence is a subject of consolation; in her, I have a model of noble sentiments and piety; I have a happy pledge for the future in the development of my children; my heart then ought to cease to suffer, but God alone can calm it; I await this benefaction from him, and submit myself blindly to His will. Do we know what is in reserve for the morrow? Why then do we torment ourselves?

Tell my cousin, the queen, how much I was rejoiced at her happy deliverance, and instantly recommend my faithful P—— to her. If I knew how to place him as he merits, there would be a much less weight upon my heart. I know that this presents some difficulties; I do not wish to be importunate.

Salute the brave B——, also his wife, if you see her. I still remember the visit they made me at Eu. What an abyss between then, and now. May God shield you and grant to you and Mrs. Schubert happier and sweeter days than those in which we live. I recommend myself with my children to your prayers.

HELEN.

At the time this letter came to me, I received another from a lady of high rank, who was daily witness to the family life at Eisenach. She paints the two princes in strong colors; the count de Paris, then ten years of age, with a tall and well developed figure, graceful in his movements, easy in his bearing, ingenious in his reflections, of a sound mind and quick understanding. "His preceptor, to whom he is much attached, possesses all the gifts requisite for the exercise of the happiest influence upon the development of the prince. He climbs the mountains of the environs with his pupil, makes him collect and press the flowers sent to him from Paris to be classed by M. Germain, who taught the prince botany. An observer who should attentively notice the deep blue eyes of the count de Paris, and his regular features, in which goodness of heart, thoughtfulness and intelligence are depicted, would soon see that he is no ordinary child.

"Robert, eight years of age, who still loves to be called little Robert, is large enough for his age, but always so forward that I believe I have never seen so active a child. He develops happily, as well with regard to his disposition as to his intellect. His voice is of a penetrating strength; his blue spiritual eyes animate a physiognomy whose fine traits remind one of those of the queen Maria Antoinette, at his age. The affection of the two children for their mother is touching; how else could life be rendered supportable to her!"

After two letters written by the duchess of Orleans from Ems and Eisenach, came the following letter, from which I have abstracted several passages:

EISENACH, March 6, 1849.

I have long wished to thank you, dear professor, for the precious letter I received from you in the month of November of the last year, and for the inclosed one addressed to my eldest son, who was moved and rejoiced with it; we are now zealously studying the little book which accompanied it, with the German lessons which I give him. My correspondence is unhappily such that it is impossible for me to fulfil all my obligations; and hence a second letter from you has come to me, to which I reply much later than it was my desire to.

(She again expresses her solicitude for the faithful valet-de-chambre of her youngest son, and her gratitude for what had already been done for him by the obliging intercession of queen Maria.)

The letter you had the goodness to write to my little Paris, deeply interested me. He has been acquainted with you from his earliest infancy, as one is acquainted with a legend; the rod from the burning bush, the rose of Sharon, the bull-bull, unhappily so early dead, and finally your natural history and the many stories of which you have been the subject, have established a mysterious bond between you and his young imagination. A letter from his invisible friend, has, then, appeared to him as a marvel from fairy-land; the numerous and excellent works which you recommend to him, will become his delight, little by little. He already strongly likes Plutarch, and knows it almost as well as his catechism; it is only the school of great men, that can now elevate him. At an epoch in which humanity has fallen so low, it is very necessary to direct his attention to the past, in order that he may not lose his faith in humanity. May he see better days, when the storms which surround us shall be calmed. My mother, near whom I am now writing, begs me cordially to salute you. How many times we speak of you, and how we wish for a visit from the pilgrim in our Thuringian hermitage.

HELEN.

If the letters we have read have already given us some idea of the kind of life and feelings of the duchess during the sojourn at Eisenach, we have still more minute information upon this subject. The duchess sought to introduce the domestic arrangement and spirit which formerly reigned at Friedensburg into her new retreat. When she was alone or with her intimate friends, she frequently occupied herself with the same subjects which had been the charm of the Friedensburg circle. She frequently recalled a religious poem, which was there particularly liked, and which is to be found in the excellent work, entitled: "*Life of J. M. Sailer Feneberg.*" It had there produced such a profound impression that is was set to music, and the choir of Friedensburg frequently and willingly sung it. One may well say, that of all the persons composing that little choir, the princess Helen best understood the words of that Christian poem, and sung the melody with the most soul. At Paris, in moments of leisure, but oftener at Eisenach, she loved still to sing it, for the experience of her heart had taught her the deep meaning of that energetic and consoling poem of the good Feneberg.

The duchess of Orleans had occasion to apply it so frequently in the course of her life, that it had become a sort of rallying word with her. A poem by bishop Spangenberg was also as an amulet to her soul, when she was engaged, in consequence of her political or religious position, upon the somewhat winding path of human wisdom. This poem is entitled, "Sacred Simplicity, the Manual of Grace;" she frequently read it in the evenings at Eisenach, as at Friedensburg.

Thus, at Eisenach, when the work of the day was ended, they closed their eyes in peace and repose of soul; and, in the morning, opened them with a disposition of heart not less calm and peaceable.

XX.

CONSOLATIONS AND NEW TRIALS.

A STRIKING proof of the general consideration which the duchess of Orleans enjoyed, was given by the people of Paris, in the midst of the whirl of the revolution of February. The mob penetrated into most of the apartments of the Tuileries, and even into some of those reserved for the duchess' suite; but they were not besought to spare the Maison Pavillon, which she inhabited, for garlands were already hung over her doors, in sign of respect. Her femme-de-chambre was afterwards able to enter, and with the aid of her faithful friends, to take away all that belonged to her mistress. A part of her possessions were sent to Eisenach; the furniture that was too heavy to transport was placed in a chamber rented for the purpose. Thus the duchess preserved all her articles inviolate, and she soon found herself surrounded by all the portraits, pictures, and other objects which were of great price to her, reminding her of happier days. She also afterwards received her dowry, which, in accordance with the French law, could not be taken from her.

On the 24th of February, 1849, the day of the anniversary of the revolution, the marquis de Mornay came to Eisenach, which was the object of a constant pilgrimage. If the duchess was happy in these testimonies of affection and sympathy, she found herself in a constant state of over excitement which affected her health, already shattered by so many storms. She was nevertheless able to face the rigors of the winter without danger, and to be a spectator to the diversions of the young princes when they skated upon the pond at the foot of the Wartburg.

She took a still more active part in the exercises and occupations which were destined to strengthen, not her physical, but her intellectual life. Though the care of her health made it her duty to prolong her nightly repose, she never neglected to call her sons around her for morning worship. Family prayers were followed by conversations, in which the lively faith of the duchess made such a deep impression upon her children that it will be forever graven upon their hearts. Their differences of worship never produced evil consequences: she listened with interest to the religious lessons given to her children by a worthy Catholic ecclesiastic; and her Lutheran faith, at once firm and conciliating, inspired such profound respect in the priest, that he, perhaps of all the members of the clergy, after the death of the duchess, most forcibly recalled what she had been and what she had done.

In the summer of 1849, she saw all her Mecklenburg relations at Leipsic; in the month of March, 1850, she went to Schwerin and Ludwigslust. After having traversed Meiningen, which reminded her of hours passed in the family of the ducal mansion, and after having at Coburg enjoyed the domestic pleasures of her dear sister Clementine, she went with her and her brother-in-law to the good old city of Nuremberg. It was in the month of April, 1850. She wished her sons to see the city which had been so dear to her in her childhood; she showed them every thing, the churches, the beautiful fountains, Albert Durer's house, and the manufactories. From Nuremberg, she went to Wurtzburg, where she made personal acquaintance with the nephew of her maternal friend, Madame de Both; she visited Frankfort Museum with a particular interest, and descended the Rhine in a steamboat, to proceed to England.

She was called thither by the duty of accompanying count de Paris, who was to take his first communion under the eyes of the royal family. A chapel in which Louis Philippe had offered his devotions, during his first exile, was designated for this solemnity; he was then in the vigor of youth, and the future was unfolding itself before him; now he entered, sustained by General Dumas, and bowed under the weight of years and cares. He was followed by the queen, whose step was firm, and eye serene. The loss of a throne for which she had never been ambitious, had not troubled her; a heart sanctified by the love of God had no regrets for the smoking ruins of a terrestrial happiness; she had in Him a sure refuge, which satisfied all her desires. After the queen, came the duchess of Orleans, with her children and the rest of the family. The entire chapel was filled with friends; twenty youths of the same age as the count de Paris, occupied the first seat near the altar. They presented a precious gift to the prince, which was placed upon the altar.*

"Who could contemplate," said an eye-witness, "without emotion, that mother, whose tearful eyes rested upon her sons as if she would envelop them

* Allusion is also here made to the administrations of Abbé Guelle, and Cardinal Wiseman, at this ceremony.

with her look of love, while she was there upon her knees, and while her countenance bore the expression of innocence, humility, and devotion ?" The sobs of the spectators were not even stifled by the sound of the organ. The prince's nurse came expressly from France to witness this ceremony.

Several persons, who had not seen the royal family since the days of its prosperity, found, that of all the members which composed it, the duchess of Orleans was the least changed and bowed down. She was adorned for this fête, as in the period of her prosperity ; the expression of her countenance, was as always, sweet, benevolent, and spiritual. She then wrote to a friend :

"One often still feels so young and so sympathetic when one does not dream of years already left behind in the distance. But God and time incessantly influence us. Ah ! what a capricious thing is life, and how much more capricious the heart of man is. God must have much, much patience with regard to us."

The duchess, in successively visiting her relations in Germany, seemed to be bidding adieu to her country. She expresses this sentiment in some passages of her letters, and her arrival in England was soon to be followed by trying adieus.

The failing of Louis Philippe's health could not escape the notice of any one who had occasion to see him at certain intervals, and above all during his sojourn in England. The members of his family, who were constantly with him, did not observe it to the same extent. His firm confidence in himself, which never abandoned him in the midst of all the dangers and vicissitudes of his reign, was shaken on the 24th of February, the time of the unexpected disaster, with which it had pleased God to strike his house. Upon his departure from Paris he proceeded to Dreux, where the ashes of his father reposed, and finally embarked for England.*

The duchess of Orleans wrote at this time as follows:

"This year has so impoverished me, that I have often trouble to shake off the thoughts which oppress and harass me, so as to prevent the loss of all freshness of spirit. But this is speaking of myself and my grief. Does not the queen set me an example of spiritual strength and celestial resig-

*Mention is here made of the sojourn at Claremont, and of Louis Philippe's death; the much fuller account given in the first part of this volume, warrants the omission here. The death of the queen of the Belgians is here simply alluded to.

nation? Ought I to bear my cross less courageously than she?"

The duchess passed the winter in England near the mourning royal family. The grand-duchess wrote to me in January, 1851: "Helen loves to frequent the German Lutheran church in London, where she enjoys the preaching of an ecclesiastic who officiates alternately with the aged pastor, Steinkopf, now eighty-four years of age."

The new events which passed in France in 1851, soon announced the thick clouds which often troubled the serene horizon of the duchess.

"The repose," wrote she, "that I loved so much to find in a tranquil retreat, in a complete oblivion of the outward world, and of odious politics, that repose, I cannot obtain, because the troubles of our poor country, the hopes of some, the follies of others, and the stupidity of the majority, disturb me too much, and give my thoughts no relaxation. I keep occupied, try to divert myself with music, walk often, and am frequently with my relatives, but my heart cannot be calmed. God only can render peace, and I have the firm hope that he will."

The following passages of another letter prove to what extent she knew how to find the source of that inward durable peace:

"Gratitude towards God, is of all feelings the one that I love the most. That outpouring of the soul, does it not attract us powerfully towards Him, and does it not often establish a more intimate relation than grief? And is there a greater grief than impotence to render thanks in the midst of prosperity? Is there any thing more withering to the heart than ingratitude? No; I love to outpour the gratitude with which my heart is filled towards Him, to whom I owe every thing, towards my neighbors and friends, who afford me so many delights; towards my enemies, shall I add, for they show me the reverse of life, and press my heart to seek the aid of God, more and more. I now comprehend the double sense of the words, 'Bless those who curse you.' But I should be a hypocrite, if I said, that I have learned to be grateful towards them. I simply confess that they merit gratitude, and that in saying, 'Forgive them, Father, for they know not what they do,' I should heap coals of fire upon their head. Behold how I have passed, without transition, from my best friends to my most bitter persecutors."

XXI.

A FORETASTE OF THE TERRORS OF DEATH.

When the heart is in the state described in the previous letter, it can calmly face the terrors and judgment of death. It was reserved for the duchess to experience them, before the moment assigned in the ordinary course of nature, when God calls man to appear before Him. In the crisis to which I allude, the duchess passed through all the agonies of the dark valley through which the dying one enters another world, the splendors of which she had for an instant gained a glimpse. It is for this reason that she afterwards left this world without contest, without seeing the approach of death, or feeling its bitterness; she had already passed through this trial; she had wrestled with death, and only prevailed after having said, like Jacob to the angel, "I cannot let thee go, unless thou bless me."

At the end of the year 1852, and in the beginning of the following year, grave events, which followed the grief of the royal family, filled the heart of the duchess with agitation. I speak of the *coup d'etat* of the 2d of December, and of the confiscation of the property of the Orleans family, which further aggravated the sentence of exile. The material loss scarcely affected the duchess, but she was under the weight of another affliction, which opened an abyss between her and the future of her life. "One should not be astonished by it," wrote the grand-duchess, "she is attached as by a charm to the country which repulses her. But the Lord will deliver her from this charm. He already begins to do so."

Her health had been very much shattered for some time. Physicians prescribed a journey into Switzerland. Her noble mother wrote to me on the 8th of August, 1852:

"Helen is now at St. Gervais, upon one of the heights at the foot of Mont Blanc, in order to breathe the pure air of the country and to strengthen her nerves. Her health does not inspire serious disquietude. The children, who must have grown much, climb the surrounding mountains with the goats; they love Nature and their studies. May the Lord grant them all His benediction."

The innocent enjoyment of these solitary walks was habitually disturbed by the presence of persons who seemed to be spies attached to the steps of the duchess and her suite. Her strength of soul was to be put to a most rude test; she was to look death in the face, and was to be saved only by the hand of God. Upon the route from Geneva to Lausanne, the closed carriage in which she was with her two sons, received such a violent shock, that it was overthrown and precipitated into a river. The duchess had her collar-bone broken; but, forgetting her pain and the approach of death, which seemed certain, she thought with anguish of her children, who were already safe, while she was under the water. She makes allusion to this deliverance in a letter which she addressed to me after her return to England. I give it entire, for it mirrors the calm of her soul.

KITTLEY, DEVONSHIRE, January 15, 1853.

It is with a true emotion, that I recognized your hand-writing and opened the book which you sent me as a souvenir of the past. You should have sooner received the expression of my gratitude, if the journey of that volume had been easier and less slow; but I have only been in possession of it for a few days. I have already read your interesting narrations to my sons, and they have been happy that one who sent the bull-bull and Moses' rod from the desert, had not forgotten them.

You have the marvellous gift of making the most noble cords of my soul vibrate; your letter has not only awakened within me, that remembrance of the *past*, in which dreams were golden and hopes full of life, but it is still a voice which speaks to me of that future without end, where dreams will become truths, and where hopes, faded here below, will bloom anew. I again, from the depths of my heart, offer you my thanks for all the affectionate sympathy of which your letter gives me proof.

I deeply regret that during my frequent excursions in Germany, I had never the pleasure of again pressing your hand, and of hearing the voice which cradled my infancy with such pretty legends, and which afterwards, by the aid of the pen, led my intellect to enjoy the most serious truths. We have sometimes no need to see you, in order to hear you; and thus, dear professor, (permit me still the old title,) I have not seen you since my sixteenth year, yet have not ceased to love and respect you.

You are, without doubt, right; some tempests have passed over us; and, in the course of the ten past years, I have *from the depths* experienced the bitterness of life. The short period of my happiness was very beautiful, too much without parallel; it has been necessary for me to expiate for it. But it is above all in the midst of these hard tests that I have sensibly experienced the grace and patience of the Lord. Latterly again, when His arm guarded my children in danger and saved me from a death which appeared inevitable, without hope ot succor, I had the very evident proof of His power and goodness; I have learned to regard my life as a gift of his love and to appreciate the value of what I have so often found bitter and painful. May this feeling contribute to the glory of God, and to the salvation of my dear children!

If you would from time to time give me tidings of yourself, you would give me great pleasure. Make my cordial salutations to queen Maria, who is so dear to me, and believe me with faithful attachment, your former pupil,

HELEN.

I left the recital of this deliverance of the duchess of Orleans to my friend Schelling in Berlin. I knew his respect and affection for the princess, with whom he had personal acquaintance at Eisenach; I knew the sympathetic part he took in her destiny. In addressing me on the 8th of March, 1853, before the last letter received from his hand, he called the duchess of Orleans "the most sorely tried woman of our epoch," and added a prophetic word with regard to her children. May it be realized in all its extent.

XXII.

NEW PILGRIMAGE.

The duchess was obliged to pass several weeks at Lausanne, until her fracture permitted her to return to England; though she was much weakened by physical and mental suffering, she wrote to her friend:

"May the will of God be accomplished in me, for his glory and my salvation; may the mysterious paths through which he leads me, purify my soul and render me capable of fulfiling my maternal duties!"

"My children prosper," wrote she at another time; "they live happily in the midst of youthful dreams, and grow strong in body and mind. I hope soon to be able to accompany them to England, whither I have an ardent desire to go. Repose, repose, isolation from all politics, that is what I have need of as well as pure air."

As she could not escape political agitation in the circle in which she lived, she took refuge for several weeks in the mountains of Scotland, and regained new strength in the bosom of that grand nature, of which she understood the charm. She again took up the pencil and the pallet which she had for so long a time neglected, and set about designing pretty landscapes after nature, in company with Madame de Vins, her reader, a lady endowed with distinguished talents.

She finally arrived in her much longed for England, but grief thither also pursued her. The duchess of Altenburg, her sister, like her, lost her husband ; this death painfully affected the duchess of Orleans, though habituated to such blows by so many cruel separations. The loyal character and sound religious principles of duke George, had rendered him dear to the duchess, as to all those who intimately knew him. She suffered much physically during the winter, but she only the more actively concentrated her strength of mind upon the education of her children. Count de Paris, at this epoch, received a military tutor, in the person of General Trézelle.

"Paris," wrote she, some time after, "passed a brilliant examination ; Robert passed his at Easter, and bore it bravely.

She introduced her sons into the circle of her relations, by accompanying them to Rudolstadt, Iena and Eisenberg, where, in August, 1854, she became godmother to her sister's little granddaughter. Her mother, the grand-duchess, who had been twice deeply afflicted in the space of two months, again at Rudolstadt, lost the last of her sisters, to whom she had been devotedly attached. The duchess hastened to join her, and finally accompanied her to Eisenach. She now especially felt the blessing of possessing such a mother, since death had made new ravages in her circle of friends, for she had learned of the sudden deaths of the minister Verney and Mademoiselle de Rantzau.

"Let us be more nearly united," she wrote to her friend, "and as soldiers, who in battle seeing their comrades fall around them, press together in the ranks, in order that the vacancy may not be perceived."

She expresses to me in the following manner the happiness she experienced in having her mother preserved to her :

"Of all visits, the dearest is that made at this time by my beloved mother ; my heart is filled with an ever new gratitude. The clearness and vigor of her mind charm all who see her, and her heart is still so young, so loving, that it gives life to the most indifferent."

The war in the Crimea was a new source of grief to the duchess, for the sons of a great number of her friends in France, had fallen upon the bloody field of battle. Count de Paris, among others, followed each scene of the military drama with as lively an interest as if the troops were still under the orders of his grandfather. He acquainted himself with the towers and forts of Sebastapol, and the respective positions of the armies, as if they were under his own eyes.

"We sigh after peace; may God grant it to us; otherwise no one will return," wrote the duchess.

Sympathy for the consequent sufferings of this war, showed itself in the minutest circumstances. The sons of her valet-de-chambre fell before Sebastapol; in the coat-pocket of one of them was found a Napoleon, which was sent to his parents with his clothing. The duchess added a gold ring to this piece of gold, that the soldier's mother might wear it in remembrance of her son. She several times went to see this grief-stricken woman.

During the winters of 1854 and '55, the duchess had frequent trouble with her eyes, which did not diminish the pleasure with which she welcomed the visit of some friends from France. "Helen is calm," wrote her mother, "though it costs her much to feel that her sons have no other perspective than the isolation of exile for the rich development of their faculties." The duchess addressed the following letter to me at the same epoch, and its tone and contents confirm this observation.

EISENACH, January 9, 1855.

For a long time, dear master and friend, I have desired to express my gratitude, and to tell you how much I am touched with each proof of your remembrance. I will not permit this return of the year to pass without acquitting the debt of my heart, and without thanking you for the gift you sent me. Your work* always makes me serene, and the remembrances of our childhood furnish me with an abundant subject for meditation. My dearly beloved mother also enjoys this book very much, and I have often found her engaged in reading it. It has a charm for her that old age knows how to appreciate, namely, that of refreshing the impressions of childhood ; but, besides that, she can still sound the most profound passages as formerly, and follow the most delicate reasoning. She is admi-

* The first volume of the author's biography.

rable! You would be rejoiced and astonished at her ideas, so fresh and so striking upon the most important points. She has maintained a rare lucidity which even reacts happily upon her health · and notwithstanding all the suffering which has assailed her these latter years, her heart has still infinite elasticity. I am very thankful for having her near me, and I feel that God not only preserves her to us, but that *He gives* her *to me.* Her presence is of inestimable value to my dear children.

My dear professor, (for I must retain that old name,) accept my best wishes for the year 1855, and keep me, in turn, in your good remembrance, to which I closely cling.

HELEN.

In the spring of the same year, the king of Saxony, who came to Thuringia to make several family visits, also passed to Eisenach. There was a double spiritual tie established between the duchess and himself which arose from a conformity of trials and consolations. Indeed, what analogy was there not between the sad accident which put an end to the days of the duke of Orleans, and the event of the 9th of August, 1854, which tore king Frederick Augustus from the nation to which he was a father? And if the duchess of Orleans had found motives for joy and consolation in the thought of eternity, what heart could better understand her than that of a prince, whose conscience had been awakened by Dante's poem upon Eternity? Hence, in the evening, at the table of the grand duke, who had accompanied his host to Eisenach, the duchess, seated by the side of the king, experienced the sweet satisfaction of understanding and being understood. What chiefly struck one in the prince, was not only his fine expression, high culture, and varied knowledge, but a depth of feeling which awakened unlimited confidence.

On the 23d of May, the king again made a visit to the duchess, before he departed for Meiningen, and invited her to visit him in Dresden, with her children and suite. The duchess accepted this invitation with pleasure, and, several weeks after, went to Dresden, where the royal family welcomed her with much affection. An excursion made into Saxon Switzerland, during the finest season of the year, agreeably diverted her. But she was chiefly happy in seeing her sons as interested in works of art as she had been when in her youth at Dresden. She would have remained a much longer time in that city, if the state of her health had not suddenly forced her to shorten her visit. She hastened to return to Eisenach, where she received the care of the grand duchess, who hastened to her bed-side; the physicians counselled her to try the waters of Pfeffers. A letter from the grand duchess, on the 13th of July, says with regard to this subject:

"God be praised! Helen is preserved to us, but she is still suffering. She will then go to Ragatz, which is a branch establishment to Pfeffers. May the Lord bless this remedy! We set out on Monday and go together as far as Giessen; from there she proceeds to Switzerland and I to Hamburg. To-day, the 13th of July, the anniversary of our common grief, we have been to take the communion, the children in their church, we in ours, but all reunited in the same spiritual communion. The two children, the eldest one particularly, were deeply moved. They develop, intellectually, so happily that all around them are rejoiced. The same may be said of their bodies; the count de Paris has the figure of a man; he is very slender, but strong, graceful, and adroit in his movements, calm and modest in his nature. The duke de Chartres also grows; he learns well, and has a vivacity altogether French. Both so passionately love their mother, that one is touched and happy at the sight of their affection. Surrounded by th..

purest and most innocent delights of childhood, they know, thanks to God, neither ennui nor regret."

The following winter, the state of the duchess was insupportable ; without being ill, she had not recovered her health. She then addressed me a letter, the contents of which refer to the part of my autobiography which concerns my sojourn at Mecklenburg. (Vol. 3, first Part.)

This letter is full of fine allusions to the situation of the country and the court at that epoch ; these allusions are only of importance to him who has the key to them. She takes, she says, a lively interest in remembrances concerning her brother Albert and the years she passed with him in her early childhood.

The duchess again resolved to go to the waters, during the beautiful season of the year 1856. This time she chose Soden, not far from Frankfort, because she could frequently see her mother, who was then in the vicinity, at Hamburg. The physicians, persuaded that a prolonged sojourn in a milder climate alone would reëstablish her health, entreated her to pass the winter in Italy. Their counsel was good ; the duchess so tried by many afflictions had need to summon the strength of her heart and soul for the last contest which awaited her; Italy, rather than any other country, offered the repose of which she had need.

"In this delightful country," wrote she to her friend, "I feel animated by a new life; I am robust and more cheerful than I have ever been since I commenced to suffer."

If this little work was to be but an agreeable recreation, I could not better attain that end than by publishing the letters written by the duchess of Orleans to her mother, during her sojourn in Italy in 1856–57. But as these letters do not directly enter into the frame which I have made, I confine myself to indicating the names of the countries through which she passed, and the cities where she sojourned. Those of my readers who have made the same journey, will scarcely have trouble to place their impressions in unison with those of the duchess.

One who, after a serious malady, has the new life which circulates through all the members of the body, will understand the animation of the first letter, written from Genoa, October 5, 1856. The duchess left England about the end of September; on the 2d of October she is at Verona, crosses the plain of the Po by the railroad, and passes the Appenines. The impression that Genoa produced upon her, with its magnificent situation, its churches, its palaces, and its works of art, is so lively and attractive that she does not mind the mud of its streets. The people please her, and the sentiments of a portion of the higher class of society are the sympathetic echo of her own thoughts. While she is seeking for a country house which corresponds to her wants, she goes to see lake Maggiore and the lakes of Como and Lugano. She enthusiastically describes the splendor of the surrounding country; she dwells complacently upon the cathedral of Lugano and the Borromean Isles, seen by the magnificent light of the moon.

From Milan, where the works of art captivate her, she passes by Pavia, returns to Genoa on the 27th of October, and soon after occupies a villa near Sestra. Seated upon the terrace of that villa, she was surrounded by a southern vegetation in the midst of winter; in front of her, she had the azure sea and breathed a sweet and welcome air. She was surrounded by a circle of acquaintances, attracted to her by conformity of principles, rank, and intellectual culture. These visitors, who always arrived by the first conveyance from Genoa and Sestra, departed in the same manner in the afternoon, and thus left the duchess in the free employment of her evenings. This sojourn in Italy, contributed in various ways to strengthen the duchess and to develop the physical strength of her sons. The count de Paris passed several weeks in Sardinia in order to enjoy the pleasures of the chase.

The necessities of her heart and mind also there found their supply. In a letter of the 31st of March, 1857, the duchess describes the benevolent establishments and schools of Genoa, in which she takes a lively interest. She also writes to the grand duchess: "How many times I have thought of you during this good and peaceable week, my dear mother. I took the communion on Easter Sabbath. Our Genoese preacher, M. Vaucher, is a man of faith, whose words deeply touch the heart."

The duchess left the Gulf of Genoa, on the 8th of May. The royal family of Sardinia, who had invited her to Turin, gave her a cordial welcome. Independent of the enjoyment still reserved for her in the fine arts of Milan, she had the pleasure of receiving a visit from the archduke Maximilian in that city; he had obtained the hand of her niece, princess Charlotte of Belgium. She finally proceeded to Augsburg, passing through Hohenschwangau, where she occupied the apartments of her relative, queen Maria of Bavaria. Towards the end of May, she found herself at Eisenach, where she only wished at that time to sojourn for a few weeks.

She wrote me a letter from there, which, as elsewhere, depicts her heart and mind.

A sojourn of several years had attached her to Eisenach; the castle in which she lived, was situated at the foot of the Wartburg, and contained al the souvenirs of happier times, with which she had wished to surround herself. It was not only in an external sense that she took possession of her residence; she had erected in the hearts of the inhabitants of the city, environs, and all Thuringia, a monument more precious than a dwelling of wood and stone, more durable than the short station of a wandering life. The materials of this monument were works of love, immeasurable consolations to the poor and afflicted, and encouragements to youth; it was the pure model of all Christian virtues that she offered to those who surrounded her, and even to those who heard her life of devotion spoken of. Her name was associated with that of the holy Elizabeth, whose name had been made popular by legend and poetry, and who, at a distant epoch, had also inhabited the Wartburg.

The duchess, who now found herself happier at Eisenach than elsewhere, even found in this feeling a warning soon to leave this sojourn, and to direct her pilgrimage to another station. She was not mistaken; the advanced age of the queen Maria

Amelia, made it her duty to be more continually near her, and she left Germany for England. Before her departure, she sent me a letter, accompanied with her portrait, which is said to be a true one; a copy of it is placed in the commencement of this volume. On the 6th of July, 1857, the duchess rejoined her family.

She occupied a country-house in the vicinity of Richmond, the property of marquis de Landsdowne. In one hour, she could be at Claremont, the residence of the queen, and in half an hour, at Twickenham, the possession of the duke d'Aumale. Her sojourn at Richmond was prolonged till the end of the lease, when she was forced to take another dwelling, which, with its façade of heavy portals and sombre columns, resembled a tomb. The duchess before entering it, caused its aspect to be made less gloomy.

XXIII.

THE END.

About this epoch, the thought of death was not only awakened in the duchess by a mere external circumstance, such as the aspect of the façade of her dwelling, but it was more than ever habitual in her soul. Many subjects which previously interested her, she now began to be indifferent to. She little by little came to share the sentiments of her mother, who shuddered at the bare thoughts of "cold, frigid politics," and who did not like one to approach the questions of the day, upon which she herself maintained a profound silence. In passing through Belgium, the duchess of Orleans had been obliged for seven consecutive hours to submit to conversations of this kind, which had extremely fatigued her; at each station, the same question presented itself anew, and she was only delivered from it upon setting her foot upon the vessel which was to transport her to England. In crossing from Calais to Dover, she was assailed by a storm, the voice of which was doubtless more powerful than that of harangue; but she was not forced to reply, and her part was simply to contemplate it in silence. What she saw at that moment inspired her with serious reflections. While the entire horizon was lit up with lightning, and the thunder pealed incessantly in the midst of the clouds, driven by the tempest, the sea was more calm than ordinarily for this portion of the channel. The noble duchess then said: "My soul ought to find itself more and more calm in the midst of the storms of politics." This she attained.

Formerly, she cherished the hope of some day returning to France, which was so dear to her; now this thought no longer absorbed her. She had educated her sons in view of rendering them useful and devoted to her country; she left to God the care of deciding in what manner their patriotism should be turned to profit.

Soon after the arrival of the duchess in England, a new affliction fell upon her heart and prepared her for her end. The sudden and so unexpected death of the duchess Victoire de Nemours (Novem ber 10, 1857), burst like a thunder-clap while the sky is serene, upon the Orleans family. Let us leave the duchess Helen to relate this catastrophe:

CLAREMONT, Nov. 11, 1857.

My dear and much beloved mother, you will share our affliction. That frightful event has paralyzed us. Never did death seize a victim so quickly. The ways of God are mysterious; but life is but a valley of bitter tears! The poor queen! to submit to such a blow at her age! to see the happiness of her dear son reduced to nothing! It is too hard. And Nemours, so touching in his grief, so profoundly afflicted and yet so pious, so resigned—yes, resigned to the will of God! His dear children show much heart. Alas! they loved their mother so much!

We are persuaded that you will sympathize with our affliction, you, my dear mother, who have such heart and who love our family so much!

We cannot yet comprehend our misfortune. A minute before, our dear Victoire was so amiable, so gay, she spoke of leaving her bed to receive a visit from her aunt; Nemours was below with the queen, and Victoire was alone with the nurse; suddenly she leaned gently upon the shoulder of the woman and said in a low voice, "Oh! I am ill!" She was no more! Nemours, the queen, all ran, and endeavored in vain to recall her to life; but, between the moment when we believed her in a swoon and the one in which the frightful truth flashed upon us, there was an abyss of despair. Poor Nemours was beside himself; he does not leave the chamber where his dear Victoire sleeps. Alas! she has still an expression so sweet, so calm; she is like a broken lily, still so white, so beautiful; there is shed such peace over her features! one almost believes that she breathes, and that she is going to speak! The queen is full of strength and courage; but she often says: "O that I was in her place!" I am established here in order to be with her as much as possible. My dear children appear very well, and show much feeling. Aumale is very useful to Nemours. Alas! what a winter is before us, who were hoping for some bright days!

I am going to give still a few more letters; we shall then see the reflection of the impressions produced upon the heart of the duchess by that unexpected blow, and the meditations which it suggested.

RICHMOND, Dec. 24, 1857.

DEAR MOTHER:

I write to you upon the evening of a very solemn day; upon the evening which reminds me of sc many proofs of love, goodness, and solicitude which you gave me in my childhood. It is a peaceful evening, serious, yet cheerful, for it is the anniversary of the birth of the Saviour who has ransomed fallen humanity, and who consoles and raises stricken hearts. The external fête which ravished my childhood, has given place to more grave remembrance ; we light no trees in our houses, and our children have no demonstrative joy as formerly. This year, death has cast a veil of mourning over the fete of the nativity, and over life, and our hearts seek elsewhere for joy and consolation.

We are all seeking to prepare for the holy communion. This evening, at midnight, the queen goes to commune with several members of her family ; to-morrow, early in the morning, will be my sons' turn ; afterwards, I shall go to my church in London. It is a very solemn thought ; I always tremble, and nevertheless, take courage, for the grace and mercy of the Lord are inexhaustible. It seems to me, dear and good mother, that I need to go to you and to read a canticle again with you, in order to receive strength, light, and benediction from you. My heart is with you in this hour of such a peaceful evening, when each one lives in retirement, and when you are in enjoyment of a sweet repose in the presence of the Lord. I am assured that you also think of me, with my dear sons—that you ask God not to withdraw his hand from us, and to bless the recent and painful trials which he has allotted us. There is, as dear Schubert always repeats, a gift of presentiment which never misleads, which draws hearts together notwithstanding distances ; hence I am now certain that we are near one another, my dearly beloved mother !

I conclude ; I will write a line to you to-morrow, after my return from London.

AFTERNOON OF CHRISTMAS-DAY

I have had a delightful morning, my dearly beloved mother, and I have thought much of you. I have returned from London, where I communed after having heard the preparatory service and the sermon. May God grant me his benediction, and above all, holy joy, which, on account of my feeble faith, fails me much. If you knew how far my depression goes, you would be pained. It is properly an evil, and a lack of faith ; but acquaintance with oneself always produces this discouragement.

The good Steinkopf, in his eighty-sixth year, was very ill and in bed ; he begged me to come near him, and spoke to me with so much heart that I was touched. He has always a word upon his lips which penetrates the soul. He told me to-day, that I did not meditate enough upon the words, "Give thanks." "If God has tried you," he added, "you are nevertheless always guided and protected by His hand, and He has beside left you many possessions. Hope in one who alone is immutable, when every thing disappears around you. You are acquainted with the nothingness of human greatness, the vanity of luxury and the glory of the world; and you are also acquainted with one who is not submitted to any change; hope, then, in Him, and lean upon Him." The excellent lady de —— took the communion at the same time with me. We returned to Richmond under a bright spring sun, and found my two sons upon our arrival, who had received the host. I am writing to you while they are gone to the evening service, which combines the vespers and the benediction, and I from time to time cast a glance upon the setting sun, which tints half of the horizon with purple. I have a magnificent spectacle before me, which reminds me of the beautiful evenings at Genoa and my timid attempts to reproduce that strange color with my brush. It is a beautiful and peaceable Christmas-eve, in which there would be nothing wanting, if you were here, dear mother.

Another letter, written at the end of 1857,

breathes the same confidence in God, and she seeks to raise the veil which covers the destinies of the ensuing year. This letter also interests by the narration of the gracious reception made at Windsor to the duchess and her two sons, by the queen of England and prince Albert. One sees that she is often penetrated by an indefinable melancholy, which externally manifests itself by the need she experiences of casting herself into the arms of her excellent mother. It was not only love for her native place that agitated the heart of the duchess; her soul had more profound and elevated aspirations; she already felt herself attracted towards that eternal country, which seems to reveal itself more distinctly to men, when the hour of departure seems about to strike. The following letter gives us a proof of this; it is the last I received from her hand, and one of the last addressed to Germany; for it is three days posterior to that which terminated the correspondence of the duchess with her mother. A few weeks after, the questions which she raises and which absorb her, received a dazzling solution in eternity.

RICHMOND, EASTER, April 4, 1858.

DEAR PROFESSOR:

I confide these lines to your grandson, in the

hope that the joy of seeing the bearer will give them some value. I have long had the intention of writing to you, and of thanking you for your kind gift, which came to me only lately, but which has not the less procured for me a great and durable joy. I read your last production * with prolonged interest, and have devoted particular attention to the chapters which treat of death and of that which follows. Those leaves could not have found me in a better condition than that which followed the sudden death of my beloved sister, the duchess de Nemours; that disposition will follow me, I hope, all the rest of my life, for it is the fruit of the serious call which has been addressed to us all by that unexpected loss. The fragility of human life and the variety of interests here below have never so seriously struck me as in these latter months, though the voice of God has been so often heard in my afflicted heart, and the strokes from His hand have showed me the instability of greatness and the inconstancy of the purest earthly happiness. In this state of mind, I ardently wished a nourishment which suited the state of my soul; your book appeared to me like a stream in the desert; and it has consoled me by the instructive relation of the experiences of pious men in trial or upon their death-beds. A multitude of

* The first volume of the Author's *Collections*.

questions incessantly press themselves upon my mind. What does the soul feel at the moment of death? Does it feel itself in the presence of God, or does it fall into a kind of lethargy until the hour of the resurrection? Does it suffer at the moment when it abruptly leaves the body and the external world? Does it regret those whom it has loved, and who weep? Does it know what they do in this world, or are all the ties to earth broken? Do we love only the Lord on high? and are we entirely absorbed in a feeling of adoration, which excludes all other feeling, and renders us strangers to what passes in the world which we have left? This is what I ask of those for whom I weep and whose image is always living before me: but I obtain no response. I well know that if God had found it good to satisfy such a natural desire of the heart, He would have revealed to us what pertains to the soul after death, and would have cleared the sombre mystery of the future life! but this persuasion does not tranquillize me, and if I believe that *acquaintance* with that future, *ought* to remain hidden from us, I shall often have an inexpressible desire to have a presentiment of it. If this desire appears culpable to you, tell me frankly; if it proceeds from a want of faith, God grant to strengthen my faith, that I may no longer be absorbed by these questions.

My sister apprises me that you labor without relaxation, very dear professor, and that you will soon send us a new work, provided your strength does not exhaust itself in this incessant activity, and that you remain for a long time upon our poor earth, where you are so useful! This wish your grandson, the doctor, will express to you especially in my name. I regret that he leaves England. I have had pleasure in seeing him and in conversing with him, for he appears to be a gifted young man, full of energy, goodness of heart, and piety; such ought to be the son of your Selma. I cannot tell you with what interest I heard many details from his mouth concerning all your family. I should doubtless enjoy a greater pleasure in seeing you again here below, and in expressing to you by word of mouth, after *forty years*, my filial respect. God grant me this joy.

HELEN.

One might say that in writing this letter, the duchess not only wished to express in words her thoughts upon the uncertainty of life, and upon that eternity to which she was so near; but, that she still felt the need of joining a visible pledge of her good-will with this last letter of adieu. She said in the postscript:

"I pray Madame de Schubert to accept a little souvenir; it is a pin, the twin-sister of which I often wear. As it is very plain, and of sombre color, I hope that your wife, who cares little for the toilet, will not disdain this modest onyx, and that she will sometimes wear it in remembrance of me."

A few days before the date of this letter, he who was charged with it again saw the duchess in the little Lutheran church, where she was taking the communion in the midst of the members of the community, and thus proved that fidelity to the end which was an essential trait of her nature and entire life.

She also had occasion to give a last testimony of it, in the accomplishment of her maternal duties.*

At its departure, the soul often leaves upon the countenance, the reflection of the eternal light which inundates it the moment it leaves the body.

Those who had seen the duchess of Orleans for the first time saluting her husband at Châlons-sur-Marne, again distinguished upon her features after death, the same indefinable expression of love, joy,

* The account here given by Professor Schubert concerning the illness of the duke de Chartres, the duchess' care of him, her illness, and peaceful death, is almost precisely the same, as the one previously given in this volume.

and humility. That fugitive instant of happiness, that sweet terrestrial dream, had received its accomplishment; faith was changed to sight.

The joy which transports the born blind, when in consequence of a skilful operation, he suddenly sees himself enveloped in a flood of light, and for the first time distinguishes the features of those who have tenderly watched over him, is well the expression of the greatest happiness which the heart of man can contain. But, at the sight of the mortal remains of the duchess, our thoughts carry us to a happiness which no eye has seen, which no ear has heard, and which it has not entered into the heart of man to conceive, and to the inexpressible felicity that God has promised to those who love Him here below, even that of contemplating Him face to face in the midst of the dazzling light of the abode of the blessed, and of being admitted to that feast of the ransomed which has no end.

APPENDIX.

POEMS BY THE DUCHESS OF ORLEANS

Herzlich lieb hab ich Dich, o Herr!
Ich bitt, wollst seyn von mir nicht fern
Mit deiner Hülf und Gnaden.
Die ganze Welt erfreut mich nicht,
Nach Himmel und Erden frag ich nicht,
Wenn ich nur Dich kann haben.
Und ob mir gleich das Herz zerbricht,
So bleibst Du doch meine Zuversicht,
Mein Heil und meines Herzens Trost,
Der mich durch sein Blut hat erlöst.
Herr Jesu Christ, mein Gott und Herr,
Mein Gott und Herr!
In Schanden lass mich nimmermehr.

Es ist ja, Herr! Dein Geschenck und Gab,
Mein Leib, Seel und Alles, was ich hab
In diesem armen Leben,
Auf dass ich's brauche zum Lobe Dein,
Zum Nutz und Dienste der Nächsten mein
Wollst mir Deine Gnade geben

Behüt mich Herr vor falscher Lehr',
Des Satans Mord und Lügen wehr,
In allem Kreuz erhalte mich,
Auf dass ich's trag' geduldiglich!
Herr Jesu Christ, mein Herr und Gott,
Mein Herr und Gott!
Tröst' mir meine Seel' in der letzten Noth.

Ach, Herr! lass Deine lieben Engelein
Am letzten Ende die Seele mein
In Abrahams Schooss tragen.
Den Leib in seinem Schlafkämmerlein
Gar sanft ohn' alle Noth und Pein
Ruh'n bis am jüngsten Tage
Alsdann vom Tod erwecke mich,
Dass meine Augen sehen Dich
In aller Freud', o Gottes Sohn,
Mein Heiland und mein Gnadenthron.
Herr Jesu Christ, erhöre mich,
Erhöre mich!
Ich will Dich preisen ewiglich!

DAS SCHWÆNELIED

Könnte meines Herzens Sehnen,
Könnte meine süsse Lust
Durch der Sprache leises Tönen
Dringen aus der vollen Brust!

Mächtig treibt in mir ein Wehen,
Dass die Seele mir belebt,
Unaufhaltsam im Entstehen
Ist die Macht, die mich durchbebt.

Mit des Stromes Silberwogen
Sehn' ich mich—wer weiss wohin?
Wie von mag'scher Kraft gezogen
Schwäne in die Ferne zieh'n.

Doch es tönen Zauberklänge
Tief im Innersten mir zu,
Eines Engelchors Gesänge
Wiegen mich in süsse Ruh:

"Glücklich bist du, Kind der Träume,
"Dem das Leben froh erscheint,
"Schwingst den Geist in freie Räume,
"Wo das Auge nie geweint.

"Wie mit goldnen Adlerschwingne
"Schwebst du durch der Lüfte Blau,
"Lässt dein Lied schon früh erklingen
"Mit dem hellen Morgenthau.

"Horch', des Weltalls goldne Leier
"Tönet süsse Harmonie,
"Und sie stimmt zur stillen Feier
"Deine sel'ge Phantasie.

"Und die ew'gen Lustgestalten,
"Deren Reize nie verblüh'n,
"Deinem Auge sich entfalten,
"Möchtest gern mit ihnen zieh'n!"

DOBBERAN, 1830.

ZURUF.

Zieh' dahin wie Silberschwäne
Nach dem unbekannten Dorf,
Selbst die still vergoss'ne Thräne
Schwellt die Fluth und hilft Dir fort.

Fürchte nie wenn Wogen schäumen
An des Felsenthales Rand,
Schwäne ziehen ohne Säumen
Nach dem herzbekannten Land.

Wagen kühn sich auf die Wogen
Wo sie hoch und sicher sind.
Wer das Flache sucht—betrogen
Ist ein solches armes Kind!

THE END.

STANDARD AND POPULAR BOOKS

PUBLISHED BY

PORTER & COATES, PHILADELPHIA, PA

WAVERLEY NOVELS. By Sir Walter Scott.

*Waverley.
*Guy Mannering.
The Antiquary.
Rob Roy.
Black Dwarf; and Old Mortality.
The Heart of Mid-Lothian.
The Bride of Lammermoor; and A Legend of Montrose.
*Ivanhoe.
The Monastery.
The Abbott.
Kenilworth.
The Pirate.
The Fortunes of Nigel.
Peveril of the Peak.
Quentin Durward.
St. Ronan's Well.
Redgauntlet.
The Betrothed; and The Talisman.
Woodstock.
The Fair Maid of Perth.
Anne of Geierstein.
Count Robert of Paris; and Castle Dangerous.
Chronicles of the Canongate.

Household Edition. 23 vols. Illustrated. 12mo. Cloth, extra, black and gold, per vol., $1.00; sheep, marbled edges, per vol., $1.50; half calf, gilt, marbled edges, per vol., $3.00. Sold separately in cloth binding only.

Universe Edition. 25 vols. Printed on thin paper, and containing one illustration to the volume. 12mo. Cloth, extra, black and gold, per vol., 75 cts.

World Edition. 12 vols. Thick 12mo. (Sold in sets only.) Cloth, extra, black and gold, $18.00; half imt. Russia, marbled edges, $24.00.

This is the best edition for the library or for general use published. Its convenient size, the extreme legibility of the type, which is larger than is used in any other 12mo edition, either English or American.

TALES OF A GRANDFATHER. By Sir Walter Scott, Bart 4 vols. Uniform with the Waverley Novels.

Household Edition. Illustrated. 12mo. Cloth, extra, black and gold, per vol., $1.00; sheep, marbled edges, per vol., $1.50; half calf, gilt, marbled edges, per vol., $3.00.

This edition contains the Fourth Series—Tales from French history—and is the only complete edition published in this country.

CHARLES DICKENS' COMPLETE WORKS. Author's Edition. 14 vols., with a portrait of the author on steel, and eight illustrations by F. O. C. Darley, Cruikshank, Fildes, Eytinge, and others, in each volume. 12mo. Cloth, extra, black and gold, per vol., $1.00; sheep, marbled edges, per vol., $1.50; half imt. Russia, marbled edges, per vol., $1.50: half calf, gilt, marbled edges, per vol., $2.75.

*Pickwick Papers.
*Oliver Twist, Pictures of Italy, and American Notes.
*Nicholas Nickleby.
Old Curiosity Shop, and Reprinted Pieces.
Barnaby Rudge, and Hard Times.
*Martin Chuzzlewit.
Dombey and Son.
*David Copperfield.
Christmas Books, Uncommercial Traveller, and Additional Christmas Stories.
Bleak House.
Little Dorrit.
Tale of Two Cities, and Great Expectations.
Our Mutual Friend.
Edwin Drood, Sketches, Master Humphrey's Clock, etc., etc.

Sold separately in cloth binding only.

*Also in Alta Edition, one illustration, 75 cents.

The same. Universe Edition. Printed on thin paper and containing one illustration to the volume. 14 vols., 12mo. Cloth, extra, black and gold, per vol., 75 cents.

The same. World Edition. 7 vols., thick 12mo., $12.25. (Sold in sets only.)

CHILD'S HISTORY OF ENGLAND. By CHARLES DICKENS. Popular 12mo. edition; from new electrotype plates. Large clear type. Beautifully illustrated with 8 engravings on wood. 12mo. Cloth, extra, black and gold, $1.00.

Alta Edition. One illustration, 75 cents.

"Dickens as a novelist and prose poet is to be classed in the front rank of the noble company to which he belongs. He has revived the novel of genuine practical life, as it existed in the works of Fielding, Smollett, and Goldsmith; but at the same time has given to his material an individual coloring and expression peculiarly his own. His characters, like those of his great exemplars, constitute a world of their own, whose truth to nature every reader instinctively recognizes in connection with their truth to darkness." —*E. P. Whipple.*

MACAULAY'S HISTORY OF ENGLAND. From the accession of James II. By THOMAS BABINGTON MACAULAY. With a steel portrait of the author. Printed from new electrotype plates from the last English Edition. Being by far the most correct edition in the American market. 5 volumes, 12mo. Cloth, extra, black and gold, per set, $5.00; sheep, marbled edges, per set, $7.50; half imitation Russia, $7.50; half calf, gilt, marbled edges, per set, $15.00.

Popular Edition. 5 vols., cloth, plain, $5.00.

8vo. Edition. 5 volumes in one, with portrait. Cloth, extra, black and gold, $3.00; sheep, marbled edges, $3.50.

MARTINEAU'S HISTORY OF ENGLAND. From the beginning of the 19th Century to the Crimean War. By HARRIET MARTINEAU. Complete in 4 vols., with full Index. Cloth, extra, black and gold, per set, $4.00; sheep, marbled edges, $6.00; half calf, gilt, marbled edges, $12.00.

HUME'S HISTORY OF ENGLAND. From the invasion of Julius Cæsar to the abdication of James II, 1688. By DAVID HUME. Standard Edition. With the author's last corrections and improvements; to which is prefixed a short account of his life, written by himself. With a portrait on steel. A new edition from entirely new stereotype plates. 5 vols., 12mo. Cloth, extra, black and gold, per set, $5.00; sheep, marbled edges, per set, $7.50; half imitation Russia, $7.50; half calf, gilt, marbled edges, per set, $15.00.

Popular Edition. 5 vols. Cloth, plain, $5.00.

GIBBON'S DECLINE AND FALL OF THE ROMAN EMPIRE. By EDWARD GIBBON. With Notes, by Rev. H. H. MILMAN. Standard Edition. To which is added a complete Index of the work. A new edition from entirely new stereotype plates. With portrait on steel. 5 vols., 12mo. Cloth, extra, black and gold, per set, $5.00; sheep, marbled edges, per set, $7.50; half imitation Russia, $7.50; half calf, gilt, marbled edges, per set, $15.00.

Popular Edition. 5 vols. Cloth, plain, $5.00.

ENGLAND, PICTURESQUE AND DESCRIPTIVE. By JOEL COOK, author of "A Holiday Tour in Europe," etc. With 487 finely engraved illustrations, descriptive of the most famous and attractive places, as well as of the historic scenes and rural life of England and Wales. With Mr. Cook's admirable descriptions of the places and the country, and the splendid illustrations, this is the most valuable and attractive book of the season, and the sale will doubtless be very large. 4to. Cloth, extra, gilt side and edges, $7.50; half calf, gilt, marbled edges, $10.00; half morocco, full gilt edges, $10.00; full Turkey morocco, gilt edges, $15.00; tree calf, gilt edges, $18.00.

This work, which is prepared in elegant style, and profusely illustrated, is a comprehensive description of England and Wales, arranged in convenient form for the tourist, and at the same time providing an illustrated guide-book to a country which Americans always view with interest. There are few satisfactory works about this land which is so generously gifted by Nature and so full of memorials of the past. Such books as there are, either cover a few counties or are devoted to special localities, or are merely guide-books. The present work is believed to be the first attempt to give in attractive form a description of the stately homes, renowned castles, ivy-clad ruins of abbeys, churches, and ancient fortresses, delicious scenery, rock-bound coasts, and celebrated places of England and Wales. It is written by an author fully competent from travel and reading, and in position to properly describe his very interesting subject; and the artist's pencil has been called into requisition to graphically illustrate its well-written pages. There are 487 illustrations, prepared in the highest style of the engraver's art, while the book itself is one of the most attractive ever presented to the American public.

Its method of construction is systematic, following the most convenient routes taken by tourists, and the letter-press includes enough of the history and legend of each of the places described to make the story highly interesting. Its pages fairly overflow with picture and description, telling of everything attractive that is presented by England and Wales. Executed in the highest style of the printer's and engraver's art, "England, Picturesque and Descriptive," is one of the best American books of the year.

HISTORY OF THE CIVIL WAR IN AMERICA. By the COMTE DE PARIS. With Maps faithfully Engraved from the Originals, and Printed in Three Colors. 8vo. Cloth, per volume, $3.50; red cloth, extra, Roxburgh style, uncut edges, $3.50; sheep, library style, $4.50; half Turkey morocco, $6.00. Vols. I, II, and III now ready.

The third volume embraces, without abridgment, the fifth and sixth volumes of the French edition, and covers one of the most interesting as well as the most anxious periods of the war, describing the operations of the Army of the Potomac in the East, and the Army of the Cumberland and Tennessee in the West.

It contains full accounts of the battle of Chancellorsville, the attack of the monitors on Fort Sumter, the sieges and fall of Vicksburg and Port Hudson; the battles of Port Gibson and Champion's Hill, and the fullest and most authentic account of the battle of Gettysburg ever written.

"The head of the Orleans family has put pen to paper with excellent result. . . . . Our present impression is that it will form by far the best history of the American war."—*Athenæum, London.*

"We advise all Americans to read it carefully, and judge for themselves if 'the future historian of our war,' of whom we have heard so much, be not already arrived in the Comte de Paris."—*Nation, New York.*

"This is incomparably the best account of our great second revolution that has yet been even attempted. It is so calm, so dispassionate, so accurate in detail, and at the same time so philosophical in general, that its reader counts confidently on finding the complete work thoroughly satisfactory."—*Evening Bulletin, Philadelphia.*

"The work expresses the calm, deliberate judgment of an experienced military observer and a highly intelligent man. Many of its statements will excite discussion, but we much mistake if it does not take high and permanent rank among the standard histories of the civil war. Indeed that place has been assigned it by the most competent critics both of this country and abroad."—*Times, Cincinnati.*

"Messrs. Porter & Coates, of Philadelphia, will publish in a few days the authorized translation of the new volume of the Comte de Paris' History of Our Civil War. The two volumes in French—the fifth and sixth—are bound together in the translation in one volume. Our readers already know, through a table of contents of these volumes, published in the cable columns of the *Herald*, the period covered by this new installment of a work remarkable in several ways. It includes the most important and decisive period of the war, and the two great campaigns of Gettysburg and Vicksburg.

"The great civil war has had no better, no abler historian than the French prince who, emulating the example of Lafayette, took part in this new struggle for freedom, and who now writes of events, in many of which he participated, as an accomplished officer, and one who, by his independent position, his high character and eminent talents, was placed in circumstances and relations which gave him almost unequalled opportunities to gain correct information and form impartial judgments.

"The new installment of a work which has already become a classic will be read with increased interest by Americans because of the importance of the period it covers and the stirring events it describes. In advance of a careful review we present to-day some extracts from the advance sheets sent us by Messrs. Porter & Coates, which will give our readers a foretaste of chapters which bring back to memory so many half-forgotten and not a few hitherto unvalued details of a time which Americans of this generation at least cannot read of without a fresh thrill of excitement."

HALF-HOURS WITH THE BEST AUTHORS. With short Biographical and Critical Notes. By CHARLES KNIGHT.

New Household Edition. With six portraits on steel. 3 vols., thick 12mo. Cloth, extra, black and gold, per set, $4.50; half imt. Russia, marbled edges, $6.00; half calf, gilt, marbled edges, $12.00.

Library Edition. Printed on fine laid and tinted paper. With twenty-four portraits on steel. 6 vols., 12mo. Cloth, extra, per set, $7.50; half calf, gilt, marbled edges, per set, $18.00; half Russia, gilt top, $21.00; full French morocco, limp, per set, $12.00; full smooth Russia, limp, round corners, in Russia case, per set, $25.00; full seal grained Russia, limp, round corners, in Russia case to match, $25.00.

The excellent idea of the editor of these choice volumes has been most admirably carried out, as will be seen by the list of authors upon all subjects. Selecting some choice passages of the best standard authors, each of sufficient length to occupy half an hour in its perusal, there is here food for thought for every day in the year: so that if the purchaser will devote but one-half hour each day to its appropriate selection he will read through these six volumes in one year, and in such a leisurely manner that the noblest thoughts of many of the greatest minds will be firmly in his mind forever. For every Sunday there is a suitable selection from some of the most eminent writers in sacred literature. We venture to say if the editor's idea is carried out the reader will possess more and better knowledge of the English classics at the end of the year than he would by five years of desultory reading.

They can be commenced at any day in the year. The variety of reading is so great that no one will ever tire of these volumes. It is a library in itself.

THE POETRY OF OTHER LANDS. A Collection of Translations into English Verse of the Poetry of Other Languages, Ancient and Modern. Compiled by N. CLEMMONS HUNT. Containing translations from the Greek, Latin, Persian, Arabian, Japanese, Turkish, Servian, Russian, Bohemian, Polish, Dutch, German, Italian, French, Spanish, and Portuguese languages. 12mo. Cloth, extra, gilt edges, $2.50; half calf, gilt, marbled edges, $4.00; Turkey morocco, gilt edges, $6.00.

"Another of the publications of Porter & Coates, called 'The Poetry of Other Lands,' compiled by N. Clemmons Hunt, we most warmly commend. It is one of the best collections we have seen, containing many exquisite poems and fragments of verse which have not before been put into book form in English words. We find many of the old favorites, which appear in every well-selected collection of sonnets and songs, and we miss others, which seem a necessity to complete the bouquet of grasses and flowers, some of which, from time to time, we hope to republish in the 'Courier.'"—*Cincinnati Courier.*

"A book of rare excellence, because it gives a collection of choice gems in many languages not available to the general lover of poetry. It contains translations from the Greek, Latin, Persian, Arabian, Japanese, Turkish, Servian, Russian, Bohemian, Polish, Dutch, German, Italian, French, Spanish, and Portuguese languages. The book will be an admirable companion volume to any one of the collections of English poetry that are now published. With the full index of authors immediately preceding the collection, and the arrangement of the poems under headings, the reader will find it convenient for reference. It is a gift that will be more valued by very many than some of the transitory ones at these holiday times."—*Philadelphia Methodist.*

THE FIRESIDE ENCYCLOPÆDIA OF POETRY. Edited by HENRY T. COATES. This is the latest, and beyond doubt the best collection of poetry published. Printed on fine paper and illustrated with thirteen steel engravings and fifteen title pages, containing portraits of prominent American poets and fac-similes of their handwriting, made expressly for this book. 8vo. Cloth, extra, black and gold, gilt edges, $5.00; half calf, gilt, marbled edges, $7.50; half morocco, full gilt edges, $7.50; full Turkey morocco, gilt edges, $10.00; tree calf, gilt edges $12.00; plush, padded side, nickel lettering, $14.00.

"The editor shows a wide acquaintance with the most precious treasures of English verse, and has gathered the most admirable specimens of their ample wealth. Many pieces which have been passed by in previous collections hold a place of honor in the present volume, and will be heartily welcomed by the lovers of poetry as a delightful addition to their sources of enjoyment. It is a volume rich in solace, in entertainment, in inspiration, of which the possession may well be coveted by every lover of poetry. The pictorial illustrations of the work are in keeping with its poetical contents, and the beauty of the typographical execution entitles it to a place among the choicest ornaments of the library."—*New York Tribune.*

"Lovers of good poetry will find this one of the richest collections ever made. All the best singers in our language are represented, and the selections are generally those which reveal their highest qualities. . . . . The lights and shades, the finer play of thought and imagination belonging to individual authors, are brought out in this way (by the arrangement of poems under subject-headings) as they would not be under any other system. . . . . We are deeply impressed with the keen appreciation of poetical worth, and also with the good taste manifested by the compiler."—*Churchman.*

"Cyclopædias of poetry are numerous, but for sterling value of its contents for the library, or as a book of reference, no work of the kind will compare with this admirable volume of Mr. Coates It takes the gems from many volumes, culling with rare skill and judgment."—*Chicago Inter-Ocean.*

THE CHILDREN'S BOOK OF POETRY. Compiled by HENRY T. COATES. Containing over 500 poems carefully selected from the works of the best and most popular writers for children; with nearly 200 illustrations. The most complete collection of poetry for children ever published. 4to. Cloth, extra, black and gold, gilt side and edges, $3.00; full Turkey morocco, gilt edges, $7.50.

"This seems to us the best book of poetry for children in existence. We have examined many other collections, but we cannot name another that deserves to be compared with this admirable compilation."—*Worcester Spy.*

"The special value of the book lies in the fact that it nearly or quite covers the entire field. There is not a great deal of good poetry which has been written for children that cannot be found in this book. The collection is particularly strong in ballads and tales, which are apt to interest children more than poems of other kinds; and Mr. Coates has shown good judgment in supplementing this department with some of the best poems of that class that have been written for grown people. A surer method of forming the taste of children for good and pure literature than by reading to them from any portion of this book can hardly be imagined. The volume is richly illustrated and beautifully bound."—*Philadelphia Evening Bulletin.*

"A more excellent volume cannot be found. We have found within the covers of this handsome volume, and upon its fair pages, many of the most exquisite poems which our language contains. It must become a standard volume, and can never grow old or obsolete."—*Episcopal Recorder.*

THE COMPLETE WORKS OF THOS. HOOD. With engravings on steel. 4 vols., 12mo., tinted paper. Poetical Works; Up the Rhine; Miscellanies and Hood's Own; Whimsicalities, Whims, and Oddities. Cloth, extra, black and gold, $6.00; red cloth, paper label, gilt top, uncut edges, $6.00; half calf, gilt, marbled edges, $14.00; half Russia, gilt top, $18.00.

Hood's verse, whether serious or comic—whether serene like a cloudless autumn evening or sparkling with puns like a frosty January midnight with stars—was ever pregnant with materials for the thought. Like every author distinguished for true comic humor, there was a deep vein of melancholy pathos running through his mirth, and even when his sun shone brightly its light seemed often reflected as if only over the rim of a cloud.

Well may we say, in the words of Tennyson, "Would he could have stayed with us." for never could it be more truly recorded of any one—in the words of Hamlet characterizing Yorick—that "he was a fellow of infinite jest, of most excellent fancy." D. M. MOIR.

THE ILIAD OF HOMER RENDERED INTO ENGLISH BLANK VERSE. By EDWARD, EARL OF DERBY. From the latest London edition, with all the author's last revisions and corrections, and with a Biographical Sketch of Lord Derby, by R. SHELTON MACKENZIE, D.C.L. With twelve steel engravings from Flaxman's celebrated designs. 2 vols., 12mo. Cloth, extra, bev. boards, gilt top, $3.50; half calf, gilt, marbled edges, $7.00; half Turkey morocco, gilt top, $7.00.

The same. Popular edition. Two vols. in one. 12mo. Cloth, extra, $1.50.

"It must equally be considered a splendid performance; and for the present we have no hesitation in saying that it is by far the best representation of Homer's Iliad in the English language."—*London Times.*

"The merits of Lord Derby's translation may be summed up in one word, it is eminently attractive; it is instinct with life; it may be read with fervent interest; it is immeasurably nearer than Pope to the text of the original. . . . . Lord Derby has given a version far more closely allied to the original, and superior to any that has yet been attempted in the blank verse of our language."—*Edinburg Review.*

THE WORKS OF FLAVIUS JOSEPHUS. Comprising the Antiquities of the Jews; a History of the Jewish Wars, and a Life of Flavius Josephus, written by himself. Translated from the original Greek, by WILLIAM WHISTON, A.M. Together with numerous explanatory Notes and seven Dissertations concerning Jesus Christ, John the Baptist, James the Just, God's command to Abraham, etc., with an Introductory Essay by Rev. H. STEBBING, D.D. 8vo. Cloth, extra, black and gold, plain edges, $3.00; cloth, red, black and gold, gilt edges, $4.50; sheep, marbled edges, $3.50; Turkey morocco, gilt edges, $8.00.

This is the largest type one volume edition published.

THE ANCIENT HISTORY OF THE EGYPTIANS, CARTHAGINIANS, ASSYRIANS, BABYLONIANS, MEDES AND PERSIANS, GRECIANS AND MACEDONIANS. Including a History of the Arts and Sciences of the Ancients. By CHARLES ROLLIN. With a Life of the Author, by JAMES BELL. 2 vols., royal 8vo. Sheep, marbled edges, per set, $6.00.

COOKERY FROM EXPERIENCE. A Practical Guide for Housekeepers in the Preparation of Every-day Meals, containing more than One Thousand Domestic Recipes, mostly tested by Personal Experience, with Suggestions for Meals, Lists of Meats and Vegetables in Season, etc. By Mrs. SARA T. PAUL. 12mo. Cloth, extra, black and gold, $1.50.

Interleaved Edition. Cloth, extra, black and gold, $1.75.

THE COMPARATIVE EDITION OF THE NEW TESTAMENT. Both Versions in One Book.

The proof readings of our Comparative Edition have been gone over by so many competent proof readers, that we believe the text is absolutely correct.

Large 12mo., 700 pp. Cloth, extra, plain edges, $1.50; cloth, extra, bevelled boards and carmine edges, $1.75; imitation panelled calf, yellow edges, $2.00; arabesque, gilt edges, $2.50; French morocco, limp, gilt edges, $4.00; Turkey morocco, limp, gilt edges, $6.00.

The Comparative New Testament has been published by Porter & Coates. In parallel columns on each page are given the old and new versions of the Testament, divided also as far as practicable into comparative verses, so that it is almost impossible for the slightest new word to escape the notice of either the ordinary reader or the analytical student. It is decidedly the best edition yet published of the most interest-exciting literary production of the day. No more convenient form for comparison could be devised either for economizing time or labor. Another feature is the foot-notes, and there is also given in an appendix the various words and expressions preferred by the American members of the Revising Commission. The work is handsomely printed on excellent paper with clear, legible type. It contains nearly 700 pages.

THE COUNT OF MONTE CRISTO. By ALEXANDRE DUMAS. Complete in one volume, with two illustrations by George G. White. 12mo. Cloth, extra, black and gold, $1.25.

THE THREE GUARDSMEN. By ALEXANDRE DUMAS. Complete in one volume, with two illustrations by George G. White. 12mo. Cloth, extra, black and gold, $1.25.

There is a magic influence in his pen, a magnetic attraction in his descriptions, a fertility in his literary resources which are characteristic of Dumas alone, and the seal of the master of light literature is set upon all his works. Even when not strictly historical, his romances give an insight into the habits and modes of thought and action of the people of the time described which are not offered in any other author's productions.

THE LAST DAYS OF POMPEII. By Sir EDWARD BULWER LYTTON, Bart. Illustrated. 12mo. Cloth, extra, black and gold, $1.00. Alta edition, one illustration, 75 cts.

JANE EYRE. By CHARLOTTE BRONTÉ (Currer Bell). New Library Edition. With five illustrations by E. M. WIMPERIS. 12mo. Cloth, extra, black and gold, $1.00.

SHIRLEY. By CHARLOTTE BRONTÉ (Currer Bell). New Library Edition. With five illustrations by E. M. WIMPERIS. 12mo. Cloth, extra, black and gold, $1.00.

www.ingramcontent.com/pod-product-compliance
Lightning Source LLC
LaVergne TN
LVHW020113110826
845151LV00001B/146

* 9 7 8 1 4 2 5 5 4 3 6 5 5 *